ITALY IN THE GOLDEN CENTURIES

italy in the golden centuries

Indro Montanelli and Roberto Gervaso

Translated by Mihaly Csikszentmihalyi

HENRY   REGNERY   COMPANY · CHICAGO

Originally published in Italy in 1967 under the title *L'Italia dei Secoli d'Oro*. Copyright © 1967 Rizzoli Editore, Milan. All rights reserved. Translation copyright © Mihaly Csikszentmihalyi. All rights reserved. Manufactured in the United States of America. Library of Congress Catalog Card Number: 78-88849.

Table of CONTENTS

Part I

THE ITALIAN SCENE

Chapter 1

The Renaissance and the Revival of Humanism

It was Vasari, in his *Lives of the Most Excellent Italian Architects, Painters and Sculptors,* who gave the name "Renaissance" to the period that stretches from the beginnings of the fourteenth century to the end of the sixteenth.

The dates are still very much a matter for argument. There are those who see the Renaissance as starting a little later, and those who make it end somewhat earlier. All this seems to us rather unimportant; what is more important is to deal with the arguments revolving around the meaning one should give to the term "Renaissance," since these arguments are interwoven with the causes of this extraordinary period, and with the reasons that it should have originated in Italy.

Vasari called the period *Rinascenza* because to him it appeared as nothing more than a rebirth of classical culture after a thousand years of medieval darkness. He saw it, more or less, as a vengeance taken by the Roman elements of culture over the Goth, Longobard, and Frankish hordes that had previously prevailed against them.

Such a point of view is well founded. There is no doubt that among all the provinces of the former Roman Empire, Italy was the first to absorb the German invaders, who, despite their policy of racial segregation, were converted to the sophisticated social structures that Rome had given the world. The reasons for this were partly that the flood of invasions was somewhat less overwhelming in Italy than elsewhere in Western Europe; partly that Italy was, for obvious geographic reasons, the country most deeply imbued with Roman traditions; and partly that Rome was still seat of the Church, even though the capital of the Empire had been moved to Constantinople. As the barbarians embraced Christianity, by and by they became its captives. If they wanted to talk with God or the pope, they had to learn Latin. And once they did so, they discovered the superiority of Roman law and administration, and that discovery, in turn, led them to jurists and officials of Roman origin. From then on, they were caught by a culture to which they had nothing to oppose except the primitive poetry of the sagas and the clumsy laws of the feud.

But one would belittle the Renaissance if one assumed that it was nothing more than the rediscovery of classical civilization. Rediscovery is only one stage of the whole period: the one called "humanistic revival," and its major figure is Petrarch. Humanists were the committed bookworms, the brave frogmen of the old archives who took it upon themselves to discover the classic texts that had survived the destructions and dispersions of the Middle Ages, who literally unearthed them from the cellars of monasteries, especially the cellars in Benedictine houses, where they had been preserved and often transcribed. And, of course, it was logical for this to happen more than elsewhere in Italy, where monasteries and ancient texts were more plentiful.

The revival of classical culture was perhaps the first element of the Renaissance, and it was certainly one of the most important. Italian prose writers borrowed Cicero's syntax, poets got their verse-structure from Vergil, and architects adopted their knowledge from Vitruvius. But writers, poets, architects, and such did not just limit themselves to an imitation of classical models. What was added to them is what made the Renaissance into the most powerful burst of genius in history since the Golden Century of Athens.

Among other factors that were needed for the process of revival to begin, urbanization was the foremost. Initially isolated by their own racial discrimination, the Germans lived in the countryside or in their castles far from the towns. There they had developed a "way of life," but not a civilization—a word derived from *civitas,* city. Rome and Athens were cities before they became civilizations. Macedonia, on the other hand, was never more than an army backed by a country of shepherds and farmers.

In Western Europe the Italian cities were the first to return to a prominent role in the life of the country, after the long rural parenthesis of the Middle Ages. Italy never had been wholly feudal, and therefore rural. Although decaying and depopulated, the cities had held on. Urban life always had a base from which to start.

A geographic factor, also, helped to ensure a leading position to the cities of Italy. In the fourteenth century, the Mediterranean Sea was still the main road for all commerce, cultural as well as material. Across this sea the Roman–German West met the Greek–Byzantine East and Islamic civilizations. At times the meeting of these cultures took the form of armed combat, but, more often, they were occasions for exchange. By the end of the Middle Ages, the East had attained greater progress than the West in everything from industrial production to intellectual output. Europe imported from the East its silks, damasks, spices, the secret processes for producing cloth and the chemical formulas for dyeing, and from the East came geometry, algebra, and Aristotelian logic—things that Europe had long forgotten and that the Italian coastal cities were now in the privileged position to gather anew.

All this meant wealth, which if not a sufficient condition for culture is a necessary one. During the Middle Ages, the Church had been the only noteworthy Italian industry. Tithes from all Europe converged upon Rome, to be redistributed to the rest of the Italian peninsula, where some traces of capitalism still persisted. In Italy money had become rare, but it did not disappear completely as it did in the countrified lands where commerce had regressed to barter.

Thus, rivulets of gold kept flowing to Rome, but now new currents began to appear also. Ship rentals were one of the main sources. Genoa and Venice had the best fleets of the times, the most experienced admirals, and the best-trained crews. For the serious risks they ran in defying storms and pirates the ship owners let themselves be paid well. But in return raw and manufactured materials were unloaded in Italy to feed its factories and its trade. The Renaissance cannot be imagined without the buildup of capital; it was the money of the Florentine weavers, merchants, and bankers that made it possible for Giotto and Arnolfo to do what they did.

The social ambitions of the urban plutocracy were another set of stimuli. The social world inherited from the Middle Ages was built like a pyramid with a closed caste structure. At the top of the status system was the nobility, despite the fact that it had lost much of its economic and political power. The newly rich banker or industrialist could not move up in status except by sponsoring the Arts. Because his ancestors had not garnered a coat of arms by participating in a Crusade, he had, if he wanted to receive recognition, to finance the building or the re-modeling of a church. The Renaissance owes a lot to middle-class pretensions. More than anything else, its secularisation was the result of bourgeois influence. Up to that point in time, Art had always dealt exclusively with sacred subjects, since no one but the Church could afford to pay the artists. But now that commissions began to flow from the bourgeoisie, the artist was left free to pursue ideals of beauty that did not derive exclusively from sacred themes and that did not undergo clerical censorship.

One more decisive fact caused the Renaissance to become an Italian phenomenon: the faster rate of maturation characteristic of more iso-lated systems. In the thirteenth century, France had been in the posi-tion of European leadership. Its Provençal language was much more sophisticated than the Italian *vulgate,* the poetry of its troubadours set the trend for the rest of the world, its architecture had achieved in the gothic style the highest known forms. In philosophy, Abelard had in-troduced Aristotelian rationalism filtered through the Arab culture of Spain to Europe.

But France could not sustain this momentum because its energies were diverted to the achievement of a different task; namely, the build-ing of national unity and the creation of a state—a staggering task for those times. And the effort tied down the country's resources and the energy of her kings almost to the end of the sixteenth century. And for the whole period the French intelligentsia found its field of action in the army and the civil service rather than in literature, the sciences, or the arts.

Italy never even considered the French goal of a united state, mostly on account of the Church, which wanted Italy divided so as to control it better. The *comuni* were the highest form of political organization to develop in the beginning of our period, and later these were expanded into the *principati*. But within these narrow confines the Italian elites, freed from other tasks, had a chance to integrate and to mature rapidly. What had happened in Athens now was repeated in Florence, Venice, and Milan: because they worked within the restricted circuit of their walls, in only two centuries the Italians leaped from a semi-barbaric state to the highest forms of civilization. While France, Spain, and England were busy producing generals, admirals, and administrators, Italy was producing and exporting artists to the rest of the world.

This is the reason that the present book deals more with personalities than with events. When a people is not a nation, it does not have a history. So the Italian Renaissance is nothing but a series of chronicles, in which such giants as Dante, Petrarch, and Boccaccio play the leading roles.

Chapter 2

The Legacy of Frederick

In 1250 Emperor Frederick II, wasted by dysentery, lay on his death-bed and probably reviewed in his mind the history of his failure. Although he had been born fifty-six years earlier at Iesi on the Adriatic coast, in a soldier's tent pitched in the market square, there was no trace of Italian blood in him. He was descended from the Swabian house of Hohenstaufen and from the Normans of Sicily. He was brought up as an orphan in Palermo and Sicily, then at the height of its splendor—hub of a cosmopolitan Greek–Arab–Hebrew–Phoenician civilization—haunted him all through his life. Several times he had visited Germany, but he had never succeeded in staying there more than a few months.

Germany was then a chaos of knights, princes, bishops, counts, and bishop-counts who never agreed on anything except on preventing one of their own number from prevailing over the rest and on preventing the Emperor from exercising his nominal authority. Frederick had given up on the idea of restoring order among them, not because he believed the task to be impossible—as he used to tell others and even himself—but because he didn't like to live outside of Italy. When he paid one of those rare calls on his brawling and coarse compatriots, all he asked for was a little peace, which he bought with gold, and then returned across the Alps as fast as he could. His thoughts were always full of Italy, the country he wanted to change into a nation. And his whole life was spent trying to make that dream come true.

In pursuit of that dream, Frederick had ridden up and down the Italian peninsula with his two sons, Enzo and Manfredi, defeating one army after another (the crown of Germany he entrusted to his third son, Conrad). But it was like trying to empty the sea of water. His enemies surrendered only long enough to betray him at the first opportunity. The pope excommunicated him and, hurling anathemas at Frederick, paid the German princes to start one rebellion after another. The last five years had seen a war without mercy: whoever took the emperor's side was sentenced to everlasting hell by the pope, and those who took the pope's side were tortured, blinded, and maimed by the emperor.

Now it was all over. Enzo had fallen prisoner and languished in a tower in Bologna; he would never leave alive. Manfredi went on winning battles at the head of a small army of Moorish mercenaries, but he was forced to pitch his camp outside the walls of the towns that, although defeated, denied him entrance through their gates.

The dying man must have asked himself where he went wrong. He was the first monarch to have welded his Italian kingdom (called the Kingdom of Sicily, it extended to the whole of southern Italy, Naples included) into a state with clear laws, secular courts, a well-ordered administration, a monetary system, a network of roads, a working police, and a trustworthy army. At his court the Italian language had been born. He was a great diplomat and a great general. He had won all the battles. Yet he had lost the war.

Perhaps in those last moments of his life Frederick understood the answer to this riddle; it was, after all, simple enough. He had lost the war because he had chosen the wrong country to fight it in. His love for Italy had blinded him to the fact that it could not become a nation because it carried the pope in its body. The Church was not going to share Rome with any lay power. To achieve its end, the Church constantly played off one pretender against another: it helped Byzantium against the Goths, the Longobards against Byzantium, the Franks against the Longobards, and in the last three centuries the free *comuni* against the emperor. By the time Frederick assumed the crown, it was already too late to begin the unifying process that later was to make modern nations out of France, Spain, and England, and to thrust them into leading roles in European history. The *comuni* had become too strong; some of them—Venice, Genoa, Milan, and Florence—were actually world powers. They had developed a lively civic spirit, and too many local interests had grown too strong to agree to their own dissolution in a national organism.

Even if Frederick had not formulated such thoughts quite so clearly, he must have agreed with their essence, because he had given up the struggle even before he was struck by illness. At the time, he seemed to have the advantage: his son Manfredi and his son-in-law Ezzelino were winning in northern Italy, and Louis IX, King of France, who had been captured by the Muslim in one of the Crusades, was appealing to Pope Innocent IV, asking for a truce with the emperor so that the latter could come to his rescue. And yet Frederick had not convened generals and ambassadors; he had sent for his confessor instead and asked to be absolved from his sins. Was his choice suggested by repentance or political expedience? Whatever the reason, it was the choice of a defeated general who at the approach of death entrusts his soul to the hands of his victorious foe.

Frederick, however, left a very important legacy: a system of government that was to be adopted throughout Italy. He had destroyed the privileges of the feudal lords in his kingdom in order to strengthen its central power and cut down the autonomy of the *comuni*. Everything had been leveled by a state that was embodied in his own person. Mayors, administrators, and judges were appointed by the emperor and were responsible to him only, without any intermediary power. He created a census and thereby controlled and taxed property and income. The economy had been planned, and all prices and production rates were centrally determined. He developed a new aristocracy of bureaucrats, who were selected because of personal skill rather than lineage. The members of his court were all devoted either to the law, or to sciences, or to culture.

The Renaissance lords later copied Frederick's model. Unfortunately, however, they copied him in *everything*, even his cruelty, his despotism, and his habit of hiring foreign mercenaries. For soldiers, Frederick used the Moors, who were still to be found in great numbers in Sicily. He established a strong Saracen colony at Nocera (in the hills to the south of Naples), from which he drew the core of his army. This example was later followed by the Italian lords of the fourteenth century who franchised the defense of their states to German, English, Swiss, and Hungarian troops. Thus they began, or, rather contributed to, the military decadence of Italy that lasts to today. The citizens of Italy became less and less used to bearing weapons and were always ready to make a deal with foreign adventurers who led their bands across the country, despoiling it either at the service of a lord or, having betrayed and murdered him, on their own account.

Thus it was that the last incarnation of the empire to survive the dark medieval times anticipated Italian history and set a model, for good and ill, that all its successors were to follow.

Frederick's death, however, did not put an end to the Hohenstaufen's adventure. Assured of victory, Pope Innocent IV returned from France, where he had been in hiding, and settled down in Naples, from where he annexed the kingdom to the Papal States, while his diplomats were attempting to convince the northern *comuni* to acknowledge his sovereignty. The *comuni,* although they were fighting Manfredi and Ezzelino in the name of the Church, were not at all prepared to give up their autonomy to it. It was the same old story that had begun in Charlemagne's time: the pope could count on the Italian cities as long as the goal was to resist the centralizing power of a king or emperor, but as soon as it tried to impose its own control, the cities turned against the Church.

The remainder of the tale takes little telling. Frederick's son, who had been crowned in Germany as Conrad IV, crossed the Alps with a fresh army and conquered back the kingdom without a blow. Then, however, having installed himself on his father's throne, he was killed almost immediately by malaria. Manfredi then took command of Conrad's army and annihilated the pope's unwieldy bands, whereupon Innocent died of a heart attack. Alexander IV, Innocent's successor, went to the point of announcing a Crusade against the imperials.

The first victim of this new development was Ezzelino, who, surrounded in the north, was finally beaten. A small nobleman from Verona, with a meager body and a bloodless face, Ezzelino had married one of Frederick's illegitimate daughters and become an ascetic terrorist. He dressed like a monk, was as continent as a vegetarian, slept on a hard cot, and had no other passion outside that for struggle and power. The only architecture he responded to was that of fortresses and prisons. He built them everywhere: in Vicenza, Padova, Feltre, and Belluno. He preferred to associate with hangmen and garrotters and assisted at torture sessions without flinching; his imagination was at its best when perfecting new and more sophisticated forms of inflicting pain. Blood filled him with exhilaration, even when at last his own was shed. Slashed by many blows when he was taken prisoner, he refused a doctor, or a confessor, or food; he tore off the bandages dressing his wounds with his own hands and allowed himself to die slowly of hunger and loss of blood—as his own victims themselves had died. His brother Alberic, who had seconded Ezzelino's cruelty with zeal, watched the latter's suffering without batting an eye. Alberic then assisted at the torture of his whole family before being grilled with burning thongs and dragged to his death behind galloping horses.

This left Manfredi and his army of Germans and Moors. The Ghibelline factions rallied around him, led by the Tuscan towns in revolt against the expansionist plans of Florence—which in its turn was the leading power of the Guelph faction. The armies clashed near Montaperti in 1260. The battle ended in a great defeat for Florence, partly, it seems, because the army of Siena pretended to accept a bribe but then didn't, and partly because Bocca degli Abati, one of the Florentine captains, betrayed his side. As a result, Manfredi enjoyed six years of uncontested lordship over the old kingdom.

Pope Urban IV realized that in its present state of disarray Italy could never hope to overcome the Hohenstaufen, so he fell back on the trusted Church policy of setting foreigners off against foreigners and offered the crown of Sicily to Louis IX, King of France. Louis was too tied down in his own country to accept the offer, but since he was very devout and did not want to displease the pope, he passed on the offer to his brother, Charles of Anjou. The latter descended into Italy with thirty thousand men. Although Manfredi had less than half that number, he stood his ground: the battle took place over the fields of Benevento in 1266. When he saw that his cause was lost, Manfredi rode into the thick of the slaughter and died sword in hand, thus ending his life in tune with his character of a bold and romantic warrior, the last embodiment of medieval chivalry.

Two years later Corradino, Conrad's son, rode down from the Alps on his father's quest to conquer back his grandfather's kingdom. He was only fifteen years old, and the German nobles allowed him only a few thousand soldiers. Charles of Anjou, now King of Sicily and bent on keeping that title, waited for him at Tagliacozzo and defeated him easily. "Father," he wrote to the pope, "I beg you: raise and partake of your devout son's quarry: we slaughtered such a number of enemies . . ." Corradino was taken prisoner. Led to Naples in chains, he was beheaded in the marketplace. Under the sign of this infanticide began the reign of Anjou.

Chapter 3

The Sicilian Vespers

Let us follow the Anjou kingdom through its first steps. Charles was presented with a great opportunity to accomplish the task at which Frederick and his successors had failed. The Sicilian kingdom was the only one in Italy to have a tradition of unity, a centralized government, an administrative and military structure. Palermo was the most flourishing and populous city in the whole country. Charles did not have to waste his energies to acquire or to defend an imperial crown, or to keep in check restive neighbors: his brother Louis was firmly established on his own throne guarding the rear; the papal court in Rome was ruled by French cardinals who kept passing the *tiara* to each other. Charles was the cardinals' man, nor was there in all of Europe a prince on whom the Church could call, as was its wont, to counteract his power. Germany was, more than ever, prey to internal convulsions, and the northern cities of Italy that had kept their enmity with the Hohenstaufen alive considered Charles to be a natural ally. Milan had proclaimed him its lord and asked for a vicar to be sent to rule it in Charles's name. Turin, Brescia, and Piacenza followed suit, and Florence acclaimed him as *podestà,* its chief official. The Guelph League changed its name to "Guelph-Anjou," and Rome made him a senator.

But Charles was only a clumsy soldier: brave, but oafish and dense.

Instead of concentrating on developing a realistic Italian policy, he aspired to extend his domains into Greece and Tunisia. As a result, he mismanaged the administration of his kingdom, provoking widespread discontent among his subjects, and finally through his high-handedness lost to French diplomacy its best weapon: the papacy.

After the death of Clement IV who, like Urban, was French, a conclave was called in Viterbo that lasted three years—among intrigues, swindles, and threats. At long last the inhabitants of Viterbo lost their patience, took the roof off the palace, and informed the cardinals that they would be stoned if they didn't make a choice in a hurry. But the contest between the candidates of the various European powers was so keen that at one point Guy de Monfort, the vicar of Anjou in Tuscany, knifed Henry of England during mass and dragged the corpse out into the square by the hair.

This was going a little too far, and the Italian cardinals at last agreed on Tebaldo Visconti of Piacenza, who was at the time in the Holy Land. Tebaldo, who returned shortly and took on the name of Gregory X, realized that he was running the danger of becoming the French court chaplain unless he could find a way to extricate himself from the French intrusions emanating from Paris and Naples. There was only one way to do this: to call back into play the former allies of the German emperor who had defended him against the Church and lost—the Ghibellines. It was the habitual papal diplomacy: always be ready to join forces with a defeated enemy as soon as the allies were winning too much and threatened to rule the whole country. The lords of Saluzzo and Monferrato were induced to repudiate their Anjou allegiance. Ottone Visconti, a Ghibelline, was made archbishop of Milan. Florence was asked to mediate among the two factions, thus depriving the Guelphs of a clear superiority over the Ghibellines. And the imperial crown, left without an inheritor at Corradino's death, was given to Rudolph of Habsburg—a former Hohenstaufen supporter—in an under-the-counter plot that foiled a scheme aimed at getting the crown for one of the French princes.

But the Italian interlude did not last long in Rome: Pope Gregory died in 1276 and his four successors disappeared one after the other within four years. And in the 1280 conclave the French cardinals, supported by Charles's troops, regained the upper hand and succeeded in electing one of their own kind: Simon de Brie, who became Martin IV.

Anjou was again faced with a great opportunity to subdue the entire peninsula. But the kingdom was no longer the same one that the great Frederick had left behind: its finances were in disarray, its roads ruined, its fields impoverished. Ill feeling ran highest in Palermo: Charles had moved his capital to Naples, and the old Sicilian metropolis had fallen to a provincial status. To forestall an insurrection, the Anjou police kept the city in a kind of state of siege, establishing curfews, banning any public gatherings, and routinely searching pedestrians.

During the Easter week in 1282, on March 31, a great crowd filled the squares and the churches of Palermo. A French sergeant, Douet by name, on duty in the city, applied precautionary measures to the womenfolk too—one doesn't know whether he was motivated by zeal or malice—and laid hands on a woman strolling on her husband's arm. The latter, wounded in his Sicilian pride, unsheathed the sergeant's own sword and dispatched him with it. The crowd right away took the murderer's side and shouting, "Mora, mora!" ("Kill them, kill them!"), overran the Anjou troops. All night the hunt went on, and the uprising spread to the whole island; the few Frenchmen who escaped the slaughter found haven aboard their ships. These were the famous "Sicilian Vespers," which entered history as the second great instance of Italian patriotism after the "Carroccio."* The Vespers were a grand gesture, fully justified in terms of Anjou oppression, but patriotism had nothing to do with it.

The insurgents appealed to the pope, asking him to sponsor the island's independence. But Martin would not, or could not, oppose his French compatriots who had elected him and gave Charles a free hand in quenching the rebellion. Charles sent over a fleet carrying an army estimated by a Sicilian chronicler to amount to ninety thousand

---

* This refers to the league of Italian towns against the invading German Emperor, Frederick I of Hohenstaufen, called "Barbarossa," the Redbeard. *Trans.*

foot soldiers and twenty-four thousand mounted troops—clearly an absurd figure, since with such numbers one could then conquer Europe. The correct figure is the one given by Villani—five thousand men altogether, including five hundred from Florence. Even so it was an army of fair size by current standards. Messina, where the fleet was to land, put up a brave resistance under the command of Roger di Lauria. Meanwhile, the leaders of the revolt, who saw themselves abandoned by the pope, asked the help of Peter the Great of Aragon and offered him the island's crown.

The Aragonese kingdom, which was establishing itself vigorously inside Spain, was planning to extend its influence over the Mediterranean to check French expansion. At the precise moment, Peter had decided to attempt an expedition against what was then called Barbery and is now Algeria. Instead, he ordered his ships to change course and head for Trapani. There his troops landed while the fleet proceeded to Messina, where it destroyed the ships of Anjou. Then Peter crowned himself King of Sicily.

A bizarre episode followed thereon, one that, although it left no concrete results, is typical of the crisis that the times had reached. Charles demanded that the pope excommunicate Peter and his island subjects, and the pope, trapped by French influence, agreed. But this produced no effects, so Charles, who was already in his seventies, challenged Peter to a duel to decide the argument according to the ancient codes of feudal chivalry. To him this business was a private, personal issue between two gentlemen; Sicily and its people represented only an object of dispute. The encounter was to take place in Bordeaux, a neutral city still under the sovereignty of the English crown. The contestants were to appear there on June 12, 1283, each followed by ninety-nine Knights. It was to be a great party, to which all the ladies of the European aristocracy were invited.

Charles was on time, but Peter, although he had committed himself with an oath, failed to show up. Peter, therefore, was declared a coward and to have forfeited the prize by the code of chivalry. But, in his turn, Peter answered by mail to the effect that he had been in Bordeaux since May 31, disguised and incognito, and had counted more than three thousand of Charles's henchmen roaming the streets and waiting to ambush him. Charles answered that it was all a lie.

The argument soon attracted a large following. Public opinion was split down the middle: the pope backed Anjou and Dante was for Aragon. They talked about it for years. If nothing else, the event illustrated the fact that the norms of chivalry were bankrupt. They had set the law for the entire Middle Ages, when no one would have dared to break them—they were one of the strongest supports upon which the feudal structure had been built. Now even the lords made light of it; their relationships no longer were bound by the rules of honor but followed the more prosaic and utilitarian guidelines of "national interest."

The argument developed into a full-fledged war. The following year, in the Bay of Naples, the fleet of Aragon surprised and defeated that of Anjou led by the prince heir. Immediately afterward, however, both protagonists of the feud died. Charles's place on the throne of Naples was taken by Charles II, "The Lame," who had already demonstrated his competence as an admiral by letting himself be beaten in his own harbor; Peter was succeeded by two sons: Alphonse, his firstborn, kept the kingdom of Aragon, and James got the crown of Sicily. But Alphonse felt it more convenient for his own plans to reach an understanding with France, so, unbeknown to his brother, he promised the restitution of Sicily to the Anjou. As James was getting ready to defend himself, Alphonse died, leaving the throne of Aragon vacant, and the laws of inheritance gave the succession to James. When the latter assumed the rule of Aragon, he recognized the validity of the reasons that had prompted Alphonse to give Sicily back to Anjou, so he endorsed the agreement and for good measure married Charles's daughter.

But the Sicilians rebelled at this and gave the crown to Frederick, the third in line of the sons of Peter, and entrusted their armies to Roger of Lauria, the brave captain who had stood the siege of Messina. What followed was such an intricate series of events that we fear to recite it would make our readers' heads spin. Frederick appealed to James for a fleet, but while he was getting ready to start the festivities for its landing in Palermo, he saw the ships sail by the harbor and proceed to Naples, where they were delivered to Charles's command. During a naval battle along the Calabrian coast, Roger of Lauria leaped from his flagship into the flagship of Anjou, then proceeded to lead the French against his own ships to a victory at Cape Orlando, where six thousand Sicilians died trying to figure out whose commander Roger was, their own or the enemies'. On land, however, Frederick once more defeated the Neapolitan troops led by the Prince of Valois, Charles's cousin.

Finally, in 1302, by the Treaty of Caltabellotta Frederick was at last recognized as King of Sicily, with the understanding that after his death the island would return to Angevin rule. But later events and the resolution of the Sicilians were to decree otherwise.

Chapter 4

The Italian Scene

Between the death of the great Frederick and the downfall of his successors to the breakdown of his kingdom between the Anjou in Naples and the Aragon in Sicily half a century passed, and a crucial period it was for the future of Italy. For the last time an emperor had attempted to restore imperial power within its boundaries. There would be other emperors who would cross the Alps, but these were fatuous characters whose plans were without any solid foundation. With the passing of the empire of which only the title remained, the German supremacy in Italy ended, to be replaced by the French. This was the implication of the events following upon Frederick's death; now let us see their effects on the rest of the country.

By the end of the thirteenth century, Italy was totally fragmented; yet from the dust-cloud of her small political entities some were taking flight and beginning to apply a certain gravitational force on their neighbors.

In Piedmont there were three centers contending for supremacy: Savoy, Monferrato, and Saluzzo. But, for the moment, the ups and downs of their struggle had no impact on national history, not so much for geographic reasons, but rather because they were operating on different planes, so to speak. Piedmont had kept its feudal structures; in contrast, in the rest of Italy the few that had ever existed had long before disappeared. The *comuni* of Piedmont had scarcely flourished, and the cities were rickety—even Turin was just a village of mountaineers. The city halls and free courts of the urban middle classes did not rule there; power was still in the hands of Frankish lordlings ensconced in castles where the scent of chivalry still lingered. Counts and marquises formed alliances, arranged marriages, betrayed and battled each other in order to add a province or a fortress to their domains. But all this remained within a regional circuit; beyond the banks of the Ticino a new world began—the world of the free *comuni* that had long ago overthrown the bulwarks of the aristocracy and substituted an urban, commercial society for the agrarian and military society of the Middle Ages.

In the center of the rich plains of Lombardy, Milan had already carved out for itself a leading position with its industries, when Pope Gregory X, to remove the city from Anjou influence, appointed the Ghibelline Otto Visconti archbishop. The Visconti were already a very powerful family, sharing with the Della Torres the freedom of Milan. But if the appointment decided the outcome of the rivalry between the two families, it sparked an extraordinary political and dynastic adventure. Otto had a strong personality and quickly overwhelmed both the Della Torres, whom he imprisoned in steel cages without giving the matter a second thought, and the democratic institutions of the city, which in Milan had less popular support than in Florence. The Milanese, meanwhile, accepted the cardinal's nephew, Matthew, as vicar of the Emperor Rudolph of Habsburg and also as the people's representative in the government—in other words, they gave him full powers, which Uncle Otto, the archbishop, endorsed in the name of the Almighty. Matthew, moreover, promptly began to use his powers freely to strengthen not only his own position in Milan but also Milan's position within Lombardy. And if at the turn of the thirteenth century this process of expansion had just begun, yet it already foreshadowed the future role of Milan as one of the Italian capitals.

Genoa was another important capital. It developed into a position of prominence almost on the sly, as was noted by one of its chroniclers,

Jacob of Varazze, who wrote in slightly miffed tones: "We are surprised that while there are many cities in Italy that ancient historians often mention, there is little or nothing said about Genoa, yet so famous, powerful, and noble." But the fault with this state of affairs rested with the Genoese, for they left no trace of their doings even in their documents. All we know is that Genoa began with the noble family of the Obertenghi, which later divided itself into the branches of the Spinola, Embriaci, Castello, and Vento. These families represented the agrarian interests of the hinterland, while the bishop stood for the urban interests of the sailors, fishermen, craftsmen, and merchants. But their conflicts never, or very rarely, developed into the open struggle that rocked Florence and so many other cities. The two sides merged, instead, into a *compagne,* a "company," which first helped to establish a city government and then controlled it completely, as had the Florentine craft guilds in their own city. From there on, the aristocracy of Genoa continued to be an entrepreneurial one; it stayed in command of a bourgeois society where status followed efficiency rather than a coat of arms.

The great fortune of Genoa was its location, not only because of the great natural harbor on which it was situated, but also because of the ring of mountains that protected it from the wars between emperors, popes, and *comuni*. In fact the name of Genoa almost never appears in the roster of the "Leagues" that were so often formed to fight now against one enemy, now against another. Hidden in its odd corner between the Alps and the sea, unable to seek adventures in a bleakly barren hinterland, Genoa could only turn toward the sea to build an empire, and this is what it did.

Genoa's only competitor at the time was Pisa, the great Tuscan harbor of the Middle Ages. Pisa was an old Ghibelline city in which the emperor was represented by one of his viscounts. Here, too, however, a company that united noblemen, shipbuilders, and merchants in their common interest in seafaring was founded, and in practice it ruled the state, especially since the emperor had granted Pisa autonomy to keep the city on his side, since it was a handy counterweight against neighboring Florence, which was devoted to the popes. Helped by other maritime cities, the fleet of Pisa had prevented the Sicilian Arabs from landing on the Italian peninsula, and for a whole century it had remained unchallenged lord of the Tyrrenian sea: Corsica and Sardinia were colonies ruled by its consuls. But Pisa had also to worry about its back-country, which, owing to its less favorable location than Genoa's, was exposed to the greed of its rivals, Lucca and Florence, both of which were anxious to obtain an outlet to the sea. Thus, the downfall of Pisa was that it could not concentrate on a maritime policy because of the need to guard the lands behind it. Doom, in fact, approached Pisa from both sides at once.

In 1283 Genoa declared war on Pisa, or rather it changed into "hot" the cold war that for decades had strained relations between the two fleets. The basis of the contention was Corsica and Sardinia, which Genoa felt cramped its approaches. Pisa sent seventy-two ships, under the command of the Venetian admiral Morosini, to sack Rapallo and Portofino while the Genoese fleet, led by Oberto Doria, was somewhere else. The Genoese sailed back in a hurry and laid an ambush behind the Meloria Islands, a few miles from Pisa. As he was returning to his base, Morosini was deceived by the few Genoese ships he could see, the others being hidden by the rocky islands. He attacked thoughtlessly and in the ensuing battle lost twenty-three galleons and several thousand men.

The defeat had been severe, but it would not have been final had not Florence and Lucca thought the time ripe to attack Pisa, rationalizing their action with the ideological excuse that it was time to depose that city's Ghibelline administration. To avoid the danger, the Pisans entrusted their government to a Guelph count, Ugolino della Gherardesca. But despite della Gherardesca's success, when Charles of Anjou died in 1288 and Guelph fortunes seemed on the wane, the Ghibelline Archbishop Ruggero degli Ubaldini had Ugolino jailed in a tower with two of his sons and three nephews—where they all died of hunger. This multiple murder was a fairly ordinary event for the times, and we are aware of it only because Dante told the tale with all the strength of his indignation.

The activities in Pisa caused the war against Florence and Lucca

to flare up again and it finally ended in 1293, leaving matters more or
less as they had been before. Nevertheless, the great maritime republic
that had repelled the enemy Arab fleets and destroyed that of Amalfi,
its former ally, was now exhausted. Some claim that Pisa, like Ravenna, was betrayed by its own sea, which every year retreated further,
leaving bars of sand, but this is not the case, because it was advantageous for a harbor of those times to be as far inland as possible, and
the Arno River was perfectly navigable. The truth is that it was Pisa
that betrayed the sea, embroiled as that city was with the problems of
the land behind it. Pisa closed in upon itself and became a city of art
and learning; its glory was no longer the fleet, but the university.

There were two great Italian sea powers still left at the end of the
thirteenth century—Genoa and Venice—and their fortunes anticipated
by two centuries the great imperial successes of Spain, England, Portugal, and the Netherlands. If they had acted with a common interest
instead of waging war against each other, these two cities could have
built a world empire for Italy. But this would assume the existence of
an Italy, that is, of a feeling of national solidarity that was then lacking.

Venice also owed its fortune partly to the fact that it was cut off by
its location from the essentially land-based conflicts between papacy
and empire. While the isolation of Genoa was insured by the battle-
ments of the Alps, that of Venice relied on its ring of lagoons. Safe
within the labyrinth of sandy bottoms known only to its admirals,
the Venetian fleets had sallied forth to conquer the whole Dalmatian
coast, as far as Albania and Greece.

As soon as the Venetians went beyond Greece, however, they came
in conflict with Genoese ships, also out to conquer the Eastern markets.
But Venice had been there first. During the Crusades—in which no
Venetian had shed a drop of blood—Venice enriched itself by renting
the ships that transported the troops, then by obtaining the largest
"dividends" in the sack of the various cities, and finally by leaving in
every city of the East a bank, a warehouse, and a trading center. Its
strength was a stable monetary system based on gold (the famous
ducat that rivaled the florin of Florence in purity) and the most modern banking system of the times. Thus, while Florentine banks were

spreading over continental Europe, the Venetian and Genoese banks were acquiring primacy over the Orient.

Venice and Genoa were in virtual control of everything from the Tyrrenian and the Adriatic Seas to the Black Sea. Galata on the Golden Horn and Caffa in Crimea each had a Genoese *podestà* and an "abbot of the people" whose task was to regulate exchanges with the Tartars, the Russians, and the Persians. Most Greek islands and whole sections of Constantinople were Venetian: "They are," the Frenchman Vitry described them, "powerful men, rich and well armed, brave, traveling on magnificent ships they very well know how to steer even in the worst weather." In 1261 Niccolo and Matteo Polo left Venice, followed a little later by Marco, who was to walk alone all the way to China and then sail to Japan—a feat that is no less remarkable than the one Columbus accomplished.

The struggle between these two great republics remained for a while on the plane of business competition interspersed with piracy: when a Venetian fleet encountered a Genoese cargo ship, the latter would be captured, and vice versa. There had been minor skirmishes, at Lapasso and in the Black Sea, but toward the end of the century, in 1298, the first real battle took place. Seventy-eight Genoese galleons, led by Lamba Doria, bravely entered the Adriatic and, near the island of Curzolo, attacked one hundred Venetian galleons under the command of Andrea Dandolo; the Genoese sank sixty-five enemy ships and left fifteen thousand bodies floating in the sea. Among the dead was Dandolo, who, seeing that he was about to be captured, ran with all his might toward the main mast and split his skull against it. But Venice, unlike Pisa, did not let defeat deter it; it rallied to give back as good as it got.

The history of the two cities continued to unfold outside the Italian peninsula, which was little involved in its ups and downs. At the beginning of the fourteenth century, Genoa and Venice had no political plans for a united Italy; they fought everywhere, except in their own countries and for their own countries.

Another capital was Florence, which was just beginning to establish its supremacy over the rest of Tuscany. Its internal affairs were rocked by violent clashes between the two parties that at the time were splitting Italy in half: the Guelphs and Ghibellines. But in Florence the party conflict was aggravated by social turmoils produced by the city's industrial and economic progress. Control of the city was in the hand of the *arti,* or craft guilds, and the guilds, in their turn, were controlled by the banking and trading upper-middle class.

The middle classes had been forced to strive for a long time to free themselves from the old warring, landowning nobility that from its castles spread across the countryside had ruled the city for centuries. The noblemen who threatened the city had been given their lands and privileges by the emperors, so they were Ghibellines; therefore, Florence had been Guelph right from the start.

The citizens of Florence, gathered under their banners, had assailed one castle after another and forced their occupants to live in the city for at least several months each year, thereby depriving them of control to the access roads and preventing them from upsetting trade, as they had done in the past. The lords had to submit to these conditions, but they took with them to Florence their political passions and violent dispositions. They built palaces in town that looked like fortresses, competing to see who could erect the tallest and best-outfitted towers, and each formed his own *consorteria,* which was a kind of a small Mafia.

After a while the nobility underwent an ideological division: some, such as the Guidi counts, remained Ghibelline; many others turned Guelph in order to participate more effectively in the politics of a Guelph city and then, partly because of financial needs, slowly began to mingle with the upper-middle classes. The two parties fought each other with every weapon and seldom were hampered by the government, which was a thicket of institutions each of which paralyzed the other. According to law, the two highest officials of the city, the *podestà* and the *Captain of the People,* had to be strangers, in order to avoid bloodshed when one of the parties prevailed over the other. But violence occurred anyway, because the state had no means of preventing it. Indeed, the state itself became prisoner of the strongest side.

Every change meant slaughter or exile for the losing party. Thus,

in 1260, after the battle of Montaperti in which Manfredi's Ghibelline
armies led by Siena defeated the Guelph forces led by Florence, the
Ghibelline exiles returned to the city while the Guelphs left in droves.
But it did not last long: the arrival of Charles of Anjou in Italy and the
death of the two last Hohenstaufens, Manfredi and Corradino, delivered a fatal blow to the Ghibelline idea and to its supporters in
Florence.

Yet, despite all of its internal turmoils, Florence continued to expand
its supremacy over Tuscany. Pisa, its most powerful rival, had failed to
recover after the defeat of Maloria. Siena, after a period of ascendance
following its victory at Montaperti, waned with the decline of the
Hohenstaufen and of the empire. Moreover, Florence succeeded, by
dint of clever diplomacy, in enlisting the support of Lucca and Pistoia, leaving uncommitted only the city of Arezzo, a bastion of the
old landowning aristocracy, where everyone was a Ghibelline, even
the bishop. However, the decisive battle eventually took place, in
1290 at Campaldino. The Florentines won, becoming the leaders of
the Guelph coalition of central Italy. Thereafter, they could devote
all of their energies to their manufactures, banks, and internal quarrels.

Briefly, then, this was the picture of Italy at the start of its golden
centuries. Genoa, Milan, Venice, Florence, and Naples were its centers.
The existence of Rome was meaningful only in terms of the papal
court, and when the popes moved to Avignon, as they were about to
do, the *urbs* fell back among cities of the second class, which it remained until the end of the fourteenth century. Rome was a shabby
hamlet of between twenty and thirty thousand malaria-ridden inhabitants, with unpaved roads and crumbling monuments, its air wafted
once in a while by the breezes of a little rhetoric inspired by Augustan
memories.

This mosaic of states divided and struggling against each other
shared a condition that was common to all: the failure of civic institutions. Rivers of ink have been spilled to account for its causes, but
the causes were actually quite simple. The most immediate reason for
the failure of the city states was that their elective executive branches
had not been able to ensure order, the basic condition for civilized

coexistence. Everywhere, civic freedom had been compromised by quarrels among factions, as in Florence. And the tired populace was ready to exchange freedom for security, even if the latter was spiced with some oppression.

The second reason was that although the urban democracies had become more and more liberal, they still failed to give any executive power to the masses, which, therefore, felt estranged. In a city such as Florence, for instance, the fully enfranchised citizens who had any voice in government numbered between five and ten thousand, no more. The other sixty to seventy thousand inhabitants were "subjects."

A third cause had to do with the enlargement and increasing complexity of the economic processes. The *comuni* were born in the Middle Ages, which was a phase of suspended animation in the life of Italy and of Europe as a whole. They were a small world of closed-circuit craft shops that provided the countryside with manufactured items and received in exchange raw materials and foodstuff. But the advent of capitalism and the occurrence of an "economic miracle" had as their consequences an increase in production—which meant a necessity for an import-export market larger than the surrounding countryside. The ancient closed circuits were blown open; their self-sufficient structures fell into pieces: some "central planning" with a wider scope was in order. At first the *comuni* attempted to create federations, economic unions with strictly limited goals in which the townships participated on an equal footing, but the attempt failed. Thus, each *comune* was left to compete against all surrounding ones in an effort to develop its centripetal force or to gain the role of a "leader-state" among them. And when power was held in a single firm hand, it seemed that such goals were reached more successfully than when it was held by the precarious elective bodies, even if the firm hand was that of a tyrant.

To these substantive causes one should add one of ideological origin: the failure of Guelphism. Guelphs were the free *comuni* at the time they had fought the emperors and the feudal nobility that was trying to keep its fiscal authority over the townships. Florence was Guelph, not because it was devoted to the Church, but because its prelates blessed its flags when the citizens moved to dislodge the noblemen from the manors in which the emperors had placed them. After the death of Frederick and his two sons, the conflict was to all intents and purposes ended; the empire, reduced to the status of an honorific title, presented no more dangers, and the Ghibelline aristocracy was uprooted and scattered. Nevertheless, the Guelph ideal remained the myth of the townpeople's revolution, a "sacred principle" analogous to those of liberty, equality, and fraternity that lingered after the French Revolution. But this situation was reversed with the arrival of the Anjou, who, although lacking the imperial title, were threatening to accomplish what the real emperors had failed to do, namely, to institute a central lay power across the whole peninsula. The *comuni* had always fought such attempts when they had been initiated by Henry IV, Barbarossa, and Frederick, and they also had done so in the name of Guelphism, that is, of the Church. But now the Church had called in Anjou: How could the towns fight him in the name of the Church?

This dramatic problem came to a head as the new century was being opened by a papal Jubilee, and as we shall see later, its main characters were two extraordinary men: Pope Boniface VIII and Dante Alighieri. But, in the meantime, we may note that the ambiguities of the Italian situation had contributed to the bankruptcy of the city governments left without the flags under which they had been first formed. And flags have their importance, too.

Toward the end of the thirteenth century, the transition from *comuni* to *signorie* was already gaining momentum. Twenty cities in Piedmont and Lombardy submitted themselves to the Marquis of Monferrato. The Visconti were already lords of Milano, and the Della Scala of Verona. Da Comino were getting established in Treviso, Colleoni in Bergamo, Este in Ferrara, Bonacolsi in Mantua and Modena, Comeggio in Parma, Malatesta in Rimini, Ordelaffi in Forli. The age of the free townships was ending; that of the despots was just beginning.

Part II

THE BABYLONIAN CAPTIVITY

Chapter 5

Boniface VIII

THE FOURTEENTH CENTURY was ushered in by a splendid holiday: the Church Jubilee. This feast had not existed in the Church calendar and had never been held before; it was the brainchild of the pope then sitting on the throne: Boniface VIII.

It was a psychologically appropriate time for the Church, which in the past decades had gone through some harsh trials and temporary crises, to give a show of strength even if it was limited to the organization of a spectacle. With the death of Frederick II, whom Dante wistfully called "the last power of the Empire," the danger of being eclipsed by a lay state had practically disappeared. A number of vigorous popes had followed each other from 1198, when Innocent III had assumed the tiara, to Gregory X, who had died in 1276, and they had given strength and prestige to the papacy.

Boniface seemed to be the most appropriate successor for reaping the fruits of this long period of consolidation. He was a Roman of the proud and overbearing house of the Caetani counts, and he proved it by the method he used to ascend the throne. The Church had been left without official leadership for two and a half years after the death of Nicholas IV because the cardinals could not agree on a successor. And as often happens in such situations, they finally compromised on a colorless person whom everyone thought to be innocuous: a poor little

33

friar of the Abruzzi called Pietro da Morrone, who had never left his mountain hermitage near Sulmona.

When Pietro found out what was about to happen, he tried his best to escape, but he was captured and dragged to Naples, where they crowned him as Celestine V. The holy man was completely at a loss among the intrigues of the Papal Curia. At night he heard a voice booming through his room: "I am the angel sent to talk with you, and in the name of Gracious God I order that you cease to be a pope and forthwith return bein' a hermit."

That voice belonged not to an angel but to Cardinal Caetani, who had installed a primitive loudspeaker system in the walls of the bedroom. Poor Celestine would have liked nothing better than to "return bein' a hermit," but ignorant as he was of canon law, he had no idea how to go about the resignation that had no precedents in Church history. Caetani, on the other hand, a master of canon law more at ease in the statutes than the Gospels, gladly provided the arguments for what Dante later called "The great refusal." Thus six months after having taken up the tiara, Celestine laid it down again and became Friar Peter once more without ever having set foot in Rome. Fifteen days later Caetani replaced him as Boniface VIII, and his first order was to send for the arrest of Friar Peter, who had in the meantime returned to his mountains. The unlucky Peter attempted to flee across the Adriatic but was captured and locked up in the castle of Fumone, where shortly afterward he died of debilitation.

There is no record that Boniface felt the least pang of guilt at this, perhaps because he was not burdened by the weight of a conscience that could make him feel guilty. He openly denied the likelihood of a divine justice to which one's acts were accountable: heaven and hell, he used to say, are right here on earth. Hell is old age, ailments, and impotence; heaven is youth, good health, women, and handsome fellows—he had no prejudices against either sex. One day he shouted down a chaplain who was asking Jesus' help: "You fool! Jesus was a man like us. If he could do nothing to help himself, what could he do for us?"

He was a precursor of the Renaissance popes, an early Borgia full of earthy cynicism, despotic and theatrical. He improved upon every sin with great conscientiousness. He was a glutton who on a day of fast mistreated his cook for having served a dinner with only six main dishes. He was greedy of riches: his clothes were embroidered with jewels and on his table sprouted fifteen small trees made of gold. He was superstitious and practiced magic: his knives had snake-horn handles, he carried an Egyptian coin in his pocket, and on his finger he wore a ring snatched from Manfredi's corpse—all implements to ward off the evil eye. He was a confirmed gambler who played with dice made of gold, but woe to the man who dared to best him. More than everything else, he thirsted for power. The day he was elected, he donned the tiara and asked the audience whether they considered him to be God's representative to mankind. When everyone agreed to that, he changed into a crown and, wielding a sword, asked whether they also accepted him as emperor. Given his character, no one disagreed, and with this deed his politics were set on their course.

Blasphemous and unbelieving as he was, the pope was full of the Church's majesty and did not allow any doubts to be cast on its earthly supremacy either. According to Boniface, the Church owned and ruled not only souls but everything else too. Therefore the thrones of every state belonged to the Church, and the kings had only temporary franchises over them. Given his attitude, it follows that Boniface would not stand for any dissension within the Papal States. Thus when the Colonna attempted to create trouble, they were excommunicated and forced to flee. The pope confiscated their estates and razed their stronghold in Palestrina, spreading salt over the ruins to purify them. When Emperor Albert of Austria sent a humble monk as his envoy to the pope, Boniface kicked the monk in the face, breaking his nose and causing a severe hemorrhage.

But not everybody was resigned to such high-handed treatment; King Philip of France, for instance, reacted by forbidding his clergy to send on to Rome the tithes they had collected in his country. This was a sore blow to the finances of the Church, since France was its fattest single contributor, and it was also a blow to the prestige of the Papacy. It was then that Boniface announced the Jubilee: partly to recover political ground, partly to replenish his empty coffers. And the enterprise could not have been better suited to the dramatic personality of the man, to his great directorial talents.

The advertising campaign had been perfect. For months and months preachers announced the pilgrimage from every pulpit of Europe, praising the benefits to be derived therefrom: the redemption of the soul and the pleasures of travel. The constant drumming had its effects: hundreds of thousands of people, on foot, horseback, or carts, answered the call. Given the length of the trip and its dangers, most pilgrims made out their wills beforehand. And many of them actually died on the road, assured of going directly to heaven. Throughout the year, Rome witnessed a daily turnover of thirty thousand visitors. They marched in long columns to the grave of the Apostles, where they were given a blank remission of all their sins, and where the coins they were expected to drop were gathered up by two deacons armed with shovels. The average daily take was a thousand pounds, a stupendous figure for the times.

Nobody knows where all the guests slept, but it is clear that it was a good business for the Romans. At last the city could again feel it was *caput mundi* (capital of the world) and enjoy the plenty and the feasting of colorful, multilingual crowds.

Among the pilgrims, there were many big names: powerful lords and princes of royal blood. More important perhaps, there were also two Florentines whose names were not yet known beyond the walls of their city. One of them was Dante Alighieri, who apparently drew the inspiration for his great masterpiece from what he saw in Rome. Whether this is in fact true or not is in doubt, but at best we are sure that he was among the pilgrims because later he remembered the event in two famous tercets, in which he also tells us that traffic in the city moved on the right. If the festivities left an indelible impression on the poet, then in his mid-thirties, his compatriot, Giovanni Villani, was not taken in by them. A merchant and a son of merchants, Villani watched the show with more realistic eyes. He wrote that in Rome he discovered the masters of rhetoric: Vergil, Livy, and Sallust—although his own style in the *Chronicles* owes little to these models. But behind the spectacular staging of the jamboree he also discovered the symptoms of Roman decadence that he accurately noted down.

There were, of course, many other men from Florence, and some of them came incognito, among them Corso Donati, head of the "Black" party, who had been banned from Florence and was now being eagerly made welcome by the pope, who was plotting the annexation of Tuscany to the Papal States. Boniface, however, had insufficient forces for the enterprise and therefore opened negotiations with King Philip of France. There was ample precedent for such a procedure; a pope, after all, had appealed to the French thirty years earlier to send an army to relieve him of the menace provided by the sons of Frederick, Manfredi and Conrad.

The deal Boniface had suggested to Philip was that the latter should send another army to help Anjou, but that, on its way through Florence, the army would subdue that city in the name of the Church. Donati's Blacks were to help the coup from within. Philip, a miserly and calculating King, was not fond of risks and detested the clergy, but his brother, Charles of Valois, was without a job and burdened with fourteen children, among them ten girls who had to be given dowries. Partly in order to get rid of him, therefore, Phillip decreed that Charles should attend the pope as Captain General and Pacifier of Tuscany. However, Philip kept his brother short of men and money. But Boniface then arranged for Charles to marry Caterine of Courtenay, theoretically heiress to the Byzantine Empire, and Charles— whom the Florentines had derisively nicknamed "No-land Charlie"— was enthralled by the imperial bait (which, incidentally, was to remain a mirage) and persuaded his brother the king, to give him stronger support.

The bargain was sealed just as the Jubilee neared its end, toward the end of the year. But instead of rallying to their own defense, the Florentines became even more divided. Quarrels, arson, and pillage wrecked the city, so that Charles was able to enter it with only a handful of men, and the citizens received him as a real peacemaker. The operation, however, ended in a massive reprisal of the Blacks against the Whites, in which Dante himself was implicated because in the meantime the emperor and the pope had had a stormy squabble and their joint plan for Florence had fallen through.

During one of his authoritarian fits, Boniface had sent a papal bull to the King of France reiterating his claims to sovereignty over all the temporal rulers of the world. Philip, who on this issue was adamant, read the message to his court, summoned the curse of God on anybody who dared to recognize an earthly ruler greater than he, and burned the letter in the public square. Boniface in his turn excommunicated Philip. Philip answered by assembling a council, which indicted the pope on charges of irreligion, traffic in holy things, sorcery, adultery, and murder. Moreover, Philip sent his minister Nogaret to Rome with the task of organizing a conspiracy against the pope with the help of the Colonna family.

Nogaret was a good man for the job: both his parents had been burned at the stake by the courts of the Inquisition so he had an old account to settle with the Church. He had no problem finding accomplices in Rome, and on the night of September 6, 1303, he entered the papal apartments in Anagni (the pope's summer estate, a dozen miles southeast of Rome) with Sciarra Colonna and summoned the pope to Philip's council. The old man, loaded with sin and vice but full also of courage and pride, answered, "Take my head, here is my neck!" but would not budge under threats or violence. It is claimed that Sciarra slapped his face, but this is doubtful. The conspirators kept him prisoner until Cardinal Freschi came to the rescue with a company of men. Meanwhile, the populace of Anagni, who up to then had had a good time shouting, "Death to Boniface, and long live the King of France!" turned about, reversed their chant, and forced Nogaret to flee in a great hurry.

Two weeks later, Boniface returned to a Rome bloodied by internal warfare. He was lacerated by kidney stones, and his howls of pain could be heard all over St. Peter's square. The crowds had pillaged the Lateran palaces (the papal residence until it was moved to the Vatican), stealing even the hay out of the stables. In his agony Boniface reviled and cursed everybody, and he died as he lived: letting out religion.

Chapter 6

HENRY VII

THE DEATH of Boniface failed to appease Philip's hatred. For seven years the vindictive king insisted on a trial of the deceased pope, and finally he succeeded. A Church tribunal was assembled at Grosean in 1310, and the indictment was opened by six ranking prelates who supported the most grievous charges with their testimony. Boniface, they alleged, had denied the resurrection of both the body and the soul. He had been of the opinion that a dogma was an expedient for keeping the populace in its place with the threat of fire and brimstone. He had declared absurd the idea that Christ was man and God at the same time. He had laughed at the virginity of Mary and at the claim that a consecrated wafer could change into the body of Christ. "Only idiots can believe such nonsense," he had said. "Intelligent people must pretend to believe, then use their brains to make sense of it all."

The charges are too much in line with the man's character to be all unfounded. But even Boniface's most ardent foes realized that if they were to be admitted publicly, this would bring a fatal blow not only to the pope's memory but to the whole of the Church and the existing social order as well. Finally, even Philip recognized the danger and allowed that the trial be adjourned to the following year's council. There the cardinals bore witness unanimously in favor of the deceased, praising his orthodoxy and good morals. Two knights flung their gauntlets on the witness stand, to challenge, according to the rules of honor, anyone who dared assert the contrary. No one took up the gauntlets—which was considered to be a conclusive proof of Boniface's innocence—and the case was dismissed.

Even so, the trial had been a disaster for the Church. In fact, that august body wouldn't have allowed it to happen in the first place, had not an event of extraordinary importance occurred in 1305: the removal of the papacy to Avignon. This development, that was to have important consequences for many centuries to come, is worth going into in more detail.

We can't say whether all the moral and ideological crimes imputed to Boniface were true, but he certainly was responsible for an involuntary offense: he had made the move to Avignon necessary, or at least possible. The rivalry among Roman nobles had been revived by his authoritarianism and nepotism. There were too many accounts to settle, too many feuds to avenge: the air of Rome had become unfit to breathe.

The successor of Boniface, Niccolo Boccasini of Treviso, Benedict XI, tried his best to restore the peace. The son of a modest family of accountants, Benedict had gone to Venice as a private tutor, and after he had entered the Dominican order, he gained a reputation as a redoubtable theologian. He also had good diplomatic sense and used it well during some missions as legate to Hungary, Silesia, and Poland. At the conclave of 1303, when he realized that his election to the throne was not assured through the inspiration of the Holy Ghost alone, he helped it along with the payment of fifty thousand florins—but this is nothing to be outraged at, since it was the habitual thing to do.

Benedict acted wisely after his election. To restore the Church's prestige he punished those responsible for the Anagni disorders and at the same time sought to pacify Philip so as to dissuade him from trying Boniface. Not being able to achieve this latter end, he waited his time and tried at least to free himself from the oppressive French tutelage that bore down on Rome and the rest of Italy from both Paris and Naples. His most dangerous "fifth column" was the Black party in Florence, which was by now in control of the city. Benedict sent one of his trusted legates to effect a reconciliation that would allow the exiled Whites to return home and help restore a measure of political balance. But the Blacks aborted the plan by setting off riots and fires, then blaming their enemies for it.

Thoroughly incensed, Benedict excommunicated the whole city and ordered the ringleaders to appear in Perugia for an inquest. The first depositions were given on July 6, 1304, and the next day the pope passed on, owing to unknown causes. According to a rumor, a young man disguised as a nun had brought him a basket of poisoned figs. The event might be fictitious, but again the characters involved make it quite credible.

The throne became again a stake in the factional rivalries that contended for it with violence and deceit. Villani claims that the 1305 election was decided by a plot between an Orsini and Niccolò of Prato, who broke the rule that forbade cardinals in a conclave to see each other privately and kept meeting at night in a lavatory. As a result, when the winner was announced, the cardinals who had voted against him shouted, "The toilet has backed up!"

The man so greeted was Bertrand of Got, Archbishop of Bordeaux, who took the name Clement V. History has not been merciful to this pope, placing the blame for the decision to move the papacy to Avignon on him and holding him responsible for its sixty years of serfdom to the kings of France. The fact is that by the time he donned the tiara, Clement was already a prisoner of Philip and the French cardinals, who had a majority in the conclave and would not permit him to return to Rome.

Clement had to comply. He was a frugal man, pious and melancholy, eaten away by insomnia and nervous disorders and threatened by a fistula that was to kill him in a few years. Yet despite all his troubles, Clement tried to do what was in the best interest of the Church, and his choice of Avignon was probably a relatively wise compromise. The city did not belong to the French crown; it was owned by the Anjou of Naples. Clement hoped to be safer there than in Rome, and to be freer than he would have been in Paris. He warded off Philip's interference as well as he could, now humoring him, now resisting for a while and then yielding part of the way. He had reluctantly endorsed Boniface's trial, but later he was able first to adjourn it and then have the charges dropped. It was a good success, and not the only one he achieved. Three years before Boniface's charges were finally dropped, he had given another proof of independence in an act that was to have wide political repercussions, especially in Italy.

The position of Holy Roman Emperor had just become vacant. Although no real power corresponded to the title any longer, it still appealed to quite a few little kings and princes without great states or strong armies, who hoped at least to enrich their coats of arms. Philip, who ruled a great nation and—considering the times—a large army, couldn't care less for the imperial crown, but he did still have to help his brother Charles to get something out of life. Charles had become a general of his Anjou cousins, but without much success. Leading their troops, he had attempted to win back Sicily, but the Aragonese had beaten him and he returned to France, more "no-land" than ever. Philip thought that the imperial crown would give his brother at least status, and above all it would relieve the court of his awkward and peevish presence.

But the last word was the pope's since he was supposed to crown the emperor. And Clement, though French himself, did not want to appoint another Frenchman. He preferred a neutral candidate instead, someone such as Henry of Luxembourg who wasn't strong enough to do much harm even if he had wanted to descend upon Italy. Weak as he was, Henry could serve as a neat counterweight to the Anjou who were scheming more and more openly all around Rome.

Unfortunately, Prince Henry, romantic and somewhat balmy, had his head definitely turned by the unexpected promotion. He decided that he had to be crowned in Rome, like Charlemagne and Barbarossa, and the pope promised to meet him there for the ceremony. The news of his coming was enough to divide the whole country immediately, as had always happened in the past and would again happen in the future whenever a foreign ruler set foot within its borders. Almost all the newly established *signorie* of the north—the Visconti, the Della

Torre, the Gonzaga, the Este, the Malatesta, the Polenta—aligned themselves on Henry's side; against him were, of course, the Anjou of Naples and the Blacks who still controlled Florence.

Those old ideological concepts Guelph and Ghibelline were trotted out again, but it was very obvious how out of touch and inappropriate they had become. It is true that Henry represented the lay power of the empire, but this time it was in alliance with the Church against another lay power: the French kings in Paris and Naples. The *comune* governments, who had achieved their independence under the pope's flag, could not rally around it any longer; and if this did not produce their downfall, it certainly contributed to it.

Henry started on his way with his wife, Marguerite of Bramant, his brothers, Valeran and Baudwin, his brothers-in-law, Amedeus of Savoy and Guy of Flanders, and other highly placed gentlemen, but without much following. The lack of armed force might not have decided the issue if it had been compensated for by a profusion of cash. But the Italians soon discovered that the emperor's treasury was also meager: it could all fit into a little cart of a size that any number of Florentine bankers could have matched without the least trouble.

In the north the reception awaiting Henry bordered on the enthusiastic: the Marquesses of Savoy and Monferrat rode out to meet him; the Milanese lit up their city; Dino Compagni, Cino da Pistoia, and Francesco da Benvenuto were among those who sent messages of warm welcome, topped only by Dante's almost biblical epistle. The festivities were marred only by a small, yet significant, incident. According to custom, Henry was supposed to be invested in Milan with the crown of Italy before he went on to don the imperial crown in Rome. The crown of the Italian kings was a crude iron contraption, but it had graced Theodoric's* brow, and it was said that its metal came from one of the nails of the Holy Cross. The crown was held as a sacred relic in the cathedral of Monza, but when they sent for it in order to crown Henry, it couldn't be found. It had disappeared; nobody knew anything about it. Only years later did a Jewish junk

* Theodoric the Great, c. 454–526, King of the Ostrogoths, conquered and ruled northern Italy from about 488 to his death. *Trans.*

dealer bring it out again; he said that Guido Della Torre had pawned it for a small loan. But the whole incident gives us an idea of how high an esteem the Italians had by now for the title of King of Italy. Henry had to make do with another crown that a goldsmith from Siena put together for him on the spot. It was much more beautiful than the one that had been lost: it had more gold, finely chased; it had more jewels; but it lacked several centuries of history.

The coronation ceremonies were not yet over when poor Henry started having troubles. He was asked to arbitrate when a disagreement ensued between the Visconti and the Della Torre families of Milan, and since he pronounced himself in favor of the former, half of the city turned against him. Henry therefore left under a cloud, and the cities of Cremona, Lodi, Pavia, and Brescia locked their gates shut at his approach. Bologna followed their example. Meanwhile, King Robert of Naples began gathering troops. The direction and financing of the resistance came from Florence, despite Dante's fiery objections.

Henry was too simple to figure out what had gone wrong. He had done no one harm, had levied no taxes or serfs. He had only asked for a formal recognition of his title and could not understand why more than half of Italy had risen in arms to deny his claim. Since Bologna and Florence were blocking all the land routes, he marched on to Genoa, planning to reach Rome by sea. He was concerned about missing his date with the pope, but on the way he found out that Clement had changed his mind, and under orders from King Philip had dispatched a cardinal to do the imperial crowning. By then all of northern Italy was in uproar, and Henry's staunchest supporters, with Cangrande Della Scala in the lead, had to abandon him precipitously to defend their own states, which were threatened by their neighbors.

At Genoa, Henry was welcomed by an epidemic of cholera that took away Marguerite, his young and handsome wife. But not even this could sober him up from his infatuation with the crown that awaited in Rome; he wanted it at all costs, with childish stubbornness, believing it possessed who knows what arcane powers. Henry had been born and raised in the Luxembourg. An upstart among the rulers of his time, a provincial aristocrat, he believed in symbols, heraldry, the rules of precedence. He left Genoa for Pisa, where all the White Florentine exiles had gathered to greet him; among them were Dante and a certain Master Petracco holding by hand a seven-year old boy, the future Petrarch. From there Henry went on to Rome, where three cardinals finally crowned him emperor in the Lateran on June 29, 1312.

But disillusion soon replaced his elation. King Robert of Naples didn't even bother to answer when asked to vow fealty to the empire. Henry therefore decided to get tough and borrowed ninety galleys from Genoa and Pisa in order to attack Naples. But the pope, under pressure from Philip, sent a veto from Avignon. As a result, Henry sent back the fleet, gathered his men, and rode against Florence, only to realize that the city had already mobilized ten thousand foot soldiers and five thousand knights, double the numbers in his own army.

Foiled again, Henry made an aboutface and headed once more toward Naples. Perhaps he was following someone's suggestion, or maybe he only wanted to end his romantic and outdated adventure with a glorious death on the battlefield. But even this was denied him. Taken ill with high fever in Buonconvento near Siena, he died on August 24. Public opinion charged a monk, Bernardino da Montepulciano, with having poisoned the wafer that the emperor took for communion. It may not be true, but the method had been used often enough before, and it would be used again.

Those in Italy who opposed France and the Anjou went into deep mourning: the northern lords sent condolences to each other, and Dante raised his personal lament in the last chapters of the *De Monarchia,* the essay he had been writing to substantiate the validity of Henry's designs. Pisa, faithful to the last, demanded the emperor's remains and rendered them solemn honor. And thus ended the last attempt to establish a lay power in Italy, which could now return undisturbed to fratricide, its true and only vocation.

Chapter 7

DANTE

DANTE was not only a witness but an active participant in these convulsive events; therefore, his version of them is to be accepted with some reservations as the partial viewpoint of a victim, and a Florentine one at that. But no poet has better embodied his times than did Dante, with all its greatness and its meanness, its faith and its superstitions. His life is a document in which one can trace the whole history, though disfigured by passion, of contemporary Italy.

Dante was born in 1265, five years after the battle of Montaperti, when the Ghibellines had regained supremacy in a Florence defeated by Siena and its imperial allies. His real name was Durante, and he belonged to a Guelph family that, given its lack of substance, did not threaten the new rulers and therefore had not been banished. The Alighieris were descended from a family called Elisei, one of whose members, Cacciaguido, had been a crusader in the Holy Land and thereby acquired a patent of nobility for his household. Later the dynasty had split into two branches, the Alighieris and the Del Bellos, but neither achieved any prominence. Dante's father, Alighiero, owned a little land and some houses, but not enough to support his family, so apparently he helped round out his income by practicing a little usury on the side, though on a very limited scale. That he must not have amounted to much we infer mainly from the fact that Dante never spoke of him; it makes one think that the son had no great respect or affection for his father.

Alighiero had married Bella, a woman about whom the only thing we know is that she died after having given life to that one son. The child was somewhere between three and five years of age at the time, and he was never to mention her, either, perhaps because he could not recall her. Instead, Dante had a stepmother Lapa, who gave Alighiero three more children: one male and two female. Many biographers hold that Dante had an unhappy childhood with a mother not his own and siblings who were half-brothers and half-sisters. But they have no evidence to offer except Dante's adult personality, which was uniformly aloof and melancholy. The few references to his relations that he did leave suggest the opposite, namely, that they were very close and helpful, especially in adversity. A passage from the *Vita Nova* relates that his half-sister, Tana, cared for him lovingly during a sickness, and that Francesco, a half-brother, loaned him quite a bit of money and then followed him into exile voluntarily.

There is still a house called "Dante's home" in Florence, but it is certainly not the one in which he was born and grew up, since that was pulled down when he was exiled; the punishment for defeated political enemies included the demolition of their homes. The house stood in the neighborhood in that section of town then called "sixth of St. Peter's Gate." What it was like, we don't know, but the houses of the time did leave a lot to be desired as far as comfort is concerned: they lacked plumbing, the floors were packed earth covered with straw that rotted and stank, the windows were made of wooden planks, lighting was taken care of by torches, and heating by small clay pots containing live coals.

Florence, then, was not the stupendous city of today. It had about fifty thousand inhabitants, and despite the fact that a second ring of walls had just been built to acquire more space, there wasn't much room to breathe and the streets were still narrow and meandering. The only imposing and artistically valuable building was St. John's Baptistry, not yet covered in marble. The city produced an overall impression of harsh severity, the result also of the tall, narrow, threatening towers built by the nobility that surrounded the city like an armed encampment. The only beautiful thing about Florence was the view: a crown of hills among which the Arno rolled. All the houses rose on the right bank of the river and were connected to the opposite bank by only one bridge, the *Ponte Vecchio*.

All the schools were run by the clergy, and they were broken up into two divisions, the lower called the *Trivium*, the upper the *Quadrivium* (*Trivium* means the place where three roads meet, *Quadrivium* where four roads meet. The *Trivium* was a curriculum that included grammar, logic, and rhetoric; the *Quadrivium* was comprised of arithmetic, music, geometry, and astronomy). Dante probably attended both divisions in the church of St. Maria Novella, which was also where Cimabue had studied. One shouldn't think that he learned much there. For a start, books were lacking: beside the Gospels few books were even known because the Latin works that had escaped the barbaric invasions were still buried in the archives of monasteries and very little had been written in the entire Middle Ages. When Dante had finished his formal education, he knew how to read and write, perform the four arithmetical operations, translate more or less accurately from corrupt medieval Latin. Perhaps he also had some vague notions of history and philosophy—which then were synonymous with theology—but nothing more.

We know of only one event in his entire childhood, the one that was to have a decisive effect on his whole life and works: the meeting with Beatrice. Historians have debated often enough the reality of her person. Some believe her to be a character of pure fancy; but it is now commonly accepted that she was the daughter of Folco Portinari, a highly esteemed banker in Florence. Almost the same age as Dante, she later married Simone de' Bardi and died in 1290, probably of childbirth.

Dante places their meeting at a children's party in 1274, when they both were nine years old. Such dates, however, are not to be completely trusted because Dante respected the superstitious meaning of numbers more than their exactness. His fondness for the number nine, the third product of three, which he believed to be the perfect number, is amply illustrated in the structure of the *Divine Comedy*: the verses are in tercets, each one of the three *cantiche* is divided into thirty-three *canti*; Hell has nine circuits and Purgatory nine cliffs, and so on. When Dante further tells us that their second meeting took place only when they were both eighteen, it suggests that he manipulated the calendar somewhat to make his numerical symbolism fit.

In his first work, the *Vita Nova*, Dante tells us that he was thunderstruck by the subdued and pure beauty of the little girl all dressed in white, to the point of being unable to forget her for the rest of his life. It is possible that it was at this meeting that Dante first experienced sexual arousal and that that is why the memory of the meeting remained so clearly imprinted in his mind. The rest might have been added by the poetic conventions of his times, of which more will be said later.

After finishing school, Dante had another teacher, from whom he learned much more. The man was Brunetto Latini, a notary who enjoyed considerable status, and not only in his professional sphere: his far-ranging culture, good breeding, and refinement singled him out as an idol of salon society and a choice diplomat. The city had employed his services more than once, even to the extent of sending him to Spain as an ambassador during the struggle against Siena and Manfredi. He was in Spain when the imperial host won at Montaperti and the Ghibellines returned to Florence to do their vengeance. A Guelph, Brunetto stayed away, between Paris and Montpellier, and wrote a *tesoretto* in French—a kind of encyclopedia that summarized the knowledge of the epoch. After the battle of Benevento, which restored his party to power, Brunetto returned home and brought with him a breath of the fresh breeze of rationalism that he had absorbed in France. His thoughts were largely unoriginal, but he had traveled and seen much, and he could talk well. He was also a good citizen, honest and efficient as a public official, and a trustworthy man of his party. Only his private life left something to be desired because of his lack of bias against either sex, but this made no great impression in the Florence of those times—or of today, for that matter.

Many have thought that Dante actually took lessons with Brunetto, since in the *Inferno*—where he had been put for the vice alluded to above—Brunetto is greeted affectionately as "master," but their relationship was not academic in a formal sense. Dante was only one of the young writers who gathered around Brunetto and formed what would now be called the "new wave" of Italian literature, which Dante himself was later to give the name that has passed into history: *stil nuovo,* or New Style.

It is perhaps useful at this point to trace down, in a parenthesis, as it were, the origins of this new literary style. Italian poetry was nothing more than an offshoot of the Provençal literature developed in France two centuries earlier. France had been the first country in Europe to recognize as a true language the tongue spoken by its people, referred to as "vulgar" from the Latin *vulgus* (people), which was a mixture of the Latin imported by the Romans, the Celtic spoken by the tribes of Vercingetorix, and the German introduced by the Franks. Actually two "vulgar" languages were developed, each taking its name from the word they used for "yes": *hoc* and *oui.*

The first literary achievements of these archaic French languages were the *chansons de geste,* a cycle of epic and religious ballads composed during the days of chivalry and the Crusades. The *chansons* did not become very popular in Italy for several reasons: first, knighthood had barely taken root in the country; second, Italians were not much involved in the Crusades; and third, Latin there had been the real language of the people, rather than an imported tongue, so it survived longer even though it was no longer commonly spoken.

But toward the end of the twelfth century, the great mystic and conquering impulse that inspired the adventures in the Holy Land exhausted itself also in France. And a new poetry became fashionable at the courts of the lords that still ruled over that country: lightly ironic, irreligious, and shot through with Arab influences. The two most exalted patrons of this poetry were William of Poitiers and Aquitaine, who had lost his faith while defending it in Jerusalem, and his daughter Eleanor, who was to become twice queen: of France first, then of England, two unrepentant libertines who devoted themselves to sensuous and intellectual pleasures with the thoroughness that their predecessors had dedicated to wars and religious zeal.

The new poetry was known as *gai saber,* or "merry science"; its bards were *trouvères,* the troubadours, who naturally reflected their protectors' tastes and world-view. In those times poets were not paid royalties; they lived at the expense of some powerful man whose whims they had to satisfy. Their life at court was, however, pretty easy. The lady of the house graced them with her sympathy and often conceded them her favors, and by dint of mixing with the gentry they began considering themselves of that number too. They wore splendid cloaks woven in gold and lined with fur and took part in hunts and tournaments. For the pleasure of their aristocratic hosts, they usually composed music as well as lyrics, and at the end of banquets they sang their songs to the accompaniment of a lute.

Their poems had several forms. The *chanson d'amour* was a love song; the *tenson* had a moral or philosophical message. The *sirventès* was a song of war, while the *complainte* sang of grief and death. The *serenade* was a nocturnal song, and the *pastourelle* consisted of a dialogue between a knight and a shepherdess. As for the pattern of composition, the highest praises went to the *sestina,* a complicated poem constructed of six six-line stanzas, the six last words of which are repeated each time in a different order in each stanza and finally in the three-line *envoi,* which concludes the poem. The form was invented by an Arnaldo Daniello, whose work Dante attentively studied and very much admired.

This poetry was much easier to transplant than the *chansons de geste,* because it relied more on technique than on inspiration, and its conventional subject-matter was rather universal. Married love was considered too commonplace and was therefore severely excluded; consequently the lady who inspired the poet had to remain featureless so as not to be recognizable by her husband. As a result, the poems were highly allusive and written in a plaintive, evasive vein. Only a few men were able to give them an original content: Bernard de Ventadour (whom Petrarch recognized, out of the goodness of his heart, second only to himself), Rambaldo de Vaqueiras, Peire Ramon, Folquet de Romans.

It was the Albigensian crusade that spread the seed of the troubadours into Italy. The Albigensian heretics had found protection on the lands of the great lords of southern France, who were also great patrons of poetry. This protection was not a result of the lords' theological inclinations; rather, since the aristocrats did not believe in anything, heresy was no obstacle to them. In fact, eventually they embraced heresy as the excuse to establish their independence from the central powers: the Church, which levied its tithes and got its fingers into every pie; and the kings of Paris, who pretended to be kings of France and tried to rule the whole country from their throne. For the Counts of Provence, Aquitaine, and so on, a break along religious lines was as good a way as any to reaffirm their autonomy from the center. Thus these lords took sides with the Albigensians. As a result, some lost their lives, others their estates; their courts were scattered; and the troubadours had to seek hospitality elsewhere. Many found it in Italy.

One of them had already lived there: Sordello da Goito, for whom Dante professed a deep admiration. The son of a small nobleman from Mantua, Sordello got tired of the country and chose the roaming life of a poet, ending up in the following of Count di San Bonifacio in Verona. He was handsome, eloquent, an untiring womanizer: to repay the count's hospitality, he seduced his wife, and after running away with her, he left her (or she him—it is not clear which). Partly to escape the wrathful count's assassins, but even more because he felt comfortable there, he emigrated to Provence, the homeland of the troubadours, and there he adopted their language and style.

Although Sordello was one of the best representatives of that school, its adoption in Italy was due not to him but to the exiles who had left France. Some of them found a haven in north Italy, where the feudal system had taken hold more deeply, producing a castle-based life style not too dissimilar from the one in Provence. The ladies, bored to tears inside their grim manors, were especially glad to open the doors to these wandering minstrels who carried with them a breath of fantasy, modernity, and eroticism, who offered what we would call nowadays an opportunity to escape. Others took to the southern roads instead, lured by Frederick's fame as a great sponsor of the arts. Frederick had a thing about poetry; he wrote some himself, and so did his sons Manfredi and Enzo, his chief advisor Pier delle Vigne, and several noblemen of his court—among them Rinaldo d'Aquino, Giacomino Pugliese, Guido delle Colonne, Jacopo de Lentini.

These men were the first to compose verses in a language that was not Latin, though it can't be said that it was Italian as yet, either. It was more a refined Sicilian dialect, especially in the hands of Cirello d'Alcamo, the most original and spontaneous of all those pioneers. But the themes were the ones brought by the troubadours, so that Sicilian poetry always kept its imitative qualities; to become thoroughly Italian, Provençal poetry had to get to Florence.

And it did arrive there shortly before Dante was born. Among the best known poets who began by imitating the Provençals were Guiltone d'Arezzo, Folcacchiero dei Folcacchieri, Arrigo Testa, Bonagiunta Orbiciani, Paolo Lanfranchi, Ciacco dell'Anguillara. But soon the unique climate of the city suggested new topics to their inspiration. In Florence, life did not revolve around the whims of a lord and his wife, but around political passions. Therefore the "message" of these first Florentine poets soon became "ideological," or "committed." Guiltone's best verses, for instance, are those that deal with the battle of Montaperti. But since it was, and is, impossible to start a school in Florence without immediately stimulating its antithesis, within a few years there developed the "new wave" in which Dante later also took part.

It is always difficult to trace with any assurance the genealogy of a school of poetry. In this case, the founder may have been Frederick's son Enzo, who, as a captive in Bologna, used to express the melancholy of his loneliness in verses that were reminiscent of those the troubadours had sung at his father's court. His voice did not reach the Florentines directly, but through Guido Guinizelli, a jurist and a philosopher, whose song "To Gentle Hearts Love Always Offers Harbor" became the *manifesto* of the New Style.

The difference between the New Style and the previous style consisted basically in the fact that, for the Provençals, love had been an aesthetic and sensuous feeling, directed towards an anonymous woman. The identity of the damsel who inspired the poem had to be disguised by the *senhal,* or pseudonym, for the very good reason that she usually was the lady of the house, and it was important to safe-guard the conjugal prestige of the husband who fed and clothed the poet. The New Stylists, on the other hand, removed all sexual content from their treatment of love, and having thus made love innocuous, they could openly address their work to any woman. Made ethereal and angelic, the poem's subject ceased to be a wife, or a daughter, or a sister; she was just a symbol of spiritual perfection, an instrument for reach-ing God. It was not the woman who counted any longer, but the feel-ing she produced, and it was this feeling that the New Stylists kept chewing on, turning it this way and that, exploring all its possibilities with a pedantic quibbling that, to tell the truth, was pretty boring.

The advocates of this new poetics were Cino da Pistoia, Guido Ca-valcanti, Lapo Gianni, Gianni Alfani, and Dino Frescobaldi. They were the kind of lovers of beauty who come up every two or three gen-erations, each time believing that they have discovered God only knows what. They preached what now is called "art for art's sake," a poetry uncommitted to anything, even to pleasing the lords who had supported the troubadours in their castles—this the New Stylists could afford to do, since they were members of aristocratic or rich merchant families. They were, in other words, the fair-haired boys of Florence.

Dante did not belong with them either by birth or by financial status. Rather thin by constitution and sulky in mood, with a shock of dark hair falling on his forehead, Dante admired from a distance those young men who had everything he lacked: a noble name and plenty of money. He especially admired Cavalcanti, ten years his senior, who belonged to one of the foremost families in Florence and was already famous as a poet. Guido was a haughty, lonely, impetu-ous man. When he was twelve years old, as a result of one of the many reconciliations between the two antagonistic parties, he had been mar-ried to the daughter of Farinata degli Uberti, the great Ghibelline leader. This political marriage did not grow into love, but Guido found ample solace with a girl by the name of Giovanna. He had quite a temper, and he often ended arguments by throwing rocks at his opponents.

Yet it was this man who opened the doors of the select circle of aesthetes to Dante, after the latter sent him a poem in the style of which Guido was considered to be the master. It is certain that Dante was moved to write this poem because poetry flowed in his blood, as future events were to clearly prove. Yet it is probable that he was also inspired by the desire to move up the social ladder. The troubadours had gone a long way to ennoble the poet's profession by living in the courts and choosing knights for the characters of their songs and by adopting the chivalrous ideals of honor, faithfulness, and justice. Thus there was created a strong relationship between aristocracy and poetry. But by now even in a commercial city such as Florence, the social class distinctions had become rigid. The 250 noble families lived by themselves and met each other in a very exclusive club called the Society of the Towers. The middle class in its snobbishness spent millions to raise itself to the nobility. Dante as a young man was no exception, and the sonnet he sent Guido was the only passport he could hope to use to gain entry into that set from which his birth had excluded him. Guido, whose own talent made him sensitive to others' abilities, gave him a hand and welcomed him into the club.

Thus began the only happy years of Dante's tempestuous life. Now he, too, was a member of the *jeunesse dorée,* the golden youth, and even though his purse was usually empty and the sleeves of his dress (which were the measure of one's social and financial rank) less colorful than his friends', the girls along the way would point him out to each other as the writer of poems that were beginning to make the rounds of the city.

His verse became popular, but more for the tunes to which it was played than for the content or the form of its lyrics. Like all his contemporaries, Dante put his poetry to music. He didn't compose the tunes himself, though apparently he knew music rather well, but he chose his partners shrewdly. Casella wrote the music to his "Love that Talks in my Mind," and Socchetto to "Oh Violetta, in Love's Shadow."

It is not known what sort of a life he led with his new friends. But it is no secret that they practiced very differently from how they preached, especially in regard to that spiritually ethereal view of womankind. When Guido got tired of enjoying Giovanna's exclusive favors, he set up a *ménage a trois* worthy of the most advanced twentieth-century French dramatic models with Lapo Gianni and a girl called Lapa. And Dino Frescobaldi's escapades, facilitated by his name, money, and athletic build, were the talk of the town.

The young poets argued the moral problems of the New Style with religious earnestness. For instance: Does a damsel betrayed by her lover have the right to take on a more faithful one? But they were also willing to pass the time in taverns involved in more frivolous endeavors.

Nevertheless, certain principles had to be upheld, and one of the tenets of courtly love dictated that Dante also elect some lady as an ideal for his poetry and his life. Probably this is why he remembered Beatrice. It wouldn't be at all strange if Dante's love developed out of his poetry, instead of the other way around, and it wouldn't take anything away from the greatness of its results.

He had had no more opportunities to speak with Beatrice. Dante claimed that in order to shelter her from gossip, he pretended to be interested in another girl, and then in still another. He must not have done this very discreetly though, because everyone in Florence was talking about his relationships as regular affairs. The rumor must have reached Beatrice too, because one day when they did pass each other in the street, she didn't return his greeting. This could make one think that she also was in love with Dante and had felt betrayed by him. But this wasn't the case. Beatrice knew that Dante had appointed her his Ideal, that he had told everybody that she was the source of all his inspiration, and it was flattering to have a poet at her feet, with no strings attached. But she was miffed to discover that as soon as he walked around the corner, he went to someone else to have a good time—and this also is quite human.

Years later, when they met again at a wedding feast—perhaps the one at which she married Simone de Bardi—Dante tells how the blood drained from his face and he began to shake so much that a friend had to drag him away while the women were winking at Beatrice, who smiled happily at her sweet revenge. They never saw each other again, apparently. Some historians say that right after this event Dante went to Bologna to finish his studies, at what was then the most prestigious Italian university. It is certain that he dwelt there, because he left behind a rusty sonnet about that city, but no one knows when. In any case, he didn't get a degree, and the only advantage he seems to have drawn from his stay was his friendship with Cino, exiled from Pistoia for political reasons.

Dante had until then kept himself aloof from politics, because among other reasons, the New Style credo discouraged any form of involvement. But Florence was continually rent by violence. Lately, the Guelphs had regained control after the collapse of the Hohenstaufen, although Pope Gregory X rescued the Ghibellines from the customary vengeances to avoid being overrun by the French. In 1273 a compromise was reached between the two parties, but Charles of Anjou made it ineffectual by intervening personally in the local strife and forcing the Ghibellines to escape. In 1279 Cardinal Latino was sent to the city to effect a final reconciliation, resulting in a new government composed of fourteen "Goodmen," eight of whom were to be Guelph and six Ghibelline—all fourteen supervised by three—later increased to six—priors.

It is impossible to keep track of all the developments in the civil administration of Florence. Each one represented a democratic gain, but the net effect was to reduce the city to impotence—as unfortunately democracy so often seems to end up doing, at least in Italy. The new government, based on a Captain of the People and a *podestà* (both aliens) and the priors—who after only a short time assumed all the Goodmen's powers—was called the *signoria*. Nobody knows how this form of government actually functioned; what we know is that it didn't work out well.

Despite its internal weakness, Florence had been able to pursue a vital foreign policy. At the head of the Guelph League of Tuscan cities, it had subdued all enemies save two: Pisa and Arezzo. After Pisa had been weakened by Genoa, the only contender to remain in the field was Arezzo, where the Ghibelline party of the whole country rallied around Bishop degli Ubertini, a priest who preferred a big stick to the Cross.

On June 2, 1289, the Florentine army under the command of an Angevin general, Amerigo di Narbona, and backed by reinforcements from the other Guelph cities of Tuscany descended on the enemy city to settle the accounts. Included in the army were twelve thousand men, among whom was Dante, then twenty-four years old. The enemy waited on the plains of Campaldino, nine thousand men strong, led by Ubertini, a Montefeltro, and a Guidi. The battle was fought on the eleventh, and according to Villani, it started badly for the Florentines, whose center was broken and dispersed by the foe. But the wings of their army held, and they closed in on the Aretines who had plunged through the opening. The latter left two thousand dead on the field, among them Bishop Ubertini, three Uberti, and Bonconte di Montefeltro—in other words the most eminent leaders. Among the Florentines who distinguished themselves in the struggle were Vieri Cerchi and Corso Donati, both of whom were destined to be talked about later.

In little towns near Campaldino people will still show you a ravine where Dante is supposed to have hidden in panic. But the story has become garbled. In fact, he had found himself in the middle of the combat and had been in grave danger. It is possible that he got scared, and it seems he admitted as much in a letter in which he described the battle and even drew its map, now unfortunately lost. However, he did not flee: the man was sensitive, but he was not a coward.

It is probable that during this campaign he met Cecco Angiolieri, a member of the army of Siena, a "beat" poet before the times who drove to despair his rich, miserly, and bigoted relatives. Cecco was about Dante's age, but he was already regular jailbait who loved only wine, dice, and whores. He regularly betrayed his ugly wife with Becchina, a cobbler's daughter who reciprocated his roguery and licentiousness blow by blow. After eating away his estate, he ended up, in Rome, a pauper so deeply lost in debt that after his death his sons refused to claim their inheritance. But he was a better poet than many of the New Stylists: behind his disheveled rhymes and boisterous tirades one senses the sadness of a man who has wasted his life. One cannot be certain that Cecco and Dante ever met in person, but if they did, they must have done so under the walls of Arezzo because that was the only time their lives overlapped. They were not made to be fond of each other. Later, Cecco was to dedicate three sonnets to Dante, jeering at the latter's inconsistency between preachment and practice —not an ill-founded charge, by any means.

After his return to Florence, Dante continued in the service: he took part in the campaign against Pisa, and by his own accounts he was in on the siege and plunder of the castle of Caprona. He was lying in bed with an illness after being discharged when he heard of the death of Folco Portinari, Beatrice's father. Florence engaged in solemn mourning for the civic-minded banker, who had, among other things, financed the hospital of Santa Maria Maggiore and was known as a "pillar of the state." A few months later his daughter followed him into the grave; she was only twenty-five years old.

Dante claims that he was absolutely undone by the news, that he expressed his grief in an open letter to the "Princes of the World," and that he became very angry watching from his window some passers-by behaving as if nothing had happened. Perhaps. But besides the passers-by he also noticed a woman leaning out of a window across the way who watched him with an expression of compassionate tenderness. Her concern kindled his gratitude. And since one thing leads to another, they ended up having a full-fledged "relationship." Many Dantean scholars assert that this woman was nothing less than the symbol of Philosophy, in which Dante immersed himself to find consolation. But whoever heard of a philosophy going by the name of Lisetta? And that she was a real woman of flesh and blood is proved also by the fact that when she attempted to take up Beatrice's place in Dante's heart, he broke off with her: something he did not need to do if she had been truly Philosophy. Then he up and got married.

Dante's first biographer, Boccaccio, tells us that his family married him off almost by force because he was dangerously losing weight and sleep, and that he acquiesced by default. Less romantic in fact, the truth emerged from a document dated 1277, which contains the notarized engagement contract between the twelve-year-old Dante Alighieri and Gemma Donati, a girl of the same age. The agreement had been prepared by their respective parents, as was customary at the time. So his marriage was not an emergency measure to save his health, but the result of long and careful planning. Gemma belonged to one of the most noble households and brought with her some dowry. Boccaccio describes her as selfish, mediocre, dull, and shrewish, but Boccaccio's hate for his own wife made him a sworn enemy of all wives. The evidence suggests that Gemma behaved very well toward her husband: helped him in need; brought up his children, whom he particularly ignored; and, as Boccaccio himself admits, might have been responsible for rescuing the first seven *canti* of the *Commedia* from oblivion.

If anyone was to blame, it was Dante. Right after the wedding he entered into a period of dissipation for which Guido in this life and Beatrice in the next were to reproach him severely. He fell in with a bad crowd, led by Forese "Bicci" Donati, Gemma's cousin. He spent his time among young ladies with such names as Fioretta, Violetta, and Pargoletta, whose virtue was not exactly unquestioned. But such activity did not prevent him from having a certain number of children by Gemma: three boys, Peter, Jacob, and, perhaps, John; and two girls, Antonia and Beatrice—although the two latter names might refer to the same person. It is not clear what he did for a living. Like everyone else who wanted to enjoy his full political rights, he too joined a guild, the guild of doctors and druggists. Why he chose that particular one, is a matter open to question; perhaps because not being engaged in any real profession, he could choose any one at random; or perhaps because anyone using chemicals belonged to that guild (Giotto belonged because he used colors, Dante because he used ink; both were guild members). At any rate, it must have been mostly Gemma's dowry that kept the family going.

Dante claims that this dissolute interlude of his life ended with a dream in which he beheld Beatrice's "wonderful vision." When he woke up, he swore to himself that he would say things about her that no other man had ever said of another woman. Perhaps this was the

beginning of the *Comedy's* taking shape in his mind. But besides the
dream, there was politics to give his life a new direction.

The conflict within the city had flared up again, although by now it
had lost all the ideological content it had had when the choice was between Church and Empire. But the empire was no more than a memory, and after the battle of Campaldino the Ghibellines were completely subdued. There remained the personal strivings for interest and
status. To preserve the peace, the city administration had resorted to
marriage as a method. Weddings were enforced by the state because
they affected national safety. Contrary evidence notwithstanding, it
was assumed that when two enemies married each other, hatred between their two families would be replaced by solidarity, a personal
interpretation of politics that has been inherited by Florentines down
to our own days.

Now that they didn't have the Ghibellines to cope with, the Guelphs
split into two camps against each other. The two factions were called
Whites and Blacks, on the model of Pistoia, where the leading Can-
cellieri family had divided itself into white and black branches and
polluted the whole city with its bloody hatred.

In Florence the quarrel broke out between two dynasties that contended with each other for socioeconomic primacy. The White party
was led by Vieri Cerchi, the Black by Corso Donati, brother of Forese
and cousin of Gemma Alighieri. The explosion of hatred was caused
by trivial status considerations. The Cerchi, who were high on money
but low on nobility, had just bought the most beautiful palace in Porta
San Pietro, the part of town where the Donati had been king of the
roost. And now Donati was being eclipsed by Cerchi's splendor.

Corso was not the kind of man who would take such an outrage
lying down. Descendant of a long line of warring ancestors, he had
kept the pride and the insolence of his caste. Handsome, brave, sar-
castic, he was nicknamed "The Baron," and his leadership in the "Society of Towers" went uncontested. He could not let the son of a
farmer such as Vieri Cerchi, who had struck it rich in business and
bought a knight's title for himself, challenge his position of eminence.

Vieri might not have had blue blood, but he knew how to use his money. Less overbearing and colorful than his competitor, he was his match in bravery and tenacity. He slowly attracted into the sphere of interest of his banking activities many of Corso's powerful allies, such as the Cavalcanti, Tornaquinci, Pazzi, and some of the Frescobaldi. For a while everything proceeded according to custom, including the bloodshed that every once in a while occurred between the two sides: Florence had always had parties that shed each other's blood. But the family feud exploded into a civil war when Boniface VIII began to exploit the conflict to further his own political ambitions. As has been pointed out before, Boniface wanted to annex Tuscany to the states of the Church, and to do so he asked the help of Charles of Valois. At that time Florence was controlled by the Whites, and Donati had been banished from the city after he had attempted to overthrow their rule by corruption and violence. Thus the pope took Donati under his protection and made him governor of one of his provinces, in this way winning over the Black party to the Church's side. Then, too, Valois was coming from France to abolish the independence of Florence, which was upheld by the Whites.

It was during this crisis that Dante, to his lasting misfortune, entered the political arena. It is not clear why he joined the Whites, when family connections should have tied him with the Black party—after all, he had married Donati's cousin. Perhaps he was angered by Corso's lawlessness, and even more he might have been attracted to the White side by his old friendship with Guido Cavalcanti, whom The Baron had tried to have murdered.

Dante had entered politics in 1295, when he was thirty, but had held only minor positions; his career began really to flourish after Cerchi's victory. The fact that he took on more and more responsibilities as the tension between the two parties increased indicates that his attitudes were quite radical—which fits well with what we know of his personality. In May, 1300, he was sent as ambassador to St. Gimignano. In the council hall of that city one can read an inscription that recalls the poet's visit, and from it one would imagine that the mission had been one of Dante's first triumphs. In reality he failed.

But this did not prevent him from being elected Prior on June 15.

It was the highest elective position in the city, and although his tenure lasted only two months, those two months were enough to involve Dante in a responsibility for which he was to pay a high price: the extermination of Pistoia's Black faction, which had been hindering White Florence's foreign policies. It is difficult to tell how much of the great quantity of blood that was let is to be attributed to Dante's decisions, but there is no doubt that he left with some of it on his conscience—a fact that probably fostered an increase in his radicalism. By now he was a sworn enemy of the pope, who had excommunicated the city, and of Valois, who was marching against it in the pope's name.

The information relayed by Dino Compagni, to the effect that Dante had been chosen by the city to go on a peace mission to Boniface, seems therefore a very unlikely one. Boccaccio, his first biographer, reports that when the Priors offered him the mission, the poet answered: "If I go, who will stay? And if I stay, who will go?" These words are of a piece with his character and its boundless pride, but we doubt they were ever spoken because it seems impossible that the mission was to be entrusted to the man least likely to succeed in it. History has accepted Compagni's version because a confrontation between Dante and Boniface evokes such a dramatic picture that no biographer can easily dismiss it. In any case, the mission was unsuccessful.

Florence could have mustered thousands of well-armed men, yet it surrendered to the few hundred horsemen of Valois. Donati returned with his Black henchmen and began a purge right away. Dante was among the first nine men to be sentenced to the stake—which shows what a major role he had played in the unsuccessful resistence movement. The sentence is dated January 22, 1302, and one can still read it in the sinister "Book of Nails" preserved in the Florentine archives. But the punishment could not be carried out because the poet had already escaped with his half-brother Francesco, his voluntary companion in exile.

Vengeance fell on the malefactor's house. According to Florentine custom, a demolition crew began to pick it apart under the vigilant eyes of the *podestà* and—we assume—the tearful gaze of Gemma.

From then on Dante entered his wandering life, the paths of which are impossible to unravel with certainty. At first he stayed in Arezzo, a haven for the Whites, and took part in some attempts to return home through the use of force. But the exiles' plans were foiled, and the blame seems to have fallen on Dante, who had suggested that his friend Scarpetta Ordelaffi be put in charge of operations. But these are only rumors; what is sure is that Dante soon abandoned "the wicked, foolish company," as he called it, and formed "a party for one's self alone," as his fate demanded—that is, as it naturally followed from his lonely and disdainful personality.

He turned north and settled in Verona, a guest of Bartolomeo Della Scala (or of his son Alboino, the record isn't clear). The elective city government of Verona had already been transformed into a *signoria* ruled by the rich and powerful Scala family. The poet was received with friendliness into the palace, and he repaid his host by performing for him diplomatic errands in neighboring cities. In Padua he happened to meet Giotto, who was there painting the frescoes in the Church of the Annunciation. The two had known each other in Florence, and their reunion was a pleasant occasion.

A short time later Dante moved to the Lunigiana Valley with the Malaspina family. Exiles were then always well received, first of all because anyone could become one from one day to the next, and so those temporarily in power were well advised to abide by the rules of hospitality; and, second, because when they were as well educated as Dante was, they came in handy—except for priests, few people knew how to read and write. In fact, Dante went on some diplomatic missions for the Malaspina to the Bishop of Luni and thus earned his board.

Boccaccio relates a strange episode from this period. According to Boccaccio, when Gemma emptied her house before its demolition, she found in a strongbox a manuscript in verse. At first she laid it away without thinking about it, but later she showed it to Dino Frescobaldi, who became enthusiastic about it and, upon finding out that Dante was in Lunigiana, sent the manuscript to him with a plea that it should be continued. It was the first seven *canti* of the *Divine Comedy* that Dante had given up as lost.

Dante could not go back to work on it right away because he was called to the Casentino region by Count Guido di Dovadola, with whom Dante had almost family ties since their great-grandfathers were apparently, good friends. And there he suffered an unpleasant emotional experience—he fell desperately in love with a "woman mean and beautiful" as well as "goitered," according to Boccaccio. Nothing else is known about her except that she made sport of the poet, now in his forties, by first wooing him and then denying herself to him, in the best teasing tradition.

After this episode one loses track of Dante; the most credible hypothesis is that he went on to spend a year in Paris. This is what both Villani and Boccaccio wrote, while his son Jacob does not mention the trip in the biographical notes he wrote about his father. In 1881 a French philologist found in the Montpellier archives the manuscript of a poem entitled "The Flower," written in Italian and signed Durante, which was Dante's real name. It was the shortened version of a long-winded and dirty French poem; Dante scholars have, of course, rejected with horror the idea that this was their hero's work. But since it includes parts of a rather lewd sonnet that the poet had written in Casentino, the issue is open to doubt.

In 1308 Dante was back in Tuscany, up to his neck in politics once more. He was attracted there by the coming of Henry VII, who, as we have seen, wanted to restore imperial power in Italy. Henry's plan was hopeless, but Dante was so enthusiastic about it that he burned all the bridges behind himself. He wrote a grave letter "to every and each King in Italy, and the senators of the nurturing cities, to the dukes and marquises and to all the peoples" inviting them to submit to the emperor. And he apparently went to Milan to hand it in person to Henry, who had no idea what the man was or why he would be entitled to speak on behalf of the whole country. How little ready the country was to submit itself became clear shortly afterward, and it was the poet's compatriots who were the most restive. So Dante wrote another letter, addressing it this time to the "most scoundrelly Florentines," expressing the hope that death and destruction would descend on their city. And he sent Henry a third message to spur him on to the punishment of the rebellious city, suggesting that after its unconditional surrender he should burn it down and butcher its inhabitants. In all likelihood, Henry never read through these dispatches, but the Florentines did. It is quite understandable, therefore, that when shortly after they put into effect an amnesty for the exiles, Dante was excluded from it. The poet then pinned all his hopes on Henry's army, but the army was weak, and Henry soon died, leaving Dante without a future to look forward to.

"Extremely poor, he spent the rest of his life living in various parts of Lombardy, Tuscany and Romagna under the subsidy of various Lords," Bruni, the most serious and best documented of Dante's first biographers, succinctly says, and regrettably, we can't add much to this statement. It is almost certain that the first of these lords was Cangrande Della Scale of Verona, one of the most splendid and colorful despots of the times. He held an open court for all the passing guests, and probably this is exactly why the peevish poet did not feel at ease there and, still in the lord's pay, withdrew to a cottage by himself, later to be joined by his children, who had been banished earlier after Dante had declined an invitation to return home on condition that he make an "offering," that is, a formal acknowledgement of his guilt and a plea for clemency. There is a letter documenting the disdainful answer of the poet, but its authenticity is doubtful; perhaps he failed to answer altogether.

Exactly when Dante left Verona is not known. Years later, when Petrarch visited the city, he collected some gossip to the effect that Cangrande got tired of Dante and amused himself by humiliating the poet. This is surely false, because the poet remained steadfastly grateful to his host, to whom he brought the first drafts of the *Comedy's canti* for inspection. The tale of their quarreling must be attributed to the fact that Dante never became popular in Verona, although some of his work attained a certain fame there. His personality did not arouse much sympathy, nor did he show any for others; he was never in the center of things at court, nor did he have friends at the university, where he had perhaps expected, in vain as it turned out, to get a faculty appointment.

These were probably the reasons that prompted Dante to accept

Guido Novello da Polenta's invitation to settle down in Ravenna. Guido was another one of those fourteenth-century lords who had succeeded, by dint of violence and cunning, in supplanting the democratic communal institutions with their personal power. This power Guido flaunted less than Cangrande and used more tact—as a youth he had been a rather adventurous military leader, but now, having matured and achieved security in his position, he became interested in culture. He lived in a much less splendid palace than the Scalas, and he surrounded himself with comfort and books. He also put together verses of his own: they were rather poor, but extremely respectful of the rules of grammar.

Perhaps Guido had known Dante while the latter was engaged in some diplomatic mission for Cangrande that brought him to Ravenna. Perhaps he took a fancy to him upon hearing a tercet of the *Inferno,* which was already beginning to be rather well-known in the small circles of the intelligentsia of the times. Or he might have been grateful to the poet for having treated with so much kindness his aunt Francesca de Rimini.*

Upon Guido's invitation Dante went to teach rhetoric—or so it seems—in the university, which was one of Guido's pet projects. The quiet and enigmatic beauty of that grave-like city, closed upon the memories of its glorious past, must have pleased him as much as the benevolence of his lord. The esteem and kindness with which he was received helped to relax a little the kinks of his tight-knit personality. It is not sure where he found a house, although it seems that he lived across from the Franciscan monastery in which he was later to be buried. In any event, he sent right away for his sons Peter and Jacob and his daughter Antonia, who supplied him with the warmth of a home.

These last years were perhaps the most serene of Dante's crowded life; they were certainly the most productive. Guido overwhelmed him with favors and his friends with affection; in their company the poet took long walks under the stupendous pines of the Chiassi forest,

---

* The main character in the fifth *canto* of the *Divine Comedy. Trans.*

across the squares of the hundred churches, among Byzantine and Gothic monuments, and made friendly calls at the palace. Once in a while Guido entrusted him with a mission, but only in cases of real emergency, so that he would have time for writing. On one occasion Dante was sent to Venice to resolve a thorny conflict that threatened to result in a war between the two cities. There is no record of how successful he had been; perhaps he didn't even have time to begin his hearings because he fell ill and, sensing the approach of his end, returned in haste. It must have been an acute case of malaria, because he had a very high fever and was delirious; by the time he reached Ravenna, he was exhausted. It is questionable even whether he recognized his sons and his friends who took turns standing around the deathbed; he died during the night of September 13, 1321.

His contemporaries were not too aware of the loss—Dante was much less admired than many a mediocre Latinist. Even among poets he was thought the inferior of someone such as Guinizelli, whom the city of Bologna crowned with everlasting laurel. Dante's greatness was not recognized until much later. Boccaccio was the first one to have a more or less accurate estimate of it, but the first serious critical studies of his work did not begin until the eighteenth century.

Dante had not scattered his talents through a large output of work. In his twenties he had made his debut with the *Vita Nova,* the poetic tale of his love for Beatrice, written according to the convention (how obvious, alas) of the New Style. Some of those poems were later included in the *Canzoniere,* together with other more fresh and original ones he wrote during that period. His first organically conceived work is the *Convivio,* which he wrote at the start of his long exile to prove his talent to those who gave him asylum; it is an omnibus that was supposed to dissect all human knowledge in fifteen treatises. Luckily, the poet gave up after the first three, probably because he became bored along the way. More important is the *De Vulgari Eloquentia,* the first systematic treatment of the Italian language. It is an unfinished work, crude from a philological point of view—Dante explained the variety of languages by pointing at the Tower of Babel—which contained, however, some amazing insights. He understood that Latin had become a dead language but feared that the "vulgar" tongue would be buried by local dialects for the lack of a central court that could nurture a refined national language. He had foreseen the tragedy of the Italian language: that it had never had a matrix in which to develop. In this treatise, in which he advocated a national unity focused around a lay court, Dante's Ghibelline feelings are better expressed than in the *De Monarchia,* which he wrote in order to contribute a philosophical and juridical ban to Henry VII's pretense at an imperial restoration. In the latter work, Dante comes through as a nostalgic dreamer of an impossible return to a medieval conception in which papacy and empire would amiably share the spiritual and temporal rule of the world.

There also remain thirteen epistles from the hundreds he must have written in his lifetime to start new friendships or, more likely, to break up old ones. Leonardo Bruni said that he saw many more of these letters and described their handwriting as "thin and long and very proper." The final remaining works of Dante are the mediocre *Egloghe,* which he exchanged with Giovanni del Virgilio, and an essay on water and earth, *Quaestio de Aqua et Terra,* which shows both his interest in and ignorance of science, which was about par for his times.

They were all thin little works that would have secured for Dante a rank similar to that occupied by Cavalcanti, were it not for the reflected light shed on them by the *Comedy.* The dates for the development of his masterpiece are uncertain: Boccaccio claimed that Dante had already finished seven *canti* before he left Florence. It is likely that the first idea for the great work came to him in Rome while he was participating in the papal Jubilee of 1300. Dante supported this supposition in the line—"Midway through the journey of my life . . . ," that is, at thirty-five years of age, which is how old he was at the time. But having conceived the idea, Dante need not necessarily have started to work on it right away; it is more likely that it matured slowly inside him for a while. One has the impression in reading the poem that it was something thought about for a long time and then poured out in white heat. The writing must have been done in the years of exile, probably between Verona and Ravenna; through the whole poem there breathes the despair of a fugitive who appeals to God's justice against the justice of man.

This is not the place to summarize the content of the *Comedy,* the main structural lines of which are well known to almost everybody. Boccaccio said that Dante had thought at first that he would write it in Latin, but this is highly unlikely, not only because it ran counter to his literary opinions, but also because he handled Latin rather poorly. This marvelous voyage in the Hereafter is divided into three *cantiche* (Hell, Purgatory, and Paradise), each consisting of thirty-three *canti* that, counting the Prologue, add up to the perfect number of one hundred. Each *canto* is made up of *terzine,* three-line-verses of eleven syllables per line—the first line rhymes with the third, the second with the first line of the following *terzina.*

Dante could not have set a more rigid or a more difficult plan for himself. But he was a contemporary of Giotto and Arnolfo, the great cathedral builders, and he wanted to erect one, too, according to the same conceptions of symmetrical relationships. He was able to carry out his plan because of an absolute mastery of the line: he often said that sometimes he had been stumped by an idea, but never by a rhyme. And his virtuosity is ample proof of this; he was able, for instance, to end all three *cantiche* with the word "stars."

The *Comedy* is not a very original work. The Middle Ages were rife with tales about trips to the beyond, drawn mostly from Arab sources. Dante distilled some of these stories and then added what only he possessed: true poetry. It cannot be found in all fifteen thousand lines of the poem, which here and there becomes boring and irrelevant, but nobody has ever written as much exalted poetry as he did. Dante makes us smile when he gets on the high horse of philosophy—he thought he was a theologian writing a *Summa.* Yet in that field he was behind the times in comparison with many of his contemporaries who had become familiar with the new rationalistic currents originating in France at Abelard's school, which were diffused in Italy by St. Thomas.

Dante was left behind in the Middle Ages, with its superstitions, its terrors, and its picture of the world as a huge mystery whose key only

God could provide. His time stopped in 1300, the year of his exile; afterward he lived only from memories, bent over himself and his past. For the rest of his life his thoughts kept turning around Florence, Boniface, Corso, Vieri, Guido, Beatrice. But the poetry he drew from that well of thoughts was sublime, in prayer as well as in cursing. His very failures as a man—pride, self-centeredness, temper—were the conditions of his greatness as a poet.

Dante was not a forerunner of the *Risorgimento* and of national unity, as some have foolishly claimed; politically, he was a reactionary dreaming an impossible dream of imperial unification. But he gave Italians the tool they most needed in order to become Italians—their language. In this country riddled with impossible Latinate rhetoric, Dante made the vulgar tongue noble; if nothing else, this contribution would have been enough to earn him his title: "Father of his Country."

Chapter 8

THE BABYLONIAN CAPTIVITY

CLEMENT V justified moving the Holy See to Avignon in 1305 with the argument that Rome no longer could offer guarantees of physical or moral safety. He stated that the city was in the hands of contentious noblemen, and that its life was rotten to the core. He was quite right, but the prospects of Avignon were not much better, since wherever the papal court settled itself, the contest between factions exploded in an effort to gain influence over the Church by whatever means available. The truth was that Clement V and the majority of the cardinals were French, and they obeyed their king, who had no desire to face another Boniface VIII. It is not completely untrue, then, to say that the pope was a prisoner during his stay in Avignon, and many have called the period the "Babylonian Captivity" of the Church.

The shy and tormented Clement was followed by John XXII, a shrewd man who looked at the Church as a large business enterprise and was very successful, on that level, at restoring the papal coffers to their previous state of prosperity. He was somewhat less outstanding as a shepherd of souls or as a theologian. Once, when he was taking part in a dispute over the divine attributes of the Virgin Mary, John declared that she, too, would have to wait for the last judgment before being admitted to heaven. Many a poor fellow had been burned at the stake for stating less controversial beliefs; John was spared because he was pope and ninety years old. But he provoked a storm of protest, and his declaration was branded as heresy by a synod that met at Vincennes, and only old age saved him from having to retract the statement.

John's successor, Benedict XII, tried to correct some of the problems that John had created by recklessly awarding titles to whoever paid most—which had been the way he had adopted to upgrade the finances of the Church—to the detriment of its organizational structure. Benedict, whose financial position was now strong, thanks to John's methods, tried to weed out the payroll, but his fight to curb the corruption of his court failed to attract popularity. Everyone was getting emotionally attached to the comfortable pattern of bribing, so there was a general sigh of relief when Benedict passed away prematurely in 1342. The consensus was that his successor ought to be someone in sympathy with the good old custom of tips and grafts.

Clement VI, another Frenchman, had been born a great gentleman and had lived as such, and he let everyone know right away that he couldn't see why he should not continue to live in the same manner while he was pope. There was plenty of money now, he said, and he invited everybody to enjoy it. One witness related that more than a hundred thousand priests responded to his call, and none departed empty-handed. But the non-clergy benefited, too, especially if they were poets, artists, ladies, or even horses. Clement was a fine breeder, and evil tongues murmured that if he had known half as much about saints as he did about fillies, he would have been a great theologian. It is understandable that Petrarch should have had a weakness for the pope, for he was an amazingly likable man: generous, liberal, scholarly, unprejudiced, and gallant—to the point of placing the Countess of Turenne in charge of all promotions within the church, a position she thoroughly exploited, leaving one to wonder at the reason of her own appointment.

But Clement concerned himself with organization and beautification as well as with his own pleasures. The Church under his leadership perfected its bureaucratic and administrative machinery; the majestic palace of the popes, begun by Benedict, expanded beyond the original plans. Clement had a refined palate and an itch for building. Giotto died before he could travel to France, but Simone Martini came instead, and his frescoes in Avignon set a model for all French artists to follow.

These grandiose efforts soon depleted the coffers that John had just refilled, and Clement was forced to increase taxes. The situation was far from being healthy: Italy, now that the pope was in France and therefore much less able to dole out favors or engage in reprisals, sent almost no money; the *signorie* were less loyal to the church than the Guelph *comuni* had been; France had become involved in a war with England that was to last a hundred years; both countries used all their resources for their armies, leaving to the clergy only eyes to weep with; the German priests were hostile to a French-speaking papacy. To overcome these obstacles, John and Benedict already had been required to increase fiscal pressure to its limits: a new bishop or abbot had to pay, in advance, one-third of his income to the pope, and an archbishop had to pay astronomical sums for his mantle, with which only the papal *Curia* was authorized to provide him. After the election of a new pope, all beneficiaries had to pay him an annuity on their incomes. When a cardinal, a bishop, or an abbot died, his whole estate reverted to the pope, who also enjoyed the profits on it until a new beneficiary was appointed—which was one reason that appointments were slow in coming. Whoever took on a title was responsible for his predecessor's debts; if anyone was bold enough to defend his rights before the pope's tribunal, he incurred such exorbitant expenses that even victory in the case was no compensation.

Ill-feeling against Avignon was nurtured more by fiscal high-handedness than by anything else. In his *Lament over the Church,* Alvaro Pelayo wrote such things as: "Every time I enter the papal court I see nothing but priests counting stolen money . . . They are the wolves who have assumed control over the church and now suck the blood of the sheep." The German clergy met in a synod, which decided to refuse payment of tithes to papal agents. The latter were delivered, to the fury of the populace, and as a result many agents were lynched. The British Parliament passed laws against the pope's taxes and forbade export of British money. Thus, as a result of these and other such measures, the situation became ripe for a more radical protest—a questioning of the Church itself rather than of its morals.

A fervor for revolt and a yearning for pure evangelical beginnings had always survived in the background, and no persecution had been able to extinguish it completely. The most violent eruptions, caused by the Albigenses, the Waldenses, and the Patarines, had occurred in the two preceding centuries and had been squelched only through the establishment of the Inquisition. But torture, stakes, and slaughter had destroyed only the organization of the heretical movements; the cause that inspired them lay untouched under the embers. It blazed up again early in the fourteenth century when a monk from Novara by the name of Dolcino arraigned the incurable cancer of the papacy in a series of revolutionary sermons. He held that since the time of Pope Silvester, who had reigned in the fourth century, there had been only one truly Christian pope—Celestine V—and that he had, of course, resigned. With his sister Margaret, Dolcino founded an "Apostolical Confraternity" in Parma; it was a coeducational sect in which each man lived with his mate in strictest chastity and absolute independence from Church hierarchy.

The pope gave orders for the Inquisition to summon the rebels. They refused to attend and, taking up arms, entrenched themselves among the Alps of Piedmont. The Inquisitors blocked all the exits from the mountains with a large army of mercenaries: Dolcino and his men ate grass, acorns, horses, and rats, but they did not surrender. About a thousand fell in the final assault; the rest were captured and sent to the stake. Despite her deprivations, Margaret was still so beautiful that one of the pope's lieutenants offered to marry and save her if she would only recant, but Margaret refused and perished among the flames. A special treatment was held in store for Dolcino and his aide Longino. They were driven in a cart through the streets of Vercelli, while a score of executioners slowly stripped their flesh with red-hot pincers and threw the pieces to the jubilant crowd.

As in previous times of peril, the Church again found some saints as a protection against heresy, just as Thomas, Francis, and Dominic had stood up in its defense when past schisms had threatened. This correlation is not a coincidence—saints and heretics are motivated by the same frustrations, and they resemble each other much more than either of them resembles the orthodox religious conformist. Indeed, the new saints were no different. For example, St. Catherine avoided Margaret's fate only by a hairbreadth. She was born in Siena, the most medieval of Italian cities. Enclosed within its walls is the stillness of a changeless time. The architects and painters who were born there—Lorenzo Maitani, Andrea Pisano, Duccio di Buoninsegna, Simone Martini—had given the city a beauty so absolute that no one had dared to touch it since. The Piazza del Campo, with its Public Palace, the Tower of Mangia, and the frame of stupendous palaces, was not an urban center but a whole world, a civilization with a clock that had stopped and has never told time since. Neighborhood and party loyalties were alive in Siena even more than in Florence, and they still are, and the air of the city was redolent with the religious mysticism and fanaticism of the Crusades.

Catherine embodied these attributes perfectly. When she turned fifteen, she joined the third order of Dominican nuns, which allowed her to live outside a cloister. Her parents, who wanted to dissuade her from this vocation, forced on her the heaviest household duties: she had to clean, wash, and fetch the firewood. She completed these tasks joyfully, rewarded by the happiness that awaited her at night in the bare little monastic room that was her own. There she reached ecstasy and had visitations; she rejoiced in feeling the nails that had pierced Christ on the cross stab through her flesh and heard Him call her His bride. When she felt strong enough to resist the snares of the world, she left home to bring help and consolation to those in need. She must have radiated an irresistible fascination, because even the most callous sinners listened reverently to her words. During the plague she assisted the diseased and caught the contagion, which disfigured her face, but she survived. The fame of her holiness spread everywhere. The city of Montepulciano called on her to restore peace among the factions that were destroying it. Pisa and Lucca appealed for her advice. Florence asked her to go as ambassador to Avignon; Catherine consented, and what she saw there filled her with horror and despair. She let Gregory XI know what she thought by crying out at one point, "Here one smells the stench of Hell!" Some of the cardinals present suggested that she be arrested, but the pope, more clearsighted than they, took her under his protection.

Back in her cell, Catherine flooded the churchly world with letters full of exalted despair. She didn't write them herself, since she was illiterate; she dictated them in a simple language ablaze with a faith that induced respect and fear even in the least receptive reader. The word "reformation" appeared again and again in her passionate appeals, and not many years later her prophecies were fulfilled. For the rest of her life she refused to leave the seclusion of her desolate cell, from which she upset popes, cardinals, bishops, and kings. Her energy remained unflagging even when, pushing asceticism to its limits, she scorned all nourishment except for the consecrated wafer. Only the schism of the Church could break her: she died of despair in 1380, at only thirty-three years of age. She was made a saint because on that famous day Gregory XI had refused to arrest her; if Boniface VIII had been in his place she would have probably shared the fate of Brother Dolcino's sister, with whom she had all her goals in common.

Chapter 9

COLA DI RIENZO

THE ROMANS soon discovered that with the loss of the papacy they had lost their only profitable business. The Church didn't manage its money well, but it did attract revenues from all over Europe. These were not invested in roads, hospitals, or schools; they were spread out in the shape of the charity and bribes to which the populace had grown accustomed. And tourism, the other main source of income, had also disappeared: nobody had a reason any longer to visit a city that was not the capital of anything.

Decay set in quickly. The cosmopolitan world of clerics and attorneys that had revolved around the *Curia,* contributing to the corruption of the city and also to its wealth and intellectual vigor, had followed the pope to Avignon. Left behind were an arrogant aristocracy and a tattered populace—not one skilled craftsman nor a penny to repair the cobblestones. A fire in the Lateran ravaged half of the palace before it extinguished itself; there were no firemen to put it out.

The rest of the Church dominions declined with the capital. The small rulers who had been managing the cities of central Italy in the pope's name were now taking advantage of his absence to assert more and more their independence. The Roman consuls and senators carried pretentious titles but had no authority to have even a sewer fixed. The poles of attraction in the Italian peninsula were elsewhere—in

Venice, Milan, Genoa, Florence, Naples. Rome had sent message upon message asking Clement and John to return. But the French popes were doing well on their home ground, and they gave evasive replies or failed to reply altogether. Even if they had wanted to, they could not have returned; they were oppressed by an overwhelming majority of French cardinals whose loyalty was first to their king, then to the Church.

In reaction to this situation the Romans welcomed with enthusiasm Ludwig IV of Bavaria, the successor of Henry VII, who had arrived in Italy in 1327 to don the two crowns: the Italian in Milan, and the imperial in Rome. Like his predecessor, Ludwig had few men and little gold, but he endeared himself to the Romans when he was excommunicated by Pope John. The Visconti, the Della Scala, and the Castracani of Lucca provided him with means in abundance; the Romans, more helpless and poor than he was, overwhelmed him with applause and honorific titles. The excommunicated Ludwig was proclaimed emperor by a bishop who, in turn, was excommunicated, then he was hailed as senator and captain of the people on Capitol Hill. Speaking to a cheering crowd in St. Peter's Square, Ludwig announced the deposition of "The Antichrist Jacob of Cahors, who calls himself John XXII," nominated as his replacement the monk Peter of Corvara, giving him the title Pope Nicholas V, and then had himself anointed by the new pope.

It was the usual flash in the pan. When the Romans heard that Robert of Anjou was marching northward with an army stronger than the Bavarian one—which wasn't at all hard to do—they began to have second thoughts about the legitimacy of Ludwig's crown and Nicholas's tiara. Their doubts became deeper as Robert kept approaching, and they changed into an absolute conviction that the real pope was John as soon as they saw the Germans break camp precipitously and take to the northern roads. Nicholas followed their example and asked for asylum in Pisa, counting on its Ghibelline faith, but the Pisans tied him up in a bundle and sent him to Avignon as a present to Pope John. Because the latter did not believe in God, he was not greatly disturbed by offenses against the title of Christ's vicar, so all Pope John did was first to ask Nicholas to repent, which the poor man willingly did, admitting to all his sins, and then to leave the poor ex-pope to die in peace in an isolated wing of the papal palace. In the meantime, Ludwig had marched up the Italian peninsula, blackmailing every city on his way to pay him gold in exchange for immunity from attack, and disappeared across the Alps leaving behind a disenchantment that applied not only to him but also to the position he had usurped.

The decay of Rome continued, and the once-proud capital became more and more like a village. Having lost hope in the ability of its noble representatives to bring the pope back, in 1343 the populace decided to take matters into its own hands and sent an embassy to Avignon. The mission was led by a young attorney named Nicholas di Rienzo Cabrini, known as Cola di Rienzo. He was the son of an innkeeper and a washerwoman, born in the poorest section of Trastevere, and he embodied the frustration and rage of an ignorant populace embittered by the comparison between ancient glories and a wretched present. He had many of Mussolini's traits: a typical Italian rabble-rouser, he got drunk on his own words and ended up believing in them, losing all sense of reality and measure.

On arriving in Avignon, Cola went to see Petrarch first, knowing that he had good contacts and influence at the Curia. The poet had always tried to avoid politics and had succeeded up to that time in steering clear of commitments, but Cola conquered him with his tales of Rome, the empire, Augustus, the arches, the columns, the eagles, the glory. Two years earlier Petrarch had been crowned with laurel on Capitol Hill, and he had cried over the ruins of the city, praying for its resurrection; now he saw in Cola, who spoke the same language, the only man who could accomplish that task and therefore took his side without reservations.

John XXII had died, and his place had been taken by Clement VI, who was as great a skeptic as he was a gentleman. He welcomed the Roman attorney with fatherly kindness and listened graciously to Cola's diatribe against the Roman nobles who had turned the city into an arena by their struggles, knowing full well that the speaker was a fanatic. The pope agreed with Cola, encouraged him to organize a revolt against Roman misrule, and, true to form, sent him back with a few of those florins that his predecessor had so stubbornly acquired.

Fortified by the pope's money and blessings, Cola took action as soon as he returned to Rome. Dressed in a white senatorial cloak and a bizarre hood embroidered with swords, he called up a popular parliament for Whitsunday, 1344, and let himself be elected regent, in conjunction with the papal vicar, as well as "Liberator of the Holy Roman Republic," though no one knew what, if any, authority the vague title involved. Cola interpreted his powers with plenty of latitude; he armed a militia to beat back the bands of the nobility, which feigned submission and withdrew into the surrounding castles to prepare a counteroffensive.

Cola at first managed quite well: he straightened out the treasury and put the courts back into working order. Even Prince Pietro Colonna was tried and imprisoned. But success turned Cola's head, and he began to refer to himself as "The Saviour of the Sacred Roman Empire by Christ's will." On the holy day commemorating the Virgin's ascension he had himself crowned in the basilica of Santa Maria Maggiore with six crowns, held high a silver ball that symbolized power over the whole world, forbade all foreign armies to set foot on Italian soil, announced that he was convening all the rulers of the world in Rome to elect an emperor (who was to be himself, of course), and began to act as if he already had been given that title. He asked to be knighted, and for that ceremony he dived in full regalia into the holy water font of the Lateran baptistry, where Emperor Constantine was supposed to have been baptized. Then he bundled himself up in his white toga and spent the night on a bed in the nave of the basilica. The next morning he proclaimed all Italian cities free, allowed them to be called "Roman," and made three signs in the air with his sword in each direction, shouting: "This belongs to me, and that, and that, too." He adopted a new silk uniform with gold trimmings, rode a white horse covered with a royal baldachin, and employed an escort of a hundred mounted soldiers. When Stefano Colonna shook his head and smirked at his passage, Cola imprisoned him and other noblemen. All the nobles were dragged in chains to Capitol Hill, where Cola obtained from parliament a sentence ordering their execution. Then he pardoned the nobles and entrusted them with government jobs, whereupon they fled to organize an army for his overthrow.

Up to that point, Pope Clement, who had no affection for the Roman nobility, had looked on Cola with some indulgence, but now he realized that he had a madman on his hands, so he made out a papal bull to the effect that if Cola remained in power, the Roman Jubilee planned for 1350 would be canceled, and that Rome would never again have the privilege to hold another. At this announcement the nobles surrounded the city with their hordes. Cola rang the bells to call the people to his defense, but almost no one came: the people, although still siding with Cola because his rhetoric had taken their minds off hunger, were afraid of missing the Jubilee, which was the only opportunity Rome still had for preserving the illusion of importance and for getting a little money from the visitors.

The despot left the city as the bands of the aristocracy were breaking through its walls. He traveled through all of Italy, encountering numerous dangerous adventures, then crossed into Germany, where he asked the protection of the Emperor Charles IV of Bohemia. Cola told his host that the anarchy in Rome was all the pope's fault, but the emperor was quite uninterested, though when Clement demanded Cola's extradition, the emperor refused to extradite the Roman. The deposed despot himself decided, after a year of idleness, to take the road to Avignon. When he arrived there, he asked right away to see Petrarch, trusting his help. The poet was in his retreat in the Vaucluse and wouldn't budge; instead, he composed a letter in Cola's defense, proclaiming him emphatically the champion of Roman greatness and freedom.

Perhaps partly because of Petrarch's sponsorship, the tribune was spared. Cola was imprisoned in a tower of the papal castle and given the Holy Scriptures to read and meditate on. Two years later another Roman commoner, by name of Baroncelli, tried to repeat Cola's caper by whipping the populace into a frenzy, chasing the noblemen away, and proclaiming himself the emperor's vicar. Innocent VI, the pope who had followed after Clement's death, thought that Cola was the man to stop this latest scourge; so he sent him to Rome as counselor and assistant to Cardinal Albornoz, who was charged with restoring papal authority.

Upon hearing the news of their former leader's return, the mob drove out Baroncelli, whom it had cheered up to that point, and raised triumphal arches for Cola's reception. Albornoz, who thought it expedient to exploit Cola's popularity, named him senator and governor of the city. When the Romans gathered on Capitol Hill to see and hear their old idol, they became somewhat disillusioned. Although he was only a few years over forty, Cola had become fat and flabby; even his eloquence had lost its edge.

Cola's first step as governor was to engage in a sort of public confession, condemning and ridiculing, rather wittily, his own youthful follies and previous superiority complex. By the end of the speech, however, he was again comparing himself to Nebuchadnezzar and announcing the return of the eagles to the fateful hills of Rome. His administration relied on a police that made arbitrary arrests and indiscriminate executions. And at every opportunity, Cola came out on his balcony to give long speeches loaded with threats and boasting, in which the most rosy hopes alternated with the direst predictions.

People began to suspect that the governor's head was not in working order. It probably never had been, but now alcohol was helping to confuse it even further. Cola drank enormous quantities, and he was beginning to show it. The chronicler Fortifiocca wrote: "He had guts like unto a whale, a glorious paunch like an abbot."

Finally, after seventy days of a government during which the most preposterous things happened, the populace of the outskirts began to riot, perhaps helped along by bribes from the nobility. Cola tried to quiet things down with one of his usual speeches but soon realized that the myth was finished. He tried to escape disguised as a shepherd and in blackface, but he was recognized by a golden bracelet that he wore around a wrist and dragged to the bottom of Capitol Hill, where so many heads had rolled by his order. He asked to speak, but a craftsman who feared his ability to enthrall the mob cut him short with a dagger. Hundreds more followed the example; Cola's body, riddled with wounds, remained two days hanging from a balcony. "Horribly fat he was," writes Fortifiocca, "Milk-white, bloodied. His obesity was such that he appeared to be an oversized buffalo, or butchered cow."

Chapter 10

PETRARCH

EARLIER we saw that in 1302, upon the coming of Charles of Valois and with Boniface VIII's blessings, the Blacks of Florence, led by Corso Donati, had settled their accounts with Vieri Cerchi and his Whites. One of the resulting exiles was a Mister Petracco, who took the road to Arezzo as Dante Alighieri had done. Petracco belonged to the solid middle class of Florence and was an attorney of good repute. He most likely had a nice estate, but he lost almost all of it when exiled. However, he was able to take with him what he probably most treasured, his beautiful wife Eletta, much younger than he, whom he had just married.

From the start, Petracco played an important role in Arezzo's "White University," a political and military body organized by the exiles to prepare a counteroffensive. In the spring of 1304, Petracco was one of the two delegates that the Whites sent to Florence to discuss with the Blacks conditions for their return. Charles Valois had left Tuscany, Boniface was dead, and Benedict XI, the new pope, had given up on the idea of annexing Florence to the Church, now only wishing for the factional struggles to end.

Petracco carried out his diplomatic mission well, and after a solemn ceremony on the square of Santa Maria Novella he exchanged the kiss of peace with the Black negotiators, amidst a festive ringing of church bells. Unfortunately, the effects of the peace treaty did not go beyond that kiss. Taking their cue from Benedict's death, the Blacks unleashed riots and looting in the city, blamed the Whites for it, and prolonged their ban. The exiles were left with violence as their last resort, but their *coup* miscarried when one of the leaders tried to carry it out by himself before the core of the army had assembled, thus squashing the attempt.

It must have been a hard blow for Petracco, who saw both his mission and his hopes for returning home dashed to pieces; his bitterness was relieved, however, by his wife, who on that very day, July 20, 1304, gave birth to a handsome baby boy whom they named Francesco. It is possible that Dante went to congratulate the mother and see the new baby in his crib, since he was also in Arezzo at the time and knew the attorney. The infant did not have a chance to become familiar with the city of his birth; he was still in his swaddling clothes when his parents moved to the village from which the Petraccos originated, Incisa Val d'Arno. He was reared there until he was about eight years of age, and it was probably there that his younger brother, Gherardo, was born. His childhood must have been rather untamed in that isolated hamlet of a few hundred souls. But when he was eight, he experienced the first of many extraordinary events that were to enrich his life: his father took him to Pisa to meet Emperor Henry VII, the last bulwark of the exiled Whites. They were all there, waiting— Dante among them. In a letter written to Boccaccio sixty years later, Petrarch tells how they first met on that occasion.

What impressed the boy more than Dante, of whose greatness he could have no idea, was the city of Pisa itself. It was not the "queen of the sea" any longer, since Genoa had destroyed its fleet and Florence had eaten away its lands, but the glorious old republic had found a second youth in art and in culture. It was there that the wonderful cathedral, the famous tower, and the splendid churchyard were being created. The University of Pisa was already famous, thanks mainly to Bartolo di Sassoferrato, a bright light of jurisprudence.

Petrarch's stay in Pisa was brief, as was Henry's adventure. After the latter died, the Florentine exiles disbanded. Dante returned to

Verona, where he already had found a job and a home with Cangrande
Della Scala, and Petracco boarded ship with his family to sail for
Avignon, where, in 1305, Clement V had moved the Holy See.
Petracco almost certainly found a job at court but could not get housing in that small town overrun with thousands of churchmen, dignitaries, and diplomats, so his family put up in the neighboring village
of Carpentras, where Francesco lived a happy and rather ignorant life
until he reached the age of fifteen.

The quiet interlude ended in 1319 when his father, who wanted
him to follow in the paternal footsteps, sent Francesco to law school—
first to Montpellier and then to Bologna, where he was to discover
his true vocation. The University of Bologna was the most prestigious
in Europe. It had ten thousand students from every corner of the
known world, and they gave that city of fifty thousand inhabitants (or
less—census figures were not to become available until later) a cosmopolitan and free-wheeling character. The students were grouped in
"nations" according to their country of origin and organized in all-
powerful "corporations" that ruled over the faculty. Professors in purple cloaks and hoods swore loyalty to the corporation, were paid by it,
were fined by it for unexcused absences, and were fired when their
lectures became boring. What gave strength and status to the school
was, besides its almost two centuries of past history, its lay orientation.
It developed at the most crucial time in the struggle between papacy
and empire: the latter had helped to finance its planning to shape in
the university a managerial class to oppose that of the Church. Secularization meant freedom, which is a prerequisite for any progress,
especially cultural progress.

There was nothing in Bologna that Petrarch failed to appreciate—
except the law courses that were the reason for his father's having
sent him there. As he was to say later, law is a profession in which dis-
honesty is ruled out, but in which honesty is impossible. So instead
of listening to the lectures in jurisprudence, he attended those in literature, especially in the classics, which were becoming fashionable again
at that time. Vergil, Cicero, and Seneca were astounding discoveries
to him; on their texts he perfected his already quite fluent Latin. And

he developed a craving for rare manuscripts, which was later to make
of him a refined collector, an explorer of archives—in other words, the
first great European *humanist*.

We know nothing else about Petrarch's life as a student. But everything points to the conclusion that there wasn't much else: he doesn't
seem to have taken part in fraternity orgies and was not a great tavern-
goer. Already he was too elegant, too exacting, and too snobbish to
feel comfortable with his fellow students. He was fastidious in his
dress and enjoyed admiration, but more by scholars than by courtesans.
Like most people, he probably had bawdy interludes, but he wasn't
cut out for them. A handsome youth, he was more sensitive than sensuous; he never let himself be carried away by passions, if one assumes
that he had any. Petrarch had already lost his mother before coming
to Bologna; she had died in 1318, and Petrarch had mourned her for
a long time, dedicating his first Latin poems to her memory. In 1326
Petracco died, too, and with him disappeared the necessity for pretending to study jurisprudence. Petrarch, relieved, threw out the law
books that had made him yawn so often and returned to Avignon. He
joined the clergy in order to make a living but took only the minor
orders that were enough to qualify him for clerical benefits. With his
education and brilliant social polish, he had no problem getting ahead
in that court of worldly cardinals, who appreciated his qualities very
much.

Petrarch was not a man who would refuse the pleasures that the
city had to offer. As always he chose the most refined among them:
the most erudite friends, the most exquisite tables, and a discreet
mistress who bore him two illegitimate sons. But his activities did not
prevent him from deploring the corruption of the clergy and insisting
that the Holy See be brought back to Rome. His stand endeared him
to the powerful Colonna brothers, Cardinal Giovanni and Bishop
Giacomo, and earned him their protection—or possibly it was their
protection that suggested his stand. Anyway, he obtained the income
to which he always had aspired and lived comfortably off it.

His liaison and children had not kept him from being a moralist,
and they did not restrain him from falling in love with Laura, the
source of inspiration for his most beautiful poems. Who she was and

whether she even existed has long been uncertain, and the facts are contested even today. But there is a note written in a volume of Vergil's *Aeneid* that had belonged to Petrarch, in which the poet himself has recorded some of the personal data about his lady love. Petrarch recorded the date and the occasion of their first meeting: Easter Mass of 1327, the year after his return to Avignon, in the church of Saint Chiara. At the same hour on the same date in 1348, he added, Laura died. From these dates, historians have deduced that she must have been the Marquise Laura de Sade, an early ancestress of another de Sade, who was to give his name to a quite common vice.

Laura, on the other hand, appears to have had no vices at all. Her features are linked by tradition to a miniature attributed to Simone Martini, now in the Laurentian Library of Florence: it is a handsome face, delicately outlined, suggestive of modesty and virtue. It is not known whether she was already married when Petrarch first saw her, but it is established that she presented her husband with twelve children. Busy as she must have been with pregnancies and nursing, she couldn't have found much time to spend with her worshiper, even if she had had a fancy to do so.

It is possible that Petrarch was not physically attracted to her either, but that he fell in love with Laura as Dante had with Beatrice—as a kind of professional duty. In Provence the influence of the troubadours was still very much alive; as Petrarch was to say later, everyone versified, even theologians, so that one was surprised when cows did not low in verse. And, of course, they continued to do it according to the old established models that required one first to choose an inspiring lady, to whom one's poems were then dedicated. Petrarch went along with the expected routine and wrote the *Canzoniere* for Laura, not even suspecting that it would become his passport to immorality. He himself believed that he would be known by posterity because of his qualities of great grammarian, Latinist, and serious academic scholar, qualities that he admittedly possessed. Instead, the 207 poems of the *Canzoniere* that were his hobby for about twenty years turned out to be his masterpiece, and they remain the only reason that he is being talked about as a poet today.

Between writing sonnets Petrarch kept living the good life; he alternated stints at Avignon, where he was a permanent guest of the Colonna, with trips that combined business and pleasure, to Paris, Flanders, and Germany. He had great tact and worldliness, and his diplomatic qualities were rounded out by a kind of sixth sense that could detect any person worth knowing. Thus, among important people in the world of culture not one escaped him. Perhaps more than knowing them Petrarch liked to be known *by* them. He kept up a thick correspondence in Latin with every man of established reputation; he was, in other words, a master of public relations, and, in fact, his name was well known in the intellectual circles of Europe well before his genius was established. Still as a guest of the Colonna, in 1336 he went to Rome, and the city impressed him with the greatness of its past and the wretchedness of its present. He wandered through the forums where sheep now grazed, was overwhelmed by the ruins of the Colosseum, and wrote fiery appeals to the pope imploring him to leave Avignon and return to Rome. Ultimately, however, he left Rome and returned to Avignon.

There, in Vaucluse, a suburb of Avignon, Petrarch bought a cottage. High society appealed to him somewhat less, his passion for Laura had been worked out in verses, and now he was ready for a simpler, more contained life. He was surrounded by two servants, one dog, many books, and nature. He made mountain-climbing fashionable by completing what was probably the first ascent of Mt. Ventoux. He went fishing, did some gardening, and, above all, he flooded the world with letters in the purest Ciceronian style; he even changed his correspondents' names into Latin, calling one Lelius, the other Scipio, or Ovid. He entreated of them to dig into the archives in pursuit of forgotten classical texts. Whenever he heard that one had been found, he had no rest until they sent him either a copy or the original, which he then copied himself. From Greece he was sent the works of Homer, but he pined in vain for Euripides. Unable to stop writing, he even wrote to the dead: Livy and Vergil were some of his addressees; classic literature was his only true passion.

His feelings for women were never so strong that he could not control them. No woman was ever given precedence over the intellectual pleasures or the quiet of his life of greatly refined selfishness. There is no record of any liaison except the purely poetic one with Laura and the one with the mother of his two illegitimate children. Having passed forty years of age, he wrote, he felt no more desires, or at least he refused to satisfy them. No vital energy could fulfill the demands both of literature and of sex, and between the two he never had any doubts as to which to choose.

Petrarch loved music and played the lute quite well. As for religious questions, he tried to avoid them as much as possible; he acted somewhat as a gadfly to the pope by disapproving the morals of the court that supported him, but he wanted no involvement with dogma. When someone asked him what he believed, Petrarch answered that he doubted everything except what was sacrilegious to doubt. In this cautious balance lay the secret of his happiness but also the limits of his poetic genius. He had much more style and education than Dante but lacked the sublime impulse, the lyrical abandon, the all-consuming thirst for the absolute that drove the other man. Petrarch must have realized this; he always spoke of Dante with respect, but with qualifications that revealed his jealousy.

In 1341 Petrarch returned to Rome to be crowned The Poet on the Capitoline Hill. The idea for the ceremony was suggested by Cardinal Giovanni Colonna, and the senate of the city, which was led by another Colonna, accepted the suggestion immediately, probably not because they admired the poet, but because the ceremony presented a good opportunity to reassert a Roman primacy, at least in the field of culture. Now that the popes had gone, the city no longer knew where to turn in order to attract the world's attention. The populace was getting really discontented; short of bread, it wanted at least to be entertained.

On his way to Rome Petrarch stopped in Naples as a guest of King Robert of Anjou, a fervent admirer of his who paid him great honors and had the poet escorted to Rome. Petrarch returned the favor by advertising the king as a learned patron of the arts—which he was not. Being well aware of the importance of ritual and stagecraft, Petrarch climbed the Capitoline Hill on April 8 clad in a red mantle obtained from Robert, followed by a long and colorful parade of senators in togas and young men in gaudy attire. On the top of the hill Stefano Colonna was waiting with a laurel crown in hand and a speech on his lips. From that moment on, Petrarch was known as "The Poet" by definition, until the title was later awarded Dante by critical acclaim.

The election of Clement VI after the death of Benedict XII drew Petrarch back to Avignon. One had to pay homage to the new pope and, if possible, get him to part with some other benefice. Clement was quite understanding: he awarded Petrarch a priorship in Pisa, a staff position in the Cathedral of Parma, and a diplomatic mission in Naples. Remaining in Naples for a few months before resuming his travels, Petrarch then visited Bologna, Parma, and Verona, where while rummaging in the archives of a church, he discovered the original manuscripts of Cicero's letters to Atticus. One year earlier, in Liége, he had unearthed another Ciceronian text—the *Pro Archia* speech. Such discoveries were the most important events in Petrarch's life, especially since he kept himself aloof from the ups and downs of politics, with the one exception of the Cola di Rienzo episode.

While it causes no wonder that the Roman mobs should have fallen under the spell of an unbalanced demagogue such as Cola, it does seem curious that a polished and cautious intellectual such as Petrarch should have experienced the same fate. Yet that is what happened; the poet was so taken with Cola that he gave up the friendship and protection of the Colonna in order to support him and in 1347 even left sheltered Vaucluse to run to Cola's aid when the latter had established his first government in Rome. It didn't work out, however, because in Genoa Petrarch met with the news of Cola's downfall. Unfortunately, however, this coincidence had brought him into Italy just when the scourge of pestilence was about to fall.

The contagion had come by sea from the Middle East, where it had already caused the death of hundreds of thousands of people. Flies and rats spread it across Europe; the population, weakened by famines resulting from several years of bad harvests, offered little resistance to the infection. The plague manifested itself in two forms: one type attacked the lungs and caused death in three days through hemorrhage, the other type, the bubonic variety, covered the sick person's body with welts and festering sores, demolishing it in five days. The descriptions left by contemporary chroniclers are terrifying. Agnolo di Tura, a historian from Siena, related that because of the overflow in the cemeteries, the corpses had to be buried in mass graves dug out hurriedly in the squares of the city, and that he himself had to do this to five of his children. Boccaccio insisted that there were a hundred thousand deaths in Florence alone—which is impossible, since that was the city's entire population. Villani quoted sixty thousand as the actual figure, but that was an exaggeration, too. However, the slaughter across Europe was indeed frightful. Among the many victims, there was one close to Petrarch's heart: Laura. And it is Petrarch's statement that she died twenty-one years to the hour after their first meeting that suggests the identity of Laura de Sade, registered among the victims of the plague in Avignon on April 3, 1348.

Petrarch escaped contagion, perhaps because of the precautions adopted by his host, Jacopo II of Carrara, Lord of Padua. Jacopo was an enlightened ruler, equally greedy of power, riches, and culture. Padua was experiencing times of splendor; it was one of the cities that had defended most strenuously its civic freedom and, because of its independence, had found itself at a disadvantage in the struggle against the despot Cangrande Della Scala, who had forced the city to become a tributary of his capital, Verona. To elude this serfdom, Padua gave itself to Jacopo I of Carrara, who defended the city with an iron hand which he later used to oppress it. In 1345, true to a family tradition that gave the murderer the privilege of disposing of the inheritance, Jacopo II succeeded his father, whom he had murdered. But Jacopo himself fell victim to the tradition, for he was knifed four years later. What Petrarch must have enjoyed most during his stay in the city was the university, which, though still quite new, was already in full bloom. He was, however, somewhat shocked by the Averroism he found there, that is, by the Aristotelian rationalism then prevalent at the university. He claimed to have heard some professors assert that the soul was not immortal, and that Christianity was a superstition fit only for the ignorant mob. Petrarch was not fond of arguments that might get him into trouble with the Church—he devoted himself to unbelief with the same strenuousness he devoted to the faith, which is to say, not much. But he felt at home in that environment of humanistic learning spiced with court festivities, and in fact he stayed there for a year, till the end of the plague. Afterward he journeyed here and there between Mantua and Ferrara, always on the lookout for important people and precious manuscripts. Finally, he decided to visit the land of his fathers and took the road to Florence.

Boccaccio, who had just begun to write the *Decameron,* was waiting for him there. They got along well together, became friends, and maintained their friendship for the rest of their lives, despite the fact that they were to meet only once more—or perhaps because of it. Given the differences in their personalities and tastes, they were bound to fall out sooner or later. But as soon as Petrarch left, Boccaccio convinced the Florentine government to return the exiled father's confiscated property to the innocent son. The government repealed the confiscation and in addition, offered Petrarch a professorship at the university. However, when Petrarch refused the job, the government took away his property once more.

In 1351 Petrarch was back in Vaucluse, busy writing a little essay entitled *De Vita Solitaria.* And for the first time he found himself involved in a bitter polemic which won him several enemies. The grounds for the quarrel were given by the ill health of Clement VI, a pope who had treated him well and with whom Petrarch had kept up a good relationship. The poet wrote to him with a warning to mistrust physicians, who were, he said, a bunch of charlatans and nothing else. This became only the prologue of a libelous tract he later composed against medicine, so bitter in tone as to suggest that there must have been some personal reasons involved. Perhaps he wasn't feeling well and took out his disappointment on the doctors who weren't able to make him feel better. This interpretation is supported by the fact that on a visit to his brother, Gherardo, who was a monk in a monastery, Petrarch, too, declared his desire to close himself off from the world. But then he relieved himself from that temptation by writing an essay on monastic life, *De Otio Religiosorum.*

The fact is that in Avignon he felt less and less at ease, especially after the death of Clement, who had kept up the tradition of munificence instituted under Pope John. Innocent VI, the new pope, was a handsome specimen of ascetic priesthood, not very responsive to the blandishments of culture. It was natural that he should dislike Petrarch, and vice versa; to the pope's nose the poet smelled of heathenism, and he threatened him with excommunication for being a follower of Vergil. Although Cardinal Talleyrand's mediation saved him, Petrarch knew that it was time for him to move on, and so he accepted with joy Giovanni Visconti's invitation to be his guest in Milan.

Giovanni was a dashing gentleman and a great seducer. When Petrarch arrived and asked how he could be of service, Giovanni answered: "With your presence only, which brings honor to me and to my country." Petrarch accepted the offer gladly and honored Giovanni's court for eight consecutive years, staying there even after the death of his host. The first mission with which he was entrusted by his new patrons was to Emperor Charles IV of Bohemia, who arrived in Italy in 1354. The poet had never met Charles, but after the fall of Cola di Rienzo, he had written him a solemn invitation to come, to restore peace, order, and glory in the "Garden of the Empire." The letter was written in a much grander style than the one Dante had sent to Henry VII, Charles's grandfather, but it lacked any trace of the fire that warmed the awkward Latin prose of the Florentine exile. The emperor and the poet met in Mantua. Petrarch repeated his invitation with magnificent eloquence, and Charles listened to it with polite agreeability. Both were aware that they were playing a comedy. The emperor, who had ice in his veins and a clear mind, knew very well that the "Garden of the Empire" was a nest of snakes, and the poet knew that the emperor knew it. They parted as good friends, and two years later Petrarch visited him in Prague on another mission.

That same year, having been given the task of mediating a reconciliation with Genoa, Petrarch journeyed to Venice as a representative of Visconti. The guerrilla war between the two maritime cities continued to rage, and in a few years it was to escalate into a deadly struggle. The poet could do little about it. But he received a deep impression of Venice, of the strength of her fleet, of the wealth and variety of her trade, and of the liveliness of her life, and so he wrote a detailed description of the city interwoven with some rather syrupy praise of two doges, who did not deserve any at all.

Even before this journey Petrarch had begun to compose a collection of poems in tercets, *The Triumphs,* perhaps as a counterweight to the *Divine Comedy,* which was fast gaining an alarming (from Petrarch's point of view) popularity. The triumphs involved are those of desire over feeling, of chastity over desire, of death over chastity, of glory over death, of time over glory, of eternity over time. It ends with a final farewell to Laura, an apology for the coarseness of his love, and an expression of hope for a definitive meeting in paradise. Unfortunately, the ambition of this work was not matched by the poet's inspiration, which puts in an appearance only rarely.

Petrarch remained a guest of Visconti for six more years, undertaking a diplomatic mission now and then, but above all composing or polishing his works. In 1362, perhaps to escape another epidemic, he returned to Padua and then to Venice, where the republic assigned him a house on the seafront. This time the plague had taken his son, Giovanni, for whom, to tell the truth, he had never cared much. He had a daughter left, Francesca, who was married and had given Petrarch a granddaughter, Eletta. After suffering a slight stroke, which reminded him of the passage of time and the closeness of his end, the poet became nostalgic for his family and called them to join him in the country on the Euganean Hills. In an earlier letter he had expressed the wish to die while reading or writing; his wish was granted, for his family found him with his head reclined over a book. And, as if in deference to his fondness for coincidence, death surprised him on July 20, 1374, his seventieth birthday. In his will he left fifty florins to buy a coat for Boccaccio, who was freezing and dying of hunger.

In Petrarch's desk were found many finished and partly finished works, since he worked on several at a time and was never through correcting and polishing them. It is difficult to understand how he found time to write while leading his wandering life full of diplomatic and cultural assignments, ceremonies, meetings, friendships, acquaintances, and conversations. He must have been a tireless worker, helped by rigid discipline and method.

His contemporaries admired his Latin verse and prose more than any other part of his work: the *Epistolae Metricae,* the *Bucolicum Carmen,* the twenty-four books of *Familiarum Rerum,* the *De Viris Illustribus,* the *Psalmi Poenitentiales,* and so on. A poem published posthumously, *Africa,* also achieved a great success; in it Petrarch attempted to refresh the forms of classical poetry. Certainly all of these are works of a very high stylistic quality. But anyone wishing to find the portrait of a man and the imprint of a unique personality in all of this Latin production needs only to read the *Secretum,* in which Petrarch, because he planned to keep it secret, left a confession of his uncertainties, his moral lapses, and the weakness of his belief in God, affected by doubts and a heavy dose of skepticism. Of his letters, the most beautiful ones are those collected under the title *Seniles,* so labeled because they were composed in the last years of his life, but even here one has the feeling that they were written more for posterity than for the people to whom they had been addressed.

The greatness of Petrarch as a poet and writer is to be found in the *Canzoniere,* which he had thought of as just a hobby, and about which he perhaps even felt embarrassed. Like Dante, who believed himself to be a theologian, Petrarch also was wrong about himself in thinking that his task was to revive classical culture and restore the Latin language. Rather, he was a modern poet, and, above all, he was a very great stylist in the Italian language, perhaps the greatest of them all. When comparing him with Dante, one cannot believe that only forty years had lapsed between them; it seems more like four hundred, so much has the inspiration changed, so much softer and more pliant has the verse become. Dante's strength—the fury, the blood, and the vision has vanished; in its place there has been born a system of beauty and of aesthetics.

But in addition to fashioning a new model of poetry, Petrarch created a new style of life as well. He was a completely new figure— the great Renaissance humanist. He was not, as some have said, just a cynical and cold careerist concerned only with his own success and profit. True, he was more concerned about the immortality of his fame than that of his soul, no matter what his *Triumphs* say; he was a clever self-promoter and did not spare flattery. But he was beset with problems, anxieties, and sadness, despite the serenity that as with Goethe, could be found more in his writings than in his mind and feelings.

Yet he differed from medieval men in that he was free inside. The world was not "God's dream" for him, but a very solid thing; life was not a penance to be endured in suffering, but an exciting adventure to be savored as pleasantly as possible. He enjoyed being liked by people because he liked people himself. He was always eager to meet them, to travel, to be involved in whatever was happening. If he never became ensnared in events to the point of suffering, as did Dante, it was more because Petrarch's interests were limited to culture, rather than for lack of courage or conviction. And he saw culture as an end in itself, a sacred calling that excused one from any other commitment. He would have sacrificed any political ideal or even his beloved Laura for a manuscript by Vergil. And although he became involved in Cola's adventure, it was perhaps because it gave him a good excuse to write epistles and appeals to the glory of Rome.

In 1342, after he already had become an important and fashionable figure, he started humbly to study Greek from a Calabrian monk, whom he later arranged to be rewarded with a bishopric. It disturbed him till the end that he did not know that language well, and out of his own money he endowed a Greek chair at the University of Florence for Leonzio Pilato, so that the latter could teach Greek to others and translate the *Iliad* and the *Odyssey* into Latin. Although he would not have risked a fine to save a pope or an emperor, he gladly would have exchanged his soul for a Homeric text. Petrarch was vain, but he was not miserly. For instance, he was very generous with Boccaccio, to the point of translating one of the stories of the *Decameron* into Latin so that readers around the world would be enabled to enjoy it, purged—he said—of its vulgarity. He never gave up his belief that only in Latin could a writer express himself with elegance. Unfortunately, he also provided a model of courtliness that was to remain engrained in the character of the Italian intelligentsia even after it lost Petrarch's redeeming talent.

Chapter 11

Boccaccio

THE FIFTY florins that Petrarch left Boccaccio came in very handy; he had reached a bad end: poor, lonely, and ill. His afflictions included an eczema that ate away his body and a psychological problem: he believed himself to be a failure and was ashamed of having written the *Decameron*.

Giovanni Boccaccio had been born sixty years earlier, in Paris, the illigitimate product of a relationship between a Florentine merchant who was there selling cloth and a woman whose name is as much in doubt as are her morals. Perhaps his bastard origins are not unrelated to the man's later character and fate. However, his father adopted little Giovanni and took him back to Certaldo, where the boy grew up rather melancholy under the infrequent care of a stepmother.

At the age of fourteen—in 1328—he was sent to Naples as an apprentice accountant in a branch office of a Florentine banker, Bardi, with whom the elder Boccaccio had business dealings. Giovanni developed the same love for bookkeeping that Petrarch had for law. But he liked Naples and remained homesick for it all his life; its noisy, colorful, and cheerful life was congenial to his outgoing and disorderly temperament.

Luckily, a literary vocation, which manifested itself very soon, helped to keep Boccaccio more or less within bounds. He became such a devotee of Ovid that he learned Latin in order to read his works in the original. Nights were spent reciting the *Metamorphoses* by heart; he arrived at the office in the mornings so sleepy and inattentive that eventually they had to fire him. His father faced the evidence: giving up on his plans to make a banker out of Giovanni, he promised him a monthly check if he entered the university to study canon law. Giovanni promised and thus kept up his affair with Ovid and literature.

During the Easter Mass of 1331—that is, under the same circumstances that Laura had appeared to Petrarch—Boccaccio saw for the first time a girl called Fiammetta, and the meeting reduced him to ashes. Hers is another identity that is difficult to pin down, and it remains one that men argue about: it seems, though, that her real name was Maria, that she was a natural child of King Robert, and that she later married the Count of Aquino.

Boccaccio, poor boy, tried to look at her through the same eyes that Dante had turned on Beatrice. This he was able to do only in his poems, which weren't very good, although he produced them in a steady stream, following the still fashionable models of the "sweet style" and the *Vita Nova,* with which he was already acquainted. But in real life it was more difficult to stay in character with the dulcet tones of his verse, partly because of the nature of his emotions and partly because of the character of the woman who had kindled them. Although Maria had been brought up in a convent, or perhaps because of it, she viewed marriage not as a responsibility but as a liberation. A few months after the wedding, the unfortunate husband had already lost count of the horns his wife had planted on his head. Maria was nevertheless a reliable woman, after a fashion; she believed that business and pleasure should be combined and chose lovers who were strong on bank accounts as well as on virility.

Limited by the small income of his father's allowance, Giovanni tried to pay his way with literary currency instead. As he could not present Maria with a fur coat, he buried her under a flood of compositions in prose and in verse. In her honor he translated the romance "Fiore and Biancofiore" into the stupefying *Filocolo.* For her he also

wrote the *Filostrato,* which was slightly better; unfortunately, however, it served as a model and paved the way for the easy and vulgar
Italian versificators that through Mestastasio and the opera lyricists
have come down to our days to write popular songs for the electronic
media. Finally, he overcame Maria's defenses by flattening them under
a ton of bricks: *La Teseide,* a ten-thousand-line poem modeled on the
Aeneid, which tells of the rivalry between two brothers, Palémone and
Arcite, for the love of a certain Emilia, who, after having received on
her bosom the last rattle of one mortally wounded brother, goes on to
bestow her favors on the victorious sibling.

Maria decided to do the same with her suitor—either to make him
quiet or to reward his five years of waiting. Unfortunately, she had
not lost her penchant for drying up a man's wallet, and Giovanni's
took only a few months to drain. She continued to be unfaithful to him
and, using typically feminine tactics, accused Boccaccio of being unfaithful to her. Tempestuous confrontations alternating with reconciliations followed. Finally, Boccaccio foundered in his debts, and even
the Bardi bank was unable to help him out, since it, too, had gone
bankrupt.

With a suitcase full of manuscripts and Fiammetta still on his mind,
but without either an accountant's diploma or a degree in canon law,
he took the road to Florence. It was a pity: Queen Giovanna was about
to be crowned and to begin in Naples an age of *dolce vita* and of
black masses. Boccaccio was just the right person to record that truly
Boccaccio-like period. Who knows what marvelous tales he could have
written about it? But he didn't have a cent to his name, and Fiammetta's infidelity tormented him too deeply. Two months after he
left Petrarch arrived in Naples as the pope's "observer"; it was another close miss for Boccaccio.

The Florence he came back to was a very different city from the one
he had left. Politically, things had not changed too much—the struggle among parties was still alive, though they fought now with less
violence than when they had been led by the Donati, the Cerchi,
or even by Dante, who, although never one of the leaders, had con-

tributed ample ideological ammunition and had finally paid the price for it. Families and interest groups continued to vie for a supremacy that continued to elude them.

But one cannot say that the city had suffered from it. Eighty banks made Florence the Wall Street of Europe. Their loans kept the finances of England and France solvent, and when a member of the banking Peruzzi or Strozzi families visited Paris or London, he was received at court with honors due sovereigns. The gross national product of the whole of England under Queen Elizabeth I was less than that of the city of Florence in the mid-fourteenth century. In the past history of the world and in its foreseeable future, there never was and never will be such a miracle.

It is difficult to say how much fiery party rivalry had contributed to fan the creative spirit of Florence. But it is easy to demonstrate that the two were not in conflict; the fighting and hatred was accompanied by a proud community spirit that challenged individuals, banks, and corporations to a contest in public expenditures. For every palace burned down by partisan hatred, two better ones were built. The millionaires of the period did not sponsor soccer teams; instead, they financed the surfacing of a street, the building of a hospital, the decoration of a church. Thus were Florentine architecture and city-planning lifted out of their medieval obscurity.

The Bardi and Peruzzi commissioned Giotto to paint in the Church of Santa Croce a cycle of frescoes telling the life story of St. Francis, St. John the Baptist, and St. John of the Gospels. A public subscription had collected funds that were to build the campanile that Giotto had designed, and that, according to the priors, was to surpass in magnificence, height, and craftsmanship anything the Greeks or Romans had wrought at the zenith of their greatness. Luca della Robbia and Andrea Pisano, who had finished carving the two bronze portals of the baptistry, were hired to decorate the bell tower. The field of sculpture was undergoing a true revolution; left behind was the sad rigidity of Byzantine art that had dominated and depressed the whole Middle Ages.

A comparable revolution had occurred in literature. The lyrical but obscure and imprecise prattle of Cavalcanti and Guinizelli had become a concrete language with a solid structure that was now turned to works of prose, which is always an indication of the maturity of a language. Nowhere in Europe was prose written with the authority that Villani wielded in his *Florentine Chronicles*. Giovanni Villani, his brother Matteo, and his nephew Filippo were the first modern historians, the first, that is, who employed economics, sociology, and statistics to explain the events they recorded. Thanks to their efforts, we know that at the beginning of the fourteenth century Florence and its suburbs had one hundred and five thousand inhabitants, of which seventeen thousand were beggars; six elementary schools with ten thousand students; and four high schools with six hundred students. Villani foreshadowed what were to become the characteristic qualities of Florentine prose: sparseness, a clinging to facts, and, above all, that objective and bitter attitude toward things that Machiavelli and Guiccardini later developed into a form of art. Realism overlay the poetic spirit in which Dante had found inspiration.

This new intellectual environment was what Boccaccio needed. It took him a while to get over Fiammetta, and for some time he kept sighing after her in verse, putting together the *Amorosa Visione* and *Ninfale Fiesolano* in tercets. Then he turned to writing prose and wrote what today would be called a psychological novel, with Fiammetta in the title role. It told the story of their loves, ending with his first seducing and then abandoning her, which leaves one in doubt as to whether he had been a rascal or a braggart.

It was only after the 1348 plague, however, that he definitely embraced his vocation as a storyteller. One can feel how deeply that horrible calamity affected him by reading his description of it in the prologue to the *Decameron*. He tells of seeing people collapse in the streets with no one to help them, not even parents their children, for fear of becoming infected; of corpses kept hidden, rotting in the attic, so that the neighbors would not set fire to the house; of people who lived in trees or at the bottom of wells, hoping to escape the contagion. As we have seen, he wrote that a hundred thousand died in Florence —according to Villani's figures, this would mean that only five thousand survived. Of course that is impossible, but the statistical exaggeration shows what a blow the epidemic had been to him. And no wonder: the plague of 1348 was a frightful catastrophe that stripped Italy of at least a third of its population and left France a desert "where one no longer hears a rooster crow."

It is from this desolate landscape that the masterpiece of Italian narrative arises, as if to counterpoint the epidemic's horrors. The *Decameron* is in fact a song of resurrection, a vengeance of life over death, a statement of faith against despair, broad laughter to drown the sobbing of survivors.

Seven young, beautiful women are leaving Mass in Santa Maria Novella. As they look over the deserted squares, the empty streets crossed only by funeral processions, their ears echoing with the mourning toll of bells, they decide to go away on a picnic to their summer homes with three young men. In the clean, germ-free air of the woods, they pass the time by each telling one story every day. And since there are ten people in this happy group and the outing lasts ten days (hence *Decameron,* from the Greek *deka hemerai,* "ten days"), there are a hundred stories in the book.

Boccaccio, like Dante, was enthralled by a medieval magic of numbers; he felt bound to respect the architectural rigor that had inspired the cathedrals. Everything was supposed to be harmonious, functional, and rigidly organized into a system. And, in fact, his "human comedy" is respectful of all proportions—ten days, ten stories per day, ten pages for each story. But underneath this traditional structure, attitudes and content are completely novel. Although Boccaccio borrows ideas from French *fabliaux* and Eastern tales, he flavors them with his own sauces. Thus, there are some vulgar stories among the hundred, which go to show that good taste and talent do not always go hand in hand. For instance, the studdish capers of Masetto, who succeeds in satisfying a whole convent of nuns, is frankly obscene; it makes one question the chastity of the seven charming ladies who listened to this bawdy tale without flinching, only blushing a very little bit. But varied as the content of Boccaccio's work is, there is in it a rhythm, breath, vigor,

humor, a fullness of invention, of muscle, and of blood, a sincerity,
and a closeness to factual experience that writers of a preceding generation would never have dreamed of, and those of future generations—
in Italy as well as abroad—would never tire of imitating. So did Sachs
and Lessing in Germany, Molière and La Fontaine in France; the
great Chaucer took from it many of his themes for *The Canterbury
Tales*. Boccaccio anticipates the fat laughter of Rabelais; he mocks
superstition, monks, and even saints. A quip he puts in the mouth of
one of his characters, the Jew Jehannat, will be repeated by Voltaire:
the Church must surely be divine if it has survived so long despite its
priesthood. And the tolerance he shows for other religions would have
seemed sacrilegious to Dante.

Boccaccio is still the great European master of the short story, yet
he himself never understood this; he wrote the *Decameron* as Petrarch did the *Canzoniere*—as a hobby. He was thirty-five when he
started writing it, and he must have published it in installments, because in his introduction to the fourth day he refutes some critical re-
views the first three days' episodes had received. It seems that the work
was completed in five years, and it earned him popularity mixed with
reproach. At the time he enjoyed the former and forgot the latter—he
was still young and hungry. Fiammetta had succumbed to the plague,
which freed Boccaccio from his obsession with her. But he replaced
her with two wives, who ruined his belief in marriage, and with various mistresses, who did not satisfy his need to look for more. The
homage he paid in the *Decameron* to the virtuous and chaste lady
characters was just a literary convention. In reality he abhorred that
type of woman, sensing that their virtue concealed coldness and du-
plicity; he much preferred the company of prostitutes.

Boccaccio lacked Dante's social ambitions and Petrarch's worldliness. But his dissipation was tempered by a disarming openness. He
was not a hypocrite or a lecher; he was a healthy sinner with passion
burning in the blood and darkening his judgment. Every adventure
ended in either a financial or an emotional loss for him, as had his first
affair with Fiammetta. But then, after stilling his desires and counting

his cash, and finding both wanting, he would erupt in violent homilies such as the *Corbaccio* against the gentle sex that have created the completely erroneous impression that he hated women.

Despite all his setbacks, Boccaccio was also able to advance in his career: sincerity and a contagious cheerfulness were apt to dispose people in his favor. They recognized a good friend in him, one incapable of any malice or jealousy. Ostasio da Polenta and Francesco Ordelaffi entrusted him with quite important jobs; the Florentines made him a chamberlain, which was a very respectable position, and sent him first as ambassador to Romagna and then to the pope in Avignon. Perhaps these responsibilities that demanded dignity and polish helped to direct Boccaccio toward more rigorous work. But the crucial thrust was given by Petrarch's visit to Florence in 1350. Friendship between writers is so rare that it is not surprising everyone quotes as an example the sincere relationship of these two; yet for Boccaccio its effects were devastating. He couldn't get over the culture, breeding, and worldly grace that Petrarch displayed with such ease. The latter appreciated Boccaccio's genius (and even more, one fears, his boundless admiration) but offered some criticism to the work it produced, especially concerning the language in which it had been couched (we know how Petrarch believed that only Latin had any validity, and that the only viable style was the imitation of the classics).

Boccaccio, who already had a few doubts of his own regarding the "vulgarity" (in both senses) of the *Decameron,* must have felt altogether embarrassed about it when he met the hallowed poet laureate who was supposed to continue Vergil's work thirteen centuries later. Consequently, to everyone's loss, he stopped writing in the vulgate, abandoning imagination and narrative in order to write useless and boring scholarly works in Latin on the genealogy of pagan gods, on the lives of famous men of antiquity, and even on the geography of mountains, seas, rivers, woods, marshes, and so on. Thus, literature lost a novelist and gained one more pedant.

It was not all Petrarch's fault, however; another bad influence was that of Pietro Petroni, a hermit monk who, as he neared his death, in 1362, sent Boccaccio a message entreating him to amend his licentious life and irreverent works, because if he would not repudiate them in time, they would cost him eternal damnation in hell. Boccaccio had always made sport of hell before, but this time he became afraid of it and decided to send there all his manuscripts, which he burned, and to sell his library. From then on he lived a perpetual Lent full of penance. Despite his meager finances, he helped pay for Leonzio Pilato's coming to Florence and, to please Petrarch, contributed to his translation of the Homeric poems. He became thoroughly respectable, a shining example to the new generation of Florentine humanists. But ailments troubled him and dampened his good cheer. Twice he traveled to Naples in the absurd hope of recapturing the times of his youth, but he was, of course, disillusioned and blamed the city for it. The *signoria* entrusted him with a few more embassies to Rome anod Avignon. But by now he disliked moving about and spent most of the year in the suburb of Certaldo. He never wrote again in the vulgate, except for a *Comment on the Divine Comedy* and a *Little Treatise in Praise of Dante*.

Neither of these works is worth much: the *Comment* is flat, and it commends Dante for all the wrong reasons, namely, for his profound philosophy, theology, and science—qualities he did not have—rather than for his poetry. But according to Boccaccio, poetry is worthless by itself; it counts only as a tool of culture and scholarship. As for the *Little Treatise,* it is a pity that "praise" took the upper hand in it over biographical accuracy. Boccaccio was still close enough in time and in place to have reconstructed Dante's life and he has left us some important facts, but these are so intermingled with gossip, legend, and flattery that even what appears to be true is made suspect.

At least these works show one of the most likable human qualities of the man: his generosity, his ability to admire competitors even to the point of becoming their promoter and copywriter. He wrote a book in Latin on Petrarch, *De Vita et Mortibus F. P.,* and it seems that the *signoria* was responding mainly to his insistence when it established a chair of Dante studies at the University of Florence. At any rate, it was he who taught from it in 1373, with great enthusiasm but not for long, for his health forced him to resign shortly afterward.

He must have been a very bad manager of his own property, as generous people usually are, because despite all the chances he had to become wealthy through his official positions, he ended up extremely poor, quite unable to make ends meet. Petrarch's fifty florins were like heavenly manna. Boccaccio died shortly before Christmas, 1375, at the age of sixty-one, full of regrets, certain of having misused the first half of his life. In fact, he had misused the second.

Chapter 12

A Renaissance Merchant

In the city of Prato there is a statue of a cloaked man, facing the city hall, a round cap on his head, and a bunch of papers in his hand. It is a monument to Francesco Datini, a fourteenth-century merchant who distinguished himself not only by making a pile of money but also by leaving it to his city, together with an archive containing one hundred and fifty thousand letters, five hundred ledgers, and sundry documents. All this material has allowed some historians, notably Mrs. Iris Onigo, to reconstruct the life of a typical businessman of that century, the ways of becoming one, and the conditions of industry and commerce. One can find everything in Datini's correspondence—he had a mania for writing and for saving what he had written—and for these reasons we decided to take him for the subject of this chapter.

Datini was born in 1335, the son of a poor innkeeper who succumbed to the plague of 1348 with his wife and two of their children. Thus Francesco was left orphaned at thirteen with a little brother, Stefano, a house, a small plot of land, and forty-seven florins.* A good-hearted neighbor, Piera Boschetti, took in the two boys and cared for them; they came to think of her as their mother from then on. In the

---

* One florin had a monetary value of approximately twenty-two dollars in present currency, although its purchasing power was, by and large, considerably higher. *Trans.*

following year Francesco went to Florence and became an apprentice clerk in a store, and there he heard the talk of merchants returning from Avignon, which, since the popes had moved there, had become the most important "territory" for Florentine trade. At fifteen he sold his share of the inheritance and with 150 florins in his pocket left for where the action was.

Avignon was indeed as it had been described to him—the center of exchanges between the two great industrial and manufacturing powers of the times, Italy and Flanders. The papal court was their best customer: for his clothes alone John XXII spent 13 hundred florins yearly, and the liveries of his servants cost eight thousand more. All the tableware was gold, worked by Florentine goldsmiths, and the cardinals refused to drink from cups that were not made of precious metal and decorated with little snakes as a precaution against being poisoned—although they did not believe in God, they did believe in magic. Even their horses' bits were of gold; "and golden" wrote Petrarch, "will soon be their hooves." And since, when young Francesco arrived, the Papal See was occupied by Clement VI, the spendthrift, lavishness knew no bounds.

Avignon itself almost had become a Tuscan city—all the artisans who supplied the court were Tuscans, thanks to their patron, Cardinal Niccolo da Prato, who had managed Clement's election. Tuscans were the painters who embellished the churches and the palaces, and foremost among them was Simone Martini, who had settled down in the city with his family and all his apprentices. From Tuscany came the bankers and money changers, the furriers who dressed the ermine pelts that John used as a border for everything, even his pillows. Tuscan was the archiater, that is, the papal physician, Naddino Bovattieri.

Datini must have felt right at home, and he found help and support for the establishment of his business venture. His first merchandise was weapons. France, weakened by the plague and the Hundred Years' War, was pillaged by robber bands—even the popes had to defend themselves from them. Being a good weapons merchant, Francesco supplied without prejudice the forces of both order and disorder; in his ledgers we find an entry recording the sale of fifty "armors for

bandits" imported from Milan and Lyons, the great hubs of war production. To the first shop he opened in the Knights' Square he soon
added three more, with a branch office in Barcelona. His books show
that business went well from the start, but Datini resisted the temptation to enlarge his company into an international outfit on the model
that other Florentines such as Soderini and Guinigi, who had even become bankers and tax collectors to the pope, had developed. True to his
origins in Prato, Datini preferred to make a lot out of a little, rather
than a little out of a lot. He lacked the broad vision of the great Florentine financiers but relished having hundreds of small enterprises run-
ing on shoestrings, so as to limit and distribute risks. For instance, his
attempt to get a corner on salt misfired, but his export of French gold-
based enamels to Florence in exchange for saffron and wine went very
well and made up for his losses.

Datini's warehouses grew in numbers and size but continued to
resemble secondhand stores; they stored everything—leather goods,
jewels, linens from Genoa, corduroy from Cremona, brides' under-
wear, traveling cases; and, above all, clerical vestments. Datini didn't
care about the quality or the origins of his merchandise, as long as
the transaction had possibilities. The mystifying sale of an altar-cloth
valued at thirty-five hundred florins makes one think that he also
dealt in stolen goods. He bought and sold paintings but was only
concerned with their sales potential: in an order he sent to his Florentine buyers, Datini asked for a large picture of Christ on the cross, a
handsome Madonna, a tree with leaves, and a pleasant view. While
his bank account increased rapidly, he remained tied down to small
business practices based on shrewdness and avarice.

He was a strange man: a mixture of courage and caution, of greatness and meanness. From his headquarters in Avignon, Datini directed
by correspondence the most disparate and complex operations taking
place in every European market. This incredible activity was goaded
on by an unremitting anxiety; he trembled at the thought of each transaction, the shipping of the goods, the dangers they faced on land and
sea, the taxes he continuously struggled against, and, especially, the
thought of being robbed by everybody, including his partners. To

prevent the latter from happening, he robbed them first of their dividends. This anxiety, which he used to call "manincony," grew worse with the passing of years and later developed into a fear of death and the hereafter. Like Rockefeller, he lived in fear of hell, and to escape it he fasted, attended pilgrimages, and even went as far as to endow churches and monasteries.

He was a graphomaniac. As if his business correspondence was not enough, he wrote letters to everybody, especially friends in Prato, whom he kept notifying of his impending return. He wanted to marry a woman from home and retire from business. Instead he kept expanding his business, and while he waited for the hometown sweetheart, he collected mistresses who gave him illegitimate children. He was around forty years of age when he finally took the plunge and married a sixteen-year-old Florentine girl, Margherita Bandini, who lived in Avignon. This deal also went well, because despite their difference in age Margherita not only remained faithful to him but put up with his unfaithfulness. And not being able to have a child of her own, she brought up the illegitimate ones he had manufactured outside the home. The wedding party was quite a feast; the menu included 406 loaves of bread, 250 eggs, 100 pounds of cheese, half a steer, 2 rams, 37 capons, 11 hens, and trimmings to boot.

In the following year, 1375, Datini had another stroke of luck. Pope Gregory XI, unwilling to return his court to Rome, had entrusted the management of the papal dominions in Central Italy to French administrators who had provoked a revolt of the population. The financial backing and support for the uprising came from Florence, the city that traditionally had been the staunchest ally of the Church. The pope's reprisal followed immediately and took the usual form of excommunication, which entitled every government to confiscate all property belonging to Florentine citizens. In Avignon, commerce and banking were run by Florentines; they had to leave their stores and companies in great haste, and to avoid losing their property, many left theirs in Datini's hand. Since he was from Prato, he did not fall under the papal sanctions, and, moreover, he had pledged allegiance to Gregory. It is not known whether he exploited this opportunity, but Sapori, one of his discerning biographers, claims that from then on his capital suddenly increased—which is not surprising, given the kind of man he was.

Upon concluding this last advantageous deal, Datini realized that when the pope returned to Rome, the Avignon market would dwindle to insignificance. Thus, he decided to leave a store there in charge of one of his clerks, loaded most of his merchandise aboard ships, and with his wife rode across the Alps, reaching Prato after a month's travel through Milan and Cremona. He arrived home just in time once more to embrace Mamma Piera, perhaps the only person he had ever really loved, or at least the only one with whom he had ever been generous, for almost immediately she died, happy for having seen him again.

Prato was then a town of twelve thousand inhabitants, mostly craftsmen and merchants. It was ruled by the Wool Guild, a labor union that enlisted weavers, spinners, clothmakers, dyers, and merchants, rather than by the constituted urban authorities. And the guild was ruled by capitalists who controlled every facet of the manufacture and monopolized the end product. Nobody could sell or buy wool on his own; no one could open an independent shop; the guild decided working hours, prices, and salaries, keeping the city in such a concentration-camp-like atmosphere that one of its inhabitants, returning to Prato after many years of absence, wrote: "Methinks one who lives here ashamed must be of living."

For Datini, a veteran of the sounds and colors of Avignon, the contrast must have been shocking. Moreover, nobody knew him any longer, and he didn't want to attract much publicity, for fear of the taxes, his constant nemesis. He declared a personal property of three thousand florins but could not resist the temptation of building for himself a house that cost six hundred, which stunned his tightfisted compatriots with its huge surrounding garden. There he installed his headquarters, his desk, and his ledgers, which bore on their frontispiece the motto of his company: "In the Name of God and of Profit." Once settled, he set about reestablishing contact with his subsidiaries in Spain, England, Germany, and the Middle East. Then he registered at the guild, becoming partner of a man who already had achieved prestige in the wool business. He left the manufacturing end to the partner and used his extensive European organization to provide a steady supply of raw material—that is, wool. The local kind was inferior in quality, and Datini secured for himself large quantities of English wool, the best in the world, thus making his products unrivaled.

Despite the profits, Datini soon came to realize that Prato was too small and reactionary to contain him. Consequently, leaving house and wife there, he moved his offices to Florence, where he registered at the Silk Guild and established a shop in Por Santa Maria that broke precedents as to equipment and efficiency. The walls were paneled in wood, and the furniture consisted of a row of benches, a desk with a chair, a safe with bolts and padlocks, a scale, two pairs of scissors, a measuring stick, a copper kettle, and one iron lantern. Windows and doors were heavily barred. In the back there was a bed for the boy who, according to the guild rules, had to sleep there at night. The personnel consisted of a scribe who stood in a corner behind a large table divided in squares, each of which was further divided into seven columns—the first for denari, the second for soldi, the third for lire, the remaining ones for twenty, a hundred, a thousand, and ten thousand lire. In addition to the scribe, who took care of all the accounting, there were two or three apprentice boys doing their practice training.

That was all: it was from such holes and with such a staff that the Florentine merchants supervised transactions involving the equivalent of millions of dollars around the world. Once in a while the guild inspector called to check the accuracy of the scale and the yardstick. Throughout the day other merchants stopped by to discuss the news and the fluctuation of prices. Every so often a courier arrived, carrying letters in his pouch—the highlight of the day.

The Florentine merchants had established a well-run express mail service that left twice a day for some of the most frequent destinations such as Venice, Flanders, and Champagne. But Datini had branches and interests as far away as in Spain and the East, so he needed private messengers as well, and in their choice he was extremely particular.

The messenger had a very difficult job: one had to be both brave and cautious, physically enduring, clever, and dependable. Datini appears to have been fortunate in his choices; the archives record that his messengers could get to Genoa in three days and to Venice in six. Nevertheless, to avoid any bad surprises, he often made several copies of each letter and sent them by different couriers. He wrote his own letters, since he mistrusted anyone else, and given the extension of his commercial network, he must have been writing from dawn to dusk—a fact amply confirmed by his files.

From his letters one can piece together the trade routes that across land and sea linked Spain to the Orient, the percentage of his losses, which were heavy, due to pirates on the sea and bandits on land, and the extent of his trade. In this latter respect, once he had established himself in Florence, to his other merchandise Datini added a new sideline: slaves. The best market for them was in Majorca, but traders were allowed to import them into Florence as long as they were "infidels," that is, Muslims or Jews. Here is what he writes about a pregnant slave: "We have talked to the priest who used to own the slave you have now; he tells you to throw her and what she carries in her belly into the sea, but she is not his chattel any longer . . ."—a small glimpse into the morals of the time and that of its clergy.

Datini worked through companies; these were at first small family concerns that included a father, his sons, and his brothers, that is, people who shared the same bread—hence the term *compagnia* (from *com pane,* "with bread"). Later they began to admit people from outside the family as "partners." Datini's companies were of the second type, but he expected his partners to hold business ties as sacred as those of kinship; of course he was always the father who, ruling over all the enterprises, brought them all together under his fist. Filial obedience was expected from his collaborators, and in exchange he dealt with them with paternalistic care. Here is what he says about one of the shop-assistants who died: "My Checco has gone to Heaven. . . . Two doctors were at all times around his bed, and all the household, ever, day and night, at his service . . . Well, it pains me; I can do no more. He was an upright youth, and faithful." But he writes to

the manager of the Barcelona branch who complained about the behavior of his nephew Maso: "Punish him every way and manner and
do not spare efforts."

By the end of the century Datini had achieved all his goals, and he
could have retired, rich, happy, and silvery-haired, in his beautiful
home in Prato. Instead, he continued to keep his wife there alone,
writing her a letter every single day, while he stayed in his shop on
Por Santa Maria to develop his business network further and further
and to follow its fortunes with the usual anxiety. He was one of the
few people who went to great expenses to insure his merchandise; yet
this was not enough to reassure him, because he knew how difficult it
was to secure refunds in case of a loss. He wrote his wife: "Sweet it is
for them to touch money when they cash in the aforementioned pre-
mium, but when a disaster strikes, each pulls his ass in . . ." They
sound like words written today. But he could draw some advantage
out of disaster, too; he would write Margherita to spread the news
around, making the misfortunes seem worse than they actually were,
so that the tax collector—his constant incubus—would take the loss into
account.

At the end of the century, perhaps to facilitate the financing of his
enterprises, Datini also joined the Guild of Changers and opened up a
bank. It caused him no end of troubles: first the internal revenue hit
him even harder than before, and then his God-fearing friends reproached him for practicing the sin of usury. An upright gentleman
by name of Lapo Mazzei acted as a kind of spiritual director to Datini,
and his affectionate yet strict letters, devoid of any servility, are documents of a friendship based on moral rectitude and human understanding. Mazzei was the only man Datini feared, and whose criticism
he would take. The letters he received from this man reveal the confusion that existed around the concept of money and of interest, thanks
mainly to the teachings of the Church. In the late Middle Ages, when
practically nobody else had any cash, the Church had been lending it
at the most outrageous interest rates. But upon the development of
private lay capitalism, the Church remembered that St. Augustine and
St. Jerome had believed that any profit derived from money itself was

usury, which was a mortal sin. This did not prevent priests from continuing to practice usury, but it allowed them to browbeat laymen who did the same. St. Thomas had tried to restore order amidst these inconsistencies by recognizing that money had its "right price," but his rule was ambiguous enough to permit any practice. One bank had evaded the stigma by asserting that sin assumes the existence of a soul, and that usury can exist only when an individual practices it, but that a bank is something impersonal without a soul, therefore it cannot sin. It is not known how this particular subterfuge worked, but we do know that popular opinion equated the terms "banker" and "usurer," and so did Lapo Mazzei, who warned Datini not to "strangle" his customers. The latter was so disturbed by it all that when his partner Cambioni died, he sold the bank, which by then had become one of the strongest in Europe.

How he found time and energy to womanize, with all the years and business weighing on his shoulders, God only knows. Yet he still had that habit. For years the only contact he had had with his wife was through his daily letters, which record more gripes than affection. Margherita had tried desperately to give him a son; she had even sent for a miraculous girdle that, according to the prescription, had to be laced on by a virgin boy, after three Our Fathers and three Hail Marys, one of each in honor of God, the Trinity, and St. Catherine. Yet not even this cure helped, and the poor woman was left disillusioned and embittered. It might have been in part to escape her nagging that Francesco transferred his business from Prato to Florence. Every Wednesday he sent word that on Saturday he would come and spend the weekend at home, but—as Margherita complained in one of her letters—"Methinks each Friday evening thou changest thy mind." It would have been better if that always had been the case. But once in a while he made it home, and then his eyes would fall on a fifteen-year-old servant girl called Ghirigora, with the result that at one point he had to spend 165 florins in dowry to find her a husband who would take on the responsibility of a child who had been conceived six months earlier and survived six more months. Datini had the infant buried inside his private chapel, at the foot of the altar, the space reserved for illegitimate children. Later Ghirigora's husband died, and she asked the old master to take her back into his house, but Datini refused. A short time afterwards, the same accident happened to another household maid, a twenty-year-old slave, Lucia. Margherita adopted the girl resulting from that liaison, and fifteen years later Datini married her off to a young man of Prato with a dowry of one thousand florins. But after the beautiful ceremony, when he was supposed to pay up, he subtracted 840 florins from the original sum to pay for the wedding expenses and pointed out in the small print of the contract the clause stating that if the bride were to die within two years, the widower had to return the thousand florins— that was the Datini business style.

The only extravagance Datini allowed himself concerned the house and his clothes. He owned six linen shirts—an unheard of luxury in those time—and each day he expected to have a clean one to wear; six pairs of trousers; four vests with cotton lining; ten fur-lined jackets, and no fewer than five floor-length overcoats. On the other hand, he didn't possess nightshirts or pajamas, and when he slept with his wife they both slept naked, except for nightcaps on their heads. His house, which still stands, could be said to be more comfortable than architecturally outstanding. Its rooms were barrel-vaulted; it had two kitchens and a few guest rooms. When illustrious guests, such as the French ambassador and Louis II of Anjou, called on Datini, he entertained with great munificence, considering the expenses helpful to the prestige of the company. His table was famous for the variety and richness of its food; Datini was a glutton, and he especially liked venison.

After his sixtieth birthday, Datini's insane working schedule had to be somewhat curtailed. But his eternal anxiety, instead of decreasing, got even worse—now he not only worried about business but about the plague as well. He had already witnessed six plagues, including the first that had killed his parents and brothers and left him shocked. Then, in 1399, another epidemic exploded. Datini dressed in the coarse robe of a monk and went on a barefoot pilgrimage, candle in hand, to be spared from the sickness. He disliked the clergy, and many were the times that he had made fun of priests, but he believed in God—or in hell, at least—had regularly gone to confession, and had often opened his purse to contribute to Church charities. He also kept abreast of sermons, especially those preached by St. Bernardine of Siena, who used to assemble an audience by imitating the crow of roosters and the croaking of frogs and then kept up its attention by spicing the Holy Writ with anecdotes and gags.

Surrounded by his brother-in-law, his partners, and other members of the household, Datini now tried to escape the danger by chanting:

> Mercy, eternal God.
> Peace, peace, pious Lord,
> Do not look at our mistakes.
> Mercy are we calling
> Mercy do not ban us
> Mercy God preserve us
> Mercy to the sinner.

But there was no mercy. Once more the black plague struck Europe, and its deadly tide washed over Prato. Datini fled on muleback across the Apennines toward Bologna, followed by Margherita, his daughter, two employees, and some servants. It was the year 1400; he remained four months of it in Bologna while the faithful Mazzei kept him supplied with news from home. They were terrifying accounts: "Yesterday 201 died here, not counting hospitals, priests, monks and convents, and others who do without carrion-pickers." Lapo's family was struck, too—two of his sons died, one after the other. His descriptions of Florence are no better than the ones Boccaccio gave of the 1348 plague: shops closed, empty streets, the death bells' constant tolling.

When the curse had passed, Datini returned to Prato and from then on remained there. As elsewhere in other Italian cities, at least one-third of the population had been wiped out. The old merchant, still sound in body, had been severely shaken. Lapo, who had miraculously escaped the epidemics, kept warning him: "This living of ours is a race towards death," and encouraged him to devote his remaining years to the Lord. Datini was moved to make his will; to his attorney he disclosed that his fortune added up to seventy thousand florins, more than the King of France could get from all his domains in a year. Listening to Mazzei's advice, he left it all to the charitable foundation called "The Poor Man's House," except for a yearly income of one hundred florins to his widow and a few smaller legacies to his daughter and servants. After this investment in heavenly real estate, he returned to managing his business and continued at it until his sudden death in 1410.

Datini had not been a great man. However, he was the perfect embodiment of the new type of capitalist produced by fourteenth-century society, and he had had the foresight to leave behind him a complete portrait of his activities in his files. In contrast to merchants and bankers of the previous century who had always belonged to a guild, a party, or a family clan, Datini was a "self-made man" who worked for himself, to an extent unknown to any Acciaioli, Bardi, Peruzzi, Cerchi, or Frescobaldi—a sign of how much the individual had become independent of social ties. Moreover, while his predecessors had been interested in money only as an instrument of power and status, he had been interested in money as a goal in itself. He had never tried to use it to buy himself a coat of arms or to start a political career. The only public office he ever held was that of Standardbearer of Justice in Prato, and that was against his wishes and only for a short time. He was uninterested in politics, or, to be more exact, he despised it as a vocation for "charlatans" who are just a nuisance to important people, namely, to those who are busy producing and hoarding gelt—a "know-nothing" attitude that, along with his business methods, Datini shares with modern capitalists. The merchants and bankers of the thirteenth century had been pioneers, adventurous fighters who had opened new trade routes single-handedly on both land and sea. They had to do everything alone, inspired by a heroic entrepreneurial spirit. Datini had been only in Avignon, Prato, and Florence and rarely had left his desk. Yet he was already plugged into a system that did not require his personal intervention; he had "vice-presidents," "branches," correspondents, messengers. Above all, he had "letters of exchange" that allowed him to move his capital with relative ease.

With Datini begins a new capitalism based more on efficiency and method than on creativity and courage. As Sapori says, with men such as Datini the business volume of the Italian economy did not decrease, but the businessmen's stature did.

Chapter 13

THE PAPACY RETURNS TO ROME

IT MIGHT be that St. Catherine's threats and entreaties influenced the decision to return the Apostolic See to Rome. However, there were two more immediate reasons. In the first place, the King of France was at the moment too weak to prevent it, having begun a war against England that was to last for a hundred years and that at the time was definitely not running in his favor. The country was being invaded by foreign armies and weakened internally by pestilence and famine. Moreover, there was no help to be expected from the Anjou subsidiary in Naples, which under Queen Giovanna's senseless rule had become incapable of exerting any political pressure.

The second reason was that the situation in Italy, and especially in the Papal States, was approaching a truly alarming level of anarchy: new *Signorie* were created, fought and destroyed each other, and were reborn under new guises. Once in a while, one of the fatuous emperors that the Germans kept electing marched into Italy, but nobody expected him to wield any power. In 1354 it was the turn of Charles IV of Bohemia, who was supported by the pope and crowned in His Holiness' name by Cardinal Bernardi. Charles, as we have seen, met with Petrarch and then scoured the country, selling to the various cities on his way the privilege of not being molested—Florence bought its safety for one hundred thousand florins. The prestige of the crown that had been worn by Charlemagne, Barbarossa, and Frederick II had never before fallen so low. The emperor had become nothing more than an odious collector of an arbitrary tax, yet many Italian princes were using the title of imperial vicar to help bolster their own unstable power. It was in the name of that illusory emperor that Cola di Rienzo had donned the cloak of Augustus and announced the return of imperial eagles to the "fateful hills" of Rome. Cola was crazy, but the many princes and princelings who grabbed for their shares of the country while all the confusion was going on knew what they were doing. The Malatesta, Ordelaffi, Montefeltro, Varano, and Trinci were slowly eating up the Papal States. The Visconti were beginning to develop a dangerously attractive power, based on Milan, over the entire peninsula; even Genoa fell into their hands by 1353. And, it was quite clear, the coalition of these two cities could well have united the rest of the country five hundred years before unification actually occurred—which was precisely what the Church most feared.

Italian unification, then, was the danger that upset the popes in Avignon, despite the fact that they were French. Clement VI had tried to restore his own authority in Rome by using Cola—which explains why the tribune, after his first fall, was treated more as a guest than a prisoner in Avignon. Then, soon afterward, Clement died, and Innocent VI, a man of very different ilk, as modest and frugal as his predecessors had been openhanded, was elected to take his place. Yet Innocent shared with Clement a firm commitment to defend the rights of the Church. It was Innocent, in fact, who, fooled by Cola's outward sanity after three years of exile in Avignon, sent back the tribune to Rome as his representative, though it is true that to avoid nasty surprises he appointed a cardinal to be always at Cola's side, a Dominican who was made on the image of St. Dominic's own lieutenants.

The cardinal, Gil Alvarez Carrillo de Albornoz, belonged to an aristocratic Spanish family and his seminary had been the military barracks. In fact, he had been made Archbishop of Toledo in recognition of his leadership in war, so when they sent him to Italy, he prepared himself for another campaign. When they stopped in Florence, Albornoz let Cola go ahead to meet his doom in Rome while he stayed behind to persuade the city to finance an army for him. The Florentines gave him a handful of men, but Albornoz used them successfully to play off against each other the various princelings who had carved up the Papal States. He would invite the enemies to parley, and during negotiations he had their fortresses demolished. Such, for example, was the fate of Giovanni Vico, who came to meet the cardinal as Lord of Viterbo, Orvieto, Amelia, Narni, and Terni. After the talks were over, he realized that he had nothing left except the title of Church Vicar in the hamlet of Corneto.

The Albornoz strategy consisted of convincing the lesser nobility that they would profit more under the patronage of a remote power such as the Church, which could defend them from the greed of their more powerful neighbors, than on their own. And the strategy worked. Thus he succeeded in isolating the two ringleaders, Malatesta and Ordelaffi, and against them there could be nothing but war.

Malatesta lost the first encounter and was cowed into suing for peace. Albornoz was magnanimous. Despite the fact that his enemy had been excommunicated, he made him the pope's representative in charge of the towns of Pesaro, Rimini, and Fano. He was less generous to Ordelaffi, a tyrant feared by his subjects for his cruelty but also respected because of his abilities. Ordelaffi's troops were led by an outstanding general—his wife, Cia degli Ubaldini. To defeat this dangerous couple Innocent resorted to excommunication, while Albornoz declared a crusade and promised the absolution of every sin, no matter how heinous, to those who took part in it. Thieves and murderers flocked to the papal army; the Ordelaffi answered by burning straw puppets representing the pope and his cardinals on the square of Forlì. "Here I am, excommunicated," the tyrant shouted, "yet meat, bread, and wine still taste as good as before."

Albornoz won the first round by conquering Cesena, which Cia had bravely defended street by street, but then he was unaccountably recalled to Avignon, and his replacement lost all of his gains. The next year—1357—Albornoz returned, and after twenty months of war Ordelaffi had to surrender. Bologna also decided to place itself in the winner's hands. But when among the festivities that accompanied the city's submission to the pope, a popular referendum, in which one voted with a black bean to express allegiance to the Church, was held, the embarrassing results showed 1644 white beans and only 5 black ones.

Since all of central Italy had returned to the Church's fold, Albornoz marched on Rome, to restore order in the city. A senator appointed by the pope was to rule it, and his most important qualification for the office was that he should not be a Roman—apparently Albornoz had learned a trick or two from past experience. The senator was supported by seven popularly elected "Reformers of the Republic," who could not be of noble birth. Then Albornoz completed his job by dictating a constitution that was to underpin the Papal States for the next five hundred years.

The road was now clear for the pope's return to the city. Innocent VI recently had died, and it was his successor, Urban V, also bent on healing and restoring the moral climate of the church, who announced the reestablishment of the Apostolic See in Rome. It is no coincidence that his decision was made when the French had suffered a beating to end all beatings and their king had been captured by the English. The still largely French cardinals were horrified by their pope's plan and accused him of having fallen for Petrarch's rhetoric and St. Catherine's threats, but Urban did not waver from his resolution.

He boarded ship in Marseilles in April, 1367, escorted by a joyous parade of Genoese galleons. Rome, deprived of popes for sixty-four years, prepared a triumphant welcome. The greatest Italian princes gathered to receive him: the Este, the Savoia, the Malatesta, some of whom held the reins of the white mule that Urban rode into the city. He was escorted to St. Peter's by a following of banners, canopies, and a crowd in shining armor and colorful uniforms. Albornoz was the only man absent: he had died on the eve of the restoration that was actually the result of his personal greatness. This Spaniard probably had been the only outstanding Italian statesman of the fourteenth century.

But when the holiday was over, the pope fell prey to misgivings.

Rome was nothing but a grandiose cemetery—St. Paul's Basilica was in ruins, St. Peter's tattooed with cracks, the Lateran was burned almost completely to the ground, palaces and hovels were caving in on each other, the unpaved roads were blistering with marshes, there was no industry, and the populace was hungry. The most arrogant and inept aristocracy in the whole of Europe had mismanaged the city almost out of existence.

Urban was unable to accustom himself to this disaster area and retired to the town of Montefiascone after handing over to the city government ample funds for the necessary emergency repairs. But even Montefiascone was not enough. Urban began to pine for France. Typically, when Petrarch found out about the pope's homesickness, he sent letter after letter entreating him not to give up. St. Bridget of Sweden predicted that Urban would die if he left Italy. Charles IV solemnly renounced the claims that the empire had held, at least in theory, over central Italy; he even called on the pope in person, humbly held the bit of Urban's horse, and then served Mass to him in St. Peter's.

Urban persevered till 1370. But when he felt the end coming, he would not rest until he saw again his beloved Avignon; he died there shortly before Christmas, dressed in a Benedictine robe, reclining on the straw of a little room that resembled a cell.

Urban's successor was Gregory XI, who had been made a cardinal by his uncle, Clement XI, at the age of eighteen, and like his uncle he preferred Cicero to the Gospels and Carnival to Lent. Gregory had no desire to follow Urban's example, and he remained in France for seven years despite Petrarch's eloquence and the despair of St. Catherine. He appointed a group of French cardinals to rule over the state that Albornoz had rebuilt, but they behaved like conquerors in an occupied territory, and the results were not long in being felt. In Perugia a nephew of the papal administrator had pursued the favors of a lady with such insistence that she finally jumped out of a window to her death rather than comply. A deputy who had come to ask for justice was answered by the arrogant legate: "What is all this? Do you think we French are eunuchs?" The city rose up in arms, followed by others in neighboring regions. By 1375 the work of Albornoz lay in ruins; of sixty-four cities that had acknowledged the pope's supremacy, only one remained faithful. And the insurrection was led by Florence, which always had stood the most rigorous guard to the papal domains. Now it was leading and financing the coalition against the pope, waving a banner embroidered with the word *Libertas*—"freedom."

Gregory attempted to cope with the problem without leaving Avignon. He excommunicated Florence, authorizing France and England to confiscate the immense possessions that Florentine merchants and bankers owned in those two countries (the two governments seized the bounty with great eagerness). But although its finances were about to collapse, Florence replied by confiscating the Church estates on its territories, closing the ecclesiastical courts, destroying the buildings of the Inquisition, jailing the resisting clergy, executing the most recalcitrant ones, and sending an invitation to Rome to join the revolt. Gregory was forced to act: he let the Romans know that if they refused Florence's plea, he would return to the city.

Such a promise assured the pope of Rome's loyalty. But now that he had promised, he had to deliver. First, however, he had to restore papal authority over the insurgents, and he lacked an Albornoz to do it. Consequently he had instead to rely on those foreign mercenary leaders who in the past dozen years had discovered what a bonanza Italy could be for them. Two of them distinguished themselves especially, by fighting for the pope and by their cruelty. One was an English adventurer called John Hawkwood, whose name the Italians changed to Giovanni Acuto but usually called "The Cutthroat." Hawkwood led a band of robbers who called themselves "The Holy Company" because they were paid by the pope. They showed their holiness in the town of Faenza, where they massacred three hundred unarmed citizens, not because they were rebels, but because they might have become such. Then Hawkwood chased all the inhabitants out of town, "keeping only those women that pleased him and his followers." Hawkwood's colleague and friend Robert of Geneva was no better, although he was a cardinal. One of his "Triumphs" occurred when, riding with a pack of Bretons, he conquered Cesena by ruse.

His actions were as bloody as Hawkwood's: he had four thousand persons killed, after which he left, taking with him, as usual, the youngest and prettiest girls.

It was then that Florence sent St. Catherine as ambassador to the pope with the result that she gave Gregory the talking-to that almost ended in her arrest and excommunication. It is impossible to say whether her violent plea affected the pope or not, but the fact is that immediately afterward Gregory sailed from Marseilles and, early in 1377, reached Rome. He didn't get the same welcome that had been extended his predecessor; in fact, he felt so insecure in the city that after a few weeks he retreated to Anagni, from where he began to try to restore peace in his dominions by the use of diplomacy rather than force. However, faith in the papacy had been so severely damaged that it took him a long time to convince the various cities to overthrow their rebellious rulers and acknowledge again the pope's sovereignty. The last to give in was Florence, and to cope with that city, the pope had to enlist Bernabò Visconti as a mediator. Visconti did his job but asked, as payment for his pains, for half of the sum Florence had to pay for reparations and for the lifting of the excommunication ban— a sum he set at eight hundred thousand florins. The pope reduced the sum to the more likely figure of two hundred fifty thousand florins, but Gregory did not live long enough to see peace entirely restored in his domains. Late in 1377 he returned to Rome, and a few months later he died, whispering one word: "France."

Thus ended the period of the pope's stay in Avignon, an era that has passed into history as "The Babylonian Captivity." There is no doubt that it had a determining influence on the coming crisis that was to lead the Church to the brink of a catastrophic schism, which even then was not avoided but simply delayed until the Reformation. The papacy of Avignon was a mistake because it nurtured the suspicion that the Church had become a tool of French political power, as the Greek Orthodox Church had become in the hands of the Byzantine rulers. The danger was that the West would now be ruled by a caesaro-papacy, with the pope's serving as the chaplain to the French king, as the Patriarch of Constantinople served his emperor. And it is more than probable that this was the goal of the King of France and that he would have achieved it had he not started the unfortunate Hundred Years' War against England. That France was planning to obtain control of the papacy and use it for political aims is shown by the fact that of 134 cardinals appointed throughout the whole interlude at Avignon, 113 were French. Naturally, the French predominance provided excellent arguments for those who, especially in England and Germany, were preparing a revolt against the centralized power of the Church, and there is no doubt that the seeds of the Reformation, which was to sunder Western Christianity, were sown in Avignon. In fact, the first assault against the totalitarian structure of the Church, led by Wycliff in England, dates from that period.

For the time being, however, the Church saved itself by moving its see back to Rome. The evidence indicated that it could not find a home anywhere else, not because God had bestowed a divine, universal mission on Rome, as her rhetoricians claimed, but because Rome was not—and has never become—the capital of a nation that could impose its lay demands over those of the Church. Any place else the Church would have had a state to contend with. But in Italy the Church successfully prevented the formation of a state, and when one eventually emerged, it became the Church's prisoner. There is a good reason that since time immemorial only Italian cardinals have been elected popes: they are truly "stateless" and thus are sure to serve only the interest of the Church.

Chapter 14

THE SCHISM AND THE COUNCIL

IT DIDN'T take the Romans long to show that they were unworthy of the papacy that they had just regained. They besieged the Lateran, where a conclave had assembled to elect a successor to Gregory, and threatened the cardinals with death if they failed to select a Roman, or at least an Italian pope. There were only sixteen cardinals, twelve of whom were foreigners, mostly French. In great haste the cardinals elected the Archbishop of Bari, Bartolomeo Prignano, and then fled in terror, nostalgic for the good times of Avignon.

The new pope assumed the name Urban VI, and he began his reign by trying to demonstrate that Providence can sometimes make use of threats and blackmail to place the right man in the right place. He appointed trusted men to consular and senatorial positions, and he organized a good police system to let the Romans know that the party was over. Next he announced a Church reform that would proceed from the top downward, beginning with the high clergy whose loose morals the pope denounced in violent public sermons. He abolished the grafts and gratuities that the prelates of the Curia demanded from everyone who had business with the Church. When Cardinal Orsini came to remonstrate, Urban turned him out, calling him a "fathead." An even worse fate awaited the Cardinal of Limoges, who was being contrary: Urban pounced on him and slapped his face. St.

Catherine wrote suggesting moderation, but Urban went ahead regardless and, to insure himself a majority in the conclave, appointed a batch of Italian cardinals.

When the French cardinals saw their ascendancy threatened, they got together in Avignon and proclaimed Urban's election void, on the ground that it had been the result of pressure from the Roman populace. Many other important prelates signed the declaration, and on September 20, 1378, Robert of Geneva was crowned pope in Avignon with the name Clement VII. The King of France, who had been behind the revolt from the beginning, immediately recognized the new pope, as did Naples, Spain, and Scotland, but the rest of Europe remained loyal to Urban. And thus began the great schism that for decades transformed the Church into a battleground.

Even the saints split up and chose sides: St. Catherine, who despite everything liked Urban's strict morality and hot temper, called Clement a Judas; St. Vincent Ferreri turned around and applied that title to Urban. Each side considered the other's sacraments void; an entire generation grew up without knowing whether it had received a bona fide baptism and died in doubt of having been genuinely absolved.

Some historians have seen in Urban a reincarnation of Boniface. It is true that both precipitated a catastrophe with their authoritarianism, but Boniface had been a cynic who used the authority of his status to achieve his personal goals, while Urban considered himself only a devout soldier of the Church and lived a frugal life without any trace of exhibitionism or ambition. Urban erred in pursuing too eagerly his beliefs but did not covet power for himself. Like all zealots, however, he could be cruel: he had seven cardinals arrested, tortured, and killed, stubbornly refusing any compromise with the opposing side.

More than the fault of single individuals, the schism was the product of a certain political situation, the progressive evolution of national states each of which wanted to have its own pope. In fact, when the two main characters died, the schism went on. To replace Urban, the Roman conclave elected Pietro Tomacelli with the name Boniface IX: to replace Clement, the conclave in Avignon elected Pedro de

Luna as Benedict XIII. The King of France suggested they both resign, but Benedict refused, and everything went on as before.

At the end of the century Boniface announced a new Jubilee. It was to be the test of strength between the two popes, and Boniface showed himself worthy of the name he had chosen—he really resembled the Boniface of a century earlier. He left no stratagem untried, however despicable, to achieve success for his plans. Foreseeing that France, Naples, and Scotland would make it difficult for pilgrims to leave for Rome, he had traveling preachers promise that a person would be absolved from all sins even without going to Rome, as long as he paid the sum needed for the expense of the trip. Some of the preachers collected the money without bothering to confess the sinners, and Boniface censored this practice. But when a preacher tried to hold back some of the money, Boniface had him tortured until the last cent was returned. Some who underwent this treatment were actually innocent and had to pay with their own money to survive. Others were lynched by the Roman populace for having exempted potential pilgrims from the trip to the city, thereby depriving its citizens from the right of fleecing their guests.

In terms of participation, the Jubilee of 1400 was less stupendous than the one of 1300, but as far as income for the pope's coffers was concerned, there was nothing to complain about. Boniface used the windfall to strengthen his personal power, but in the process he provoked the Colonna to revolt, and with French help they collected an army of eight thousand to overthrow him. Boniface retreated into St. Angel's castle and waited until the mob got tired of the siege and rebelled against the rebels. About thirty leaders were captured, and Boniface promised safety to one of them as long as he would execute the others. The unfortunate accepted the bargain and even hanged his own father and one brother.

Shortly afterward Boniface died, and when Innocent VII took his place, the Colonna returned to the offensive. The pope fled to Viterbo, and the fickle Roman mob broke into the Vatican, spread mud and excrement over the papal insignia, and threw the contents of the archives out of the windows, filling the streets with files and historic documents. Then they made peace with Innocent and recalled him to Rome, just in time to see him die.

Another conclave followed, and it elected Gregory XII, who proposed an agreement to Benedict, his rival in Avignon. The latter declared himself ready to resign, if Gregory would do the same. Gregory was about to agree, but his family made it clear to him that this was out of the question. Then some cardinals loyal to Rome announced that they were convening a council to elect a new pope that would reunite the Church in his name—this time it was Benedict's turn to refuse. But the King of France and many of the cardinals loyal to Avignon abandoned Benedict and joined with those who had left Gregory. They all decided that a council must be held and fixed its date for March 25, 1409, in Pisa.

The decision was prompted by more than the present crisis; during the past century there had developed within the Church a "conciliar movement" that questioned its monolithic and authoritarian structure. William of Occam had held that it was not the pope, nor even the clergy, but the community of believers that constituted the Church. The community can delegate its will to a council, but all power ultimately issues from it, including that of electing or deposing a pope. Marsilius of Padua had echoed the same theory—the council, he said, represents Christianity and as such cannot remain a monopoly of the clergy; the laity has a right to participate in it; and the pope is just the executor of conciliar decision.

Langenstein, a German theologian, created a great stir at the University of Paris with a treatise he had written on this topic. Whatever one might believe, he said, the facts are obvious: popes and cardinals have been unable to resolve the schism. Therefore, it is clear that when their abilities are insufficient to cope with a crisis, one needs to resort to a superior will, outside the hierarchy of the Church— that of the council. Gerson had boldly repeated these arguments in the very presence of Pope Benedict.

It was probably because of these internal attacks against the traditional structure of the Church that the cardinals of both sides agreed to hold the council. But they saw it only as an expedient to preserve the status quo of the Church, not as the beginning of a kind of democratic assembly that Occam and the other reformers wanted. It was the first act of that dramatic breach that Luther concluded a century later.

Like most councils, the one of Pisa opened in an atmosphere of misunderstanding. The old Ghibelline city, its fleet sunk by Genoa and its independence eliminated by Florence, had never experienced such a deluge of visitors; it is a mystery how the people resolved the housing shortage. There were twenty-six cardinals, four patriarchs, twelve archbishops, eighty bishops, eighty-six abbots, the generals of the great monastic orders, delegates from all the larger universities, three hundred doctors of canon law, and diplomatic missions from almost all the European governments, each with an entourage of counselors, secretaries, scribes, guards, and servants.

The council proclaimed itself "canonical," that is, qualified to draft laws binding on the whole church, and "ecumenical," that is, representative of all Christendom. Actually the representatives of the Greek Orthodox Church were missing, but for the past four centuries they had been given up as "lost brethren." Missing also were the two popes in charge, Benedict and Gregory. The council sent them a formal injunction to appear, and since they refused to comply, the council deposed them and elected the Cardinal Archbishop of Milan as Pope Alexander V, with the charge of setting up another council.

The only result of this first round was to increase the number of popes from two to three, although each pretended to ignore the other's existence. To complicate matters even further, Alexander died almost immediately. Cardinal Baldassare Cossa was elected to replace him, with the name of John XXIII.

Cossa had every attribute a priest ought to be without: he was a clever and ambitious politician, a competent but greedy administrator, an able and pitiless general. No one knows why he chose to be a priest rather than a captain of venture, and even more mysterious is the reason for his election, particularly at such a delicate juncture. According to records kept by his secretary, Cossa had seduced two hundred assorted girls, married women, widows, and nuns. Nor did he plan to relinquish that pleasurable pursuit now that he was wearing the tiara. His first responsibility, however, was the one he inherited from Alexander, that of organizing a new council. Even then he dragged his feet as long as he could, until Emperor Sigismund forced him to act.

It would be hopeless to try to unravel the knotty skein of inheritances that finally resulted in the imperial crown's falling on the brow of this king who commuted between his domains of Poland, Hungary, and Bohemia. Sigismund was one of those emperors who, like Henry VII, believed in restoring some content to his empty imperial title. He thought that the crisis of the Church would facilitate his plans, so he adopted the role of Constantine and proclaimed himself supreme umpire of its internal struggles. Perhaps to restate more clearly the parallel with the first Christian emperor, he arranged for the council to take place in Constance, in November of 1414, proclaimed himself its president, and invited to it all the ecclesiastical, aristocratic, and cultural hierarchies.

About five thousand people assembled, among whom—according to Creighton—were fifteen hundred prostitutes. The congregation (prostitutes excluded) constituted the most imposing Christian convention since the council held in 325 at Nicea. The Constance affair began, dramatically enough, with the sudden elopement of Pope John, who had heard somewhere that the council was about to charge him with adultery, murder, and impiety, and that the only way to avoid a trial would be to give up the tiara together with Benedict and Gregory. John pretended to agree, but then he fled to join Frederick, Archduke of Austria, Sigismund's enemy. When he reached safety, John wrote the "Sacrosanta" decree, which some have called "the most revolutionary official church document." It said that the council represented the militant Church and derived its authority directly from God, and therefore it should be regarded as a kind of representative congress of Christianity. Its decisions were to be binding on everybody, the pope included, concerning both dogmatic interpretation and the structural reform of the Church—which matter the council would be expected to pursue as the sole authority on the issue.

The move was worthy of the shrewdness of the man; John made it in the hope of regaining control by becoming the leader of the movement that backed the council. Even if unsuccessful, his action would have been a fitting vengeance on the cardinals who had turned against him, for they, of course, wanted to retain their autonomy and were thus loath to give broad powers to the council. In fact, the cardinals resolutely opposed the papal decree and reaffirmed their exclusive rights. But they were defeated, and for a short while it looked as if the Church was about to take a voluntary turn in the direction of democratic and anti-authoritarian reform.

The council invited John to resign. When he refused, he was called to answer to fifty-four crimes, among which were treason, theft, and simony. Sixteen even more serious accusations were not pressed. On May 29, 1415, John was officially deposed and confined in the castle of Heidelberg, which he was allowed to leave only three years later on the request of Cosimo de Medici, who kept him as a guest for the rest of his days. The official historians of the Church do not count John as a pope, and that is the reason that Cardinal Roncalli could take on the same name, John XXIII—although that was not the only reason.

The council, meanwhile, celebrated its triumph with an imposing parade. But as soon as its work was resumed, the participants found themselves facing the usual dilemma. If they were to elect a new pope, it would just exacerbate the threefold division of the Church, since Benedict and Gregory stubbornly retained their titles and both had a faithful following. Gregory, however, in a moment of generosity—or craftiness—offered to resign as long as the council would disband and then allow itself to be reconvened and consecrated by him. He said, more or less, "First you recognize me as pope, with all rights pertinent thereto, including that of convening a council. Then, I will call a council and resign into its hands all my powers." It was a subtle move intended to reaffirm that the source of all authority was the pope, and that the council could rule only by his permission. The cardinals accepted his conditions and rewarded the former Gregory with an ap-

Seal of Emperor Frederick II.

Prince Colonna seizes Pope Boniface VIII in Anagni. *Drawing by U. de Neuville.*

Dante meets Beatrice. *Painting by Henry Holiday.*

Petrarch. *From a 14th-century illuminated manuscript.*

Detail from a panoramic view of the city of Venice in 1500. *Woodcut by Jacopo de Barbari.*

Boccaccio spinning tales. *Painting by Amos Cassioli.*

Bernabò Visconti, Duke of Milan, forces two papal nuncios to eat the bull of excommunication sent him by Pope Innocent VI, in 1361. *By M. Jackson, after Giannetti.*

Death mask of Lorenzo
Medici, "The Magnificent."

Cosimo, Salviati, and Piero Medici with their following. *From
the fresco by Benozzo Gozzoli in the Medici chapel of Palazzo
Riccardi, in Florence.*

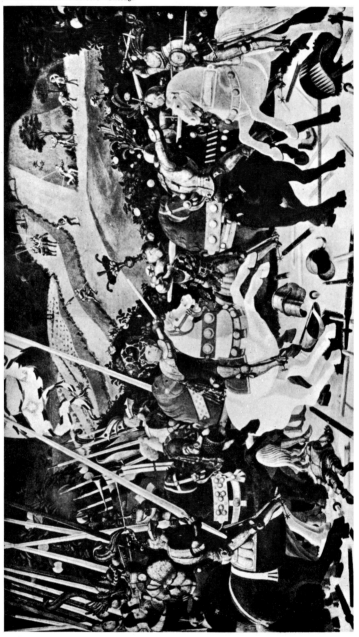

Battle of St. Egido. *Painting by Paolo Ucello.*

Interior of a Florentine banking house. *From a 15th-century woodcut.*

Lecture of Cristoforo Landino, professor of rhetoric and poetry in Florence. *From a 15th-century woodcut.*

Clothing market in Bologna. *From a 15th-century miniature painting in the statutes of the Taylors and Clothing Makers of Bologna.*

Christopher Columbus. *Engraving by T. Johnson.*

pointment as legate and governor of Ancona. It was the end of what "Sacrosanta" had stood for.

This left only Benedict; he still clung stubbornly to his title, but his followers deserted him. The council, therefore, was able to depose him without risking a secession, and the poor man withdrew to a family fortress in nearby Valencia, where everybody went on addressing him as "Holy Father." He remained there until he died at ninety years of age, never daring to leave its walls, perhaps because he dreaded that someone might not greet him with his title.

At last the road was clear to the election of a pope who would be recognized by everybody. This was Cardinal Oddone Colonna, and in 1418 he ascended the throne with the name of Martin V. The schism had finally ended.

Chapter 15

THE RESURGENCE OF THE PAPACY

BEING a good Roman pope, Martin made his first concern the taking care of his relatives, some of whom he made into cardinals, some into senators, and a few into generals. In partial justification, it should be said that he was encouraged in this course of action by the fact that Rome was in such a state of confusion that he could not return to it for the moment and had to spend his time instead between Genoa, Mantua, and Florence. He needed men to restore some order in the city, and he naturally chose them from among his own.

The job wasn't an easy one. As we saw earlier, the Papal States had broken up into a cluster of tiny *signorie* run by dictators who claimed to rule in the pope's name. But their claim involved only lip service, because in fact they acted as absolute sovereigns. All the roads that led to Rome were controlled by the chief bandit, Braccio di Montone, "Mutton Arm," who took a levy on all the supplies going into the city and could starve it at his pleasure. First the move to Avignon and then the schism had led to the deterioration of the institutions of papal government. There was no army, no police, no administration, no government officials. And, above all, there was no treasury: the vaults were empty. There wasn't even enough to feed a little bread to the hungry population accustomed to a parasitic existence.

Martin approached the difficult situation with courage and wisdom. He owed his power to a council that had entrusted it to him on condition that he would restructure it with the aim of reducing its central authority. It was strange that this task had been entrusted to a Roman cardinal, inheritor of a tradition of absolute authority. Of course, Martin had to make promises and give guarantees, but if he did not break them—he did work his way around them.

The first thing he did after the election was to ease Sigismund out of the council, telling him that now that there was a pope his presence was no longer required. Moreover, the presidency of the convention now belonged to the pope. Then, Martin opened talks with the council fathers, making sure to play off each national group against the other. Slowly, therefore, Martin succeeded in breaking down what was to be the great Church reform into a series of special deals couched in a vague language that everyone could interpret the way he liked. His methods produced some opposition, but Martin waited until it wore down. The council had lasted three years—three years of effort and expense away from home, family, and business. Eventually the opponents surrendered to that patient pope who had nothing better to do than wait while his men were putting Rome back in shape, and who had promised anyway to open a new council in five years' time.

In 1420 Martin returned to Rome, still short of money but with an army well enough organized to keep in check the marauders who roamed the plains around the city. His inaugural ceremony, in fact, featured the beheading of some of their captured ringleaders. The Romans watched the ritual with satisfaction, glad to see the good old methods at work again. Then the pope turned to replenishing his treasury, and here too he used old—if not good—methods: the sale of ecclesiastical positions and offices. He himself complained of having to do so, but there were no other resources, and necessities were growing more pressing all the time. Tottering monuments had to be propped up, bridges had to be rebuilt, and roads and sewers needed repairs. When someone reproached Martin for always worrying about money instead of thinking about the expected reforms, he answered with typical Roman good sense: "But the Church has been going fourteen centuries without reforms. Without money it might not survive one week."

He kept the word he gave to the reformers, however, and announced that a council would meet in Padua in 1423. It didn't turn out to be a grand meeting as those of Pisa and Constance had been. Another plague swept over Europe, preventing many from attending and forcing the assembly first to move to Siena and later to disband before the main issues were settled. The council again had demanded the decentralization of power, and Martin agreed, but only insofar as administrative lines were concerned. That earthly pope had other problems to think about: he worried more about the Papal States and its capital than about the Church. He had hired Gentile da Fabriano, Pisanello, and Masaccio to come to Rome and paint frescoes in the basilicas of Santa Maria Maggiore and San Giovanni in the Lateran. He had hired Poggio Bracciolini, one of the most famous humanists of the time, as his secretary, and he had replenished the College of Cardinals with people who were rather ignorant of theology but knew a great deal about literature—people such as Prospero Colonna, Giuliano Cesarini, and Domenico Capranica. In other words, while Martin was supposed to be the pope of the council, not of the Curia, he became —even though displaying tact and shrewdness—the pope of the Curia, not of the council.

Had he had enough time, perhaps Martin would have succeeded in his goal of lulling the reform movement to sleep, but he died in 1431, and the conclave elected one of the least qualified men to take his place. Gabriel Condulmer, who took the name of Eugene IV, was an Augustinian monk from Venice and a nephew of Benedict XII. There was no question about his zeal and seriousness; even as a cardinal he had led an ascetic life, following a rule of simplicity and prayer. Unfortunately, not even a strict diet prevented him from developing gout, and its pain made him impatient and unsociable. Moreover, he was obstinate—one of those pigheaded people full of humility who always talks with downcast eyes but never listens to what others say.

The cardinals who elected him had imposed some conditions in exchange for their votes, especially concerning their privileges in the matter of jobs and incomes, and they instituted thereby a practice that was to survive for centuries. The Colonna were especially insistent in asking Eugene to guarantee the privileged positions they had obtained from *their* Martin. But Eugene did not keep his commitments, thus alienating his supporters just at the time when the council called by his predecessor was assembling in Basel, more than ever ready for reform and for battle.

Eugene ordered the dissolution of the council, but the latter answered him by ordering him to appear before it, and the Colonna took the opportunity to organize a little revolution in Rome. The pope fled in a barge down the Tiber, dodging rocks that the populace threw after him and finding refuge in Florence first, then in Bologna. Once more Rome was without a pope, and thus the situation was to remain for nine years.

In the meantime, a thoroughgoing revolt was taking place in Basel. The majority of the delegates had come from France, and their goal was summarized in the clearest and most brutal way by the Archbishop of Tours: "Let us either take the Holy See away from the Italians," he said, "or let us reduce it to such a condition of impotence that it won't matter at all where its capital will be located." The delegates chose the latter course, and by decree after decree the council assumed all the papal privileges, including the award of appointments and the collection of tithes.

Eugene spoke up from Bologna, declaring invalid the council's decisions and renewing the order for its dissolution. But the council proclaimed his tenure ended and produced another pope, Amedeo di Savoia, who took the name Felix V. A new schism was in the making. Charles VII, King of France, seized the chance—as Sigismund had tried to do earlier—and convened an assembly of clergymen, princes, and jurists in Bourges. The meeting drafted a "pragmatic sanction" to supersede the one Constantine had established: it entitled the clergy of each diocese to dispose of local church appointments, on the king's "recommendation"—a procedure designed to give the king power in ecclesiastical matters comparable to the royal power in Byzantium.

On the other hand, no one was allowed to ask the pope's advice or to turn over to him the income from tithes.

It looked as if the game was over: the old monarchical structure of the Church was falling to pieces. The pragmatic sanction made an independent Gallic church possible, with the French king as its true pope, and at the same time another break was in the making in Prague, where a cardinal inveighed against the pope from the pulpit, calling him "the beast of Apocalypse." It appeared that the Reformation had succeeded even before Luther was born.

The pope, however, was momentarily saved, thanks to the intervention of his worst foes—the "lost brethren" of the Greek Orthodox Church. Constantinople was threatened by the Turks, who had assumed the leadership of the Islamic world because of their superior military organization. Emperor John and his Patriarch had concluded that only the Catholic West could save them and had therefore sent a message to Martin, shortly before the latter died, suggesting a council for the reunification of the two Christian churches. Eugene jumped at the chance: such a council would have dwarfed in importance the one being held in Basel. But the Basel assembly also understood the situation and moved accordingly.

As a result, John was met with two offers. One was from Eugene, who promised to open immediately a council in Ferrara, making it understood that he would chair it, thereby reaffirming the supremacy of his title; the other offer was from Basel, in which the council stated that it was the only legitimate party to any discussion, having, among other things, the support of Emperor Sigismund, while the pope lacked any temporal backing and thus counted for nothing. Like a proper Greek merchant, John weighed the two offers and decided to choose the first, which he thought to be the safer.

It was the end of the Basel assembly. Its best men, those for whom the reunification of the Christian world constituted a worthier goal than the fight against the papacy, moved on to Ferrara. The whole of Europe centered its hopes on the new council, since the 1054 schism between East and West had always been considered a grave loss for the true faith. Eugene belied his usual strictness and had solemn receptions made ready to welcome Emperor John, Patriarch Joseph, and the seventeen metropolitans who arrived in 1438 with a large following of bishops, monks, and theologians. The pope had won; nobody remembered the Basel council, which slowly lost all its delegates until it dissolved.

The council in Ferrara, meanwhile, bristled with problems, which were subcontracted to special commissions. The main obstacle was still the one concerning the Holy Ghost, which the Catholics thought "proceeded" from the Father *and* the Son, while the Greeks stubbornly claimed that it proceeded from the Father *through* the Son. To complicate matters further, after a few months of nitpicking arguments, the plague erupted once more in Ferrara. Fortunately, at this juncture Cosimo de Medici offered hospitality to the council in Florence, an offer that was gladly accepted, and the council reconvened on the banks of the Arno.

By 1439 a first agreement had been reached: the two sides admitted that there was, after all, no difference between their viewpoints. The Catholic phrase, *"Ex Patre Filioque procedit,"* meant the same thing as the Greek Orthodox phrase, *"Ex Patre per Filium procedit,"* and therefore both were equally valid. The only thing left to explain was why it had taken four hundred years to realize something so simple. But everybody understood right away as soon as the council began to founder on the issue of papal supremacy. The dogmatic question was child's play compared to the political one. This was the real stake, and the two parties dug in their heels in defense of their respective positions. The pope would not budge, and John had already ordered his metropolitans to pack up when Archbishop Bessarion of Nicea presented a compromise in which the ecumenical, or universal, authority of the pope was recognized, while the already established privileges of the Eastern churches were also confirmed.

The formula was accepted although, or perhaps because, nobody exactly understood what it meant. The decree proclaiming the reunion of the two great Christian churches was solemnly presented on July 6, 1439, in the majestic cathedral that only three years earlier had been crowned with Brunelleschi's stupenduous dome. Bessarion read it in

Greek, and Cardinal Cesarini in Latin. The two prelates exchanged the kiss of peace, then everybody followed the emperor's example in bending their knees to the pope, who a few months before had been in little better shape than the flotsam of a shipwreck.

Rejoicing over newly found Christian unity did not last long. The people and clergy of Constantinople welcomed their emperor and high priests with shouts, insults, and pellets of excrement. Patriarch Gregory, having endorsed the "betrayal," had to flee, and only in 1452 was he able to read the decree in the Cathedral of St. Sophia. The congregation protested by boycotting what had been their favorite church. The patriarchs of Alexandria, Antioch, and Jerusalem repudiated "The Council of Thieves," as they called the Florentine meeting. The partisans of unity, or "Uniates," found themselves in a minority and could not find added support even when the pope, faithful to his word, sent an army to relieve Constantinople. In any case, the Christian coalition, which defeated the Turks at Nish with the help of the King of Hungary and reconquered Sophia, was eventually beaten at Varna.

Uniates and orthodox went on excommunicating each other all through the next year on the subject of *Filioque,* but in 1453 Mohammed II appeared on the scene to cut the story short. Having changed the capital of the Eastern empire into the capital of Islam, he allowed Christians full freedom to pray any way they wanted and to cut each others' throats as much as they liked.

Meanwhile, the pope had returned to Rome in triumph. He had been preceded by Cardinal Vitelleschi, who had taken care to restore law and order with methods not very dissimilar from those used by Alaric or the other barbarian leaders. Nobody remembered, at least for the time being, the Basel council and its plans to substitute papal autocracy with its congressional authority.

But, leaving the papacy, let us now see what had happened during this period of ecclesiastical upheaval in the rest of Italy, where for some time the communal institutions had been going through various crises and a new form of government, the *signoria,* had been developing itself.

Part III

THE GOLDEN CIVILIZATION

Chapter 16

FROM *Comune* TO *Signoria*

THE NUCLEUS of the communal democracy had been the "neighbors' meeting" or *vicinanza,* a rudimentary popular congress that got together on the church square, and had for its symbol the elm tree that usually grew there. The participants would debate the issues arising from their relationship with the local feudal lord, who by imperial decree had almost absolute authority over the lands and people in his fief. Indeed, it was to define and to limit such authority as much as possible that the *vicinanza* would meet.

Each neighborhood elected its representatives, called "goodmen" or "rectors," and they discussed with the nobleman or with his representative, the bailiff, their common problems—the levy of taxes, duties, the setting up of *corvées,* the drafting of militias.

In larger cities every neighborhood had its *vicinanza;* in Florence there were four that took their names from the four city gates: *Duomo, San Pancrazio, Santa Maria,* and *San Pietro.* Each centered around its church, and it was more or less managed by the parish priest and a lay "rector" who was responsible for gathering taxes. Neighborhoods were also supposed to take care of their own public works and utilities —jobs such as maintaining bridges and draining sewers—but almost never agreed on a general plan for the city.

It was only much later that central authority developed, and that only against strong opposition. Even when there was such authority, it could not impose itself on the peripheral centers but existed parallel to them. This was one of the reasons for the chronic weakness and inefficiency of the communal institutions. Some unification at the top level was reached when the "rectors" were changed into "consuls," but this new form of management could never work freely because it was held in check by centers of authority below which refused to submit. Collective interest, in other words, never succeeded in prevailing over local interest.

All this did not prevent the *comune* from developing, thanks largely to the remoteness of the lords. Even at the turn of the tenth century, the powers of the nobles were not what they used to be when the Longobard or Frankish kings, in exchange for wartime service, had given them the run of a province over which they could rule as absolute masters. The lords were almost always of "barbarian," that is German, origin, and that plus their warlike training made them despise urban life. They therefore withdrew to their hulking castles out in the country, surrounded by their women, their warriors, and their horses. As long as rural society prevailed over urban life and farmlands were the only source of wealth, the lords' supremacy went unchallenged. But when the cities awoke from their lethargy, the castles were in trouble, and the lord found himself facing a new reality he hadn't anticipated and that eventually made him obsolete. The consuls took over the authority from him and his officials and became the actual masters of the city.

From the very beginning the consuls were elected on the basis of property holdings. They were the most respected and enterprising among the citizenry and usually belonged to the merchant class, which, after the new century, had initiated a new, open, dynamic, and competitive economy that spread beyond the city walls. Their base of strength rested on trading corporations, the *arti,* which were both the manufacturers' unions and the major sociopolitical organizations of their time.

Florence at the beginning of the eleventh century already had *arti* for bankers, doctors, druggists, wool and silk merchants, judges, and attorneys. Initially these unions were open to management only and determined the whole economy of the city: they set salaries, prices, and working hours and protected domestic products by imposing high duties on, or even by preventing the import of, foreign goods. As time went on, the corporations extended their hold over the food supply to the city, public works, and the urban police. They became states within the state; against them the workers' unions, then just beginning to emerge, had no legal or actual power.

Each corporation had its own palace, with offices, archives, secretaries, treasurers, and its own lower courts. Appeals were heard by ordinary magistrates; associates were bound to help each other in case of need: they paid the ransom if a member was kidnapped by bandits, they stood bail if he was jailed and paid the creditors if he went into bankruptcy. The moral code of the corporation was very rigorous, and it did not limit itself to business transactions. It prescribed even the style of dress of its members; it had a patron saint whose day was celebrated once a year with parades and lighting displays, a saint whose relics or whole remains were kept in a church sponsored by the corporation. All corporations contributed to the building and improvement of the cathedral and were punctual in their contributions to the bishop. The corporations also patronized the arts by producing stage shows and sacred pantomimes, and they maintained hospitals, orphanages, and old peoples' homes. The *arti* chiefs were due honors equal to those given to the consuls, whom they followed in citywide processions, carrying flags and banners embroidered with the crests and mottoes of their respective corporations.

The merchants' hegemony lasted till the twelfth century, when the independent workers also began to set up their own unions—saddlemakers, butchers, tanners, carpenters, ropemakers, barrelmakers, and so on. In contrast to the merchant guilds, which were known as *arti maggiori,* the latter were called *arti minori*. They also had patron saints, churches, offices, coats of arms, and codes, which prescribed prices, salaries, and working hours—no one was to work after six in the afternoon and the employment of women and children was forbidden. Every corporation, major and minor, stamped its products with a "trademark" and punished forgery severely. Members were ranked by strict status: apprentices worked ten hours a day without pay for a period ranging between three and thirteen years but received food, lodging, and clothing in exchange. Afterward, they were promoted to laborers and could own the tools of their craft. If they had some money they could open a shop, become masters, and register in the minor corporations.

It was inevitable that with time friction should develop between the major arts, whose members were called "the fat people," and the "skinny people" of the minor arts. In many towns violent social upheavals exploded during the thirteenth century. The nobility, often successfully excluded by the rich merchants from the government of the cities, also took part in the conflict. The castle-dwellers had not been able to oppose a common front to the urban forces, because of their constant internal squabbles about prestige and status. And, in fact, after they had lost ground in the cities, the nobility had also been slowly surrounded in the countryside and been forced to live in town for at least four months each year. Some compromised to the extent of swearing loyalty to the city, and in exchange ownership of part of their former lands was recognized; those who chose to fight it out had their castles destroyed and were forced to settle in town forever. Of course they were not content with a townhouse of straw and mud. They built little stone palaces like small fortresses with square towers sometimes reaching the height of 240 feet. Around them clustered the houses of relatives and clients, underscoring such groups' solidarity against the dominant bourgeois class.

With shrewd demagoguery the nobles succeeded in turning the skinny people against the merchants, allying themselves with the former to begin their climb back to power. Thus were the factions that destroyed the municipal institutions unleashed. By the middle of the twelfth century the *comuni* had been made unworkable; the executive power had drifted from the consuls into the hands of the *podestà* and the "captain of the people." The latter in wartime was the supreme commander of the troops recruited in the city and its surroundings;

the former was the official head of state, but his authority was hedged in by the "city councils" that had elected him, and since they often were divided by internal competition, they prevented him from ruling effectively. Moreover, the *podestà* himself was a party member and was therefore hindered by the opposition that aimed to curtail his activity.

To avoid this last drawback several *comuni* resorted to importing their *podestà* from abroad, since such imports would presumably be neutral in community squabbles. They were chosen from among magistrates or officials of preferably distant cities: Florence recruited many *podestà* in Milan and in Rome, Emilia got several from Tuscany, Lombardy from Venice and Genoa. When a man was chosen, he had to obtain permission from his own city, but such permission was rarely withheld. Then he gave a five- or six-day advance notice of his arrival so that the city council might have enough time to arrange suitable festivities for his welcome. The bishop and the past *podestà*, followed by an escort of notables, would ride out of the city to meet him, while the people stood on the sidelines waving flowers and olive branches—unless the new arrival was not of their liking, in which case they waved sticks and threatening signs.

Upon taking office the *podestà* had to swear to uphold the constitution before the council and the citizenry, then on the following Sunday he had to deliver an inaugural address known as the "programmatic speech." The constitution did not allow him to meet private citizens, for fear of bribes; he could not leave home after supper; he could neither visit nor receive visitors nor leave the city without a special permit. At the end of his mandate he had to submit a detailed report of his actions to the council, and only if that was approved, was he allowed to leave.

In theory this constitutional safeguard should have preserved democratic principles, but the latter had already ceased to exist some time earlier, except on paper. It could not have been otherwise, because the Italian *comune* was always run by money, corporations, and status. A few efforts were made here and there to make it popular and democratic, but they almost always died at birth or lived a very short life. The longest lasting was the experiment Giano della Bella began in Florence in 1292.

A wealthy nobleman, Giano was one of the thirteen *priors* elected every two months with the responsibility of checking the executive branch. He found support among the populace and thus was able to force upon his colleagues the so-called Ordinances of Justice, which put all the arts on the same footing and united them in a citywide federation. At the same time, Giano eliminated the leaders, or "magnates," from all directional positions in the major arts; all told almost three thousand citizens were ostracized. They were excluded from holding public office, and if any commoner denounced one of them, he could be arrested and thrown in a tower next to the Bargello palace, known thereafter as the "magnates' pallet." Five days after the accusation, the *podestà* had to open proceedings against the prisoner; if he failed to do so, the arts were supposed to call a general strike and close shops and offices.

The magnates reacted to the ordinance with bewilderment. Unable to take action against the commoners, now safely shielded by the iron laws, they vented their rage on each other. But eventually they realized that frustration was leading them nowhere and proceeded to form some sort of alliance against their common enemy.

A routine uprising toward the end of 1294 produced a corpse, and Giano was accused of having fueled the disturbance in order to gain total control of the government. The magnates rallied to the opportunity and regained mastery over the city; Giano was able to flee, but he was sentenced to death *in absentia*.

One of the causes that had made this short-lived popular reform possible was the factional struggle that rent the magnate class and paralyzed executive action. Such struggles did not take place only in Florence, but in practically every other city as well. In each case the party chiefs wielded greater authority than the elected *podestà*, and it was in such a sectarian and unsettled atmosphere that the seeds of the *signoria* germinated. The transition took place when a *podestà* or a "captain of the people," playing one party against the other, succeeded in having his mandate renewed and in obtaining full powers, thereby becoming master of the situation. The populations did not rebel. They were tired of a freedom that faded into anarchy; instead, they chose order, even though it faded into tyranny.

From contemporary documents one sees that by the mid-thirteenth century some of the *podestà* were being called *dominus civitatis,* that is, "lord of the city," and that their office had become permanent rather than temporary. Ferrara, for instance, was ruled by the Ghibelline Salinguerra for ten years between 1230 and 1240. Ezzelino da Romano was able to rouse the skinny people of Treviso against the fat ones and had himself proclaimed *signore*, or lord of the city. Similar events took place in Milan, Como, and Arezzo.

We are still far from the great *signorie* of the Renaissance, when the dying *dominus civitatis* will pass on the title to his eldest son, establishing thus the hereditary principle in city government. But the main lines and the juridical premises of the new order of things are already clearly visible.

Chapter 17

The Visconti and the Sforza in Milan

In Milan, Archbishop Ottone had appointed his nephew Matteo to succeed him, and the appointment was ratified by Henry VII for the modest sum of fifty thousand florins. As Imperial Vicar, Matteo was qualified to rule not only over Milan and its territory but also over the various cities that had asked Milan's protection to escape the turmoils of internal party struggle.

Matteo was followed by his son Galeazzo and then his nephew Azzone. But it was Luchino who laid the foundation of a true *signoria,* in the Renaissance meaning of the word, of a state that is the unified property of a single dynasty. When, upon Luchino's death, his place was taken by his brother Giovanni, the city council of Milan proclaimed the hereditability of the Visconti's supreme authority, thereby signing the death warrant of democracy and the end of communal institutions.

Giovanni followed the unfortunate Viscontian rule of inheritance, which did not recognize primogeniture, and divided his legacy between his two nephews Bernabò and Galeazzo II. The first got Cremona, Bergamo, Brescia, Lodi, Piacenza, Parma, and the district east of the river Adda; to the second went Como, Pavia, Asti, Tortona, Alessandria, Novara, Vigevano, and Bobbio. Milan itself was carved in two: Bernabò received the quarters of Porta Romana, Tosa, and

Orientale; Galeazzo those of Porta Comasina, Vercellina, and Ticinese. Bernabò established his seat in Milan, Galeazzo in Pavia.

Galeazzo died at fifty-nine, in 1378; he was succeeded by his son Gian Galeazzo, who passed into history as the Count of Virtue, not because he had ever shown much of it, but because the dowry of his wife Isabella of Valois included the title to the county of Vertus in Champagne.

Bernabò had made himself rather unpopular in Milan for having brought back some old taxes and for inventing some new ones. Gian Galeazzo saw his opportunity and marched against the city with five-hundred men, entering it without a blow. In front of the cathedral of St. Ambrogio, Gian Galeazzo met Bernabò, surrounded by his sons. Gian Galeazzo's men threw themselves on his uncle and cousins, who were tied up and dragged to the castle of Porta Giovia. Gian Galeazzo then occupied the city, greeted by shouts of "Long live the Count, death to taxes." The Milanese did not stop at that; they rushed the revenue offices, rifled the files, and burned the census lists in the city squares.

There is no need to report all the little wars that Gian Galeazzo fought to enlarge the boundaries of the duchy, which at the end of the century encompassed most of northern Italy, almost reaching Venice in the east and Tuscany in the south. Next to Naples, the Visconti land became the most powerful *signoria* in the country. Gian Galeazzo ruled it as an enlightened and astute despot. The role he played was not yet that of a Renaissance lord, but it did not belong to the Middle Ages, either. Gian Galeazzo sensed that the *comuni* had outlived their function and that the city limits were no longer wide enough to encompass the reality of the new world. He dreamed of a unified state under the Visconti's flag, but he conceived of it as private property to be managed as a family estate for the family's exclusive benefit. He organized a Secret Council and a Council of Justice. The first, a combination State and Defense Department, appointed its own ambassadors, recognized foreign ambassadors' credentials, drew up ceremonials, and dictated formal protocol.

The Secret Council also served as a high court of justice for criminal cases, while civil cases were tried by the Council of Justice—a justice, of course, tailored to the lord's designs. If evidence was lacking for the conviction of a political opponent, it was invented. The most refined forms of torture were employed to extract confessions; the most horrible one was called "Lent," during which the suspect was successively amputated of a limb, his tongue, his nose, his ears. It was known as Lent because, according to the executioner's plans, the torment was to last forty days, although the victim rarely survived the first ten.

A no lesser form of agony was reserved to Chancellor Pasquino Capelli, who had been charged of treason: Gian Galeazzo had him sewed naked into an oxhide and then immured in a cell of the castle of Pavia. He applied similar methods against the neighboring feudal lords who would not recognize his authority; the less amenable ones were imprisoned, their castles razed, their towers broken. Many of the privileges and immunities the lesser lords enjoyed were revoked, and Gian Galeazzo prohibited his vassals from keeping private jails in their manors.

Gian Galeazzo did not live long enough to uproot completely from his domains the feudal system that had entrenched itself during the long, dark centuries. But he struck it with a deadly blow. Nor was he content merely to strike at the nobility. He fought also against the privileges and franchises of the clergy, though he did not suppress the ecclesiastical courts and refrained from interfering with church affairs as long as they did not conflict with state interests. In fact he encouraged religious ceremonies, had a *Te Deum* sung after each victory, financed pilgrimages, devised harsher penalties for heresy, raised the fines for blasphemy, protected monks, and provided funds for the building of many churches including the charterhouse of Pavia, the first stone of which he laid in person (the last was to be set in place a century later). In 1383 he gave the first contribution to the works of the *Duomo* of Milan—in 13 years his support totaled 12,416 florins, not counting the free concession of the Candoglia quarries—and his example was followed by the entire population, which contributed its offerings for the construction of that grand Gothic cathedral.

Gian Galeazzo had always been fragile and delicate, and with age his complaints increased, helped along by a well-developed case of hypochondria. He spent whole days closed inside one of the inner rooms of the castle of Porta Giovia or of Pavia, lost in his thoughts or reading the classics. When he died of the plague in 1402, he left his heart to the Church of St. Michael in Pavia, and the rest of his insides to St. Anthony in Vienne—good Visconti as he was, he divided even his gizzards. He had been a hard man, grim and disagreeable. Yet despite his cruelty and arbitrariness, he made Milan into a city of European dimensions.

The city that Barbarossa had literally leveled to the ground two and a half centuries earlier had been reborn more splendid and wealthy. The best-known architects had been hired to restore it, and an authentic building boom had multiplied its neighborhoods. In Milan one could find about 14,000 houses, 200 churches, 130 bell-towers, 15 convents, and the same number of hospitals. The population approached the 250,000 mark. There were some 40 doctors and over 150 surgeons, and the attorneys numbered more than 1,500, but there were fewer than 100 grade school teachers. The city crawled with butcher shops (over 400) and bakeries (over 300), to which one must add about 1,000 other assorted stores. There was bread and work for everybody, and the ghoulish specter of famine no longer frightened people as it once did, when one bad harvest could leave the city starved for months.

Milan chose its future, that of a great trading center, from the very beginning. Merchants came to settle in the city from the whole country and from the rest of the continent as well. There was a constant traffic of English, French, German, Venetian, and Florentine businessmen. In Milan, one could buy the most diverse merchandise—spices, brocades, silks, carpets, or exotic animals. The suburbs were full of smithies, forges, armories; they produced swords, spears, shields, cuirasses and helmets that were sold all over Europe.

But the city knew how to amuse itself as well. Feasts, tournaments, and public dances cheered the life of the inhabitants, except in times of war, pestilence, or serious troubles such as followed the death of Gian Galeazzo.

As was the custom, Gian Galeazzo had partitioned the state among his various sons, bastard and legitimate. Giovanni Maria received the title of Duke of Milan, together with the cities of Milan, Como, Lodi, Cremona, Piacenza, Parma, Reggio, Bergamo, Brescia, Siena, and Perugia. Filippo Maria, the new count of Pavia, was left that city and ten other major towns. The illegitimate Gabriel got Pisa and Crema. And since the sons were under age, Gian Galeazzo's widow, Caterina, was appointed regent. Still young and handsome, she was completely inept as a ruler. Evil tongues whispered that she was having an affair with Gian Galeazzo's first chamberlain, Francesco Barbavara, to whom she entrusted the state. The court split into two factions—one supported Giovanni Maria and the other his mother, but she was defeated and fled to the castle of Pavia, where she died in 1404, apparently of poison. But Giovanni's fate was no better: he was murdered on May 16, 1412, as he was going to Mass in the church of San Gottardo.

Filippo Maria was left sole legitimate ruler. He had inherited his father's shrewdness and ambition and also his suspicious, bigoted, and glum personality. Being the son of first cousins he grew up puny and sickly and was fed only hot gruel until he reached the age of ten. When he became Count of Pavia, he buried himself in the ancestral castle, where he spent his days reading Livy and Petrarch. He spoke French fluently, and the *chansons de geste* sent him into raptures.

Filippo Maria's favorite pastimes consisted in playing ball and taking walks along the banks of the Ticino, during which he plucked flowers and branches he afterward gave as presents to the pubescent pages whom he personally chose and whose upbringing he closely supervised. They alone could approach him at any time of the night or the day, the only ones he trusted. But as soon as they entered his service, they had to cut all their ties with their families. And woe to the page who was discovered talking to a courtier without his lord's permission. Filippo Maria employed them as secretaries, counselors, sometimes as ministers and ambassadors. They never left his side. They helped him to dress, ate their meals with him, rode with him to the hunt. When Filippo Maria retreated to his apartments, they followed him.

The duke lived in constant fear of being poisoned or murdered in his sleep. He would not touch food that had not been tasted by one of his valets. He put on weight as he grew older, acquiring a dull, repulsive appearance. Every evening he had all doors and windows barred before going to sleep, and around his alcove a barrier of beds was set for his bodyguard. For fear of darkness he slept among blazing candles. He saw ghosts everywhere; often in the middle of the night he would wake up with a start, grasp a sword that he always kept under his pillow, and brandish it, slicing the air furiously, while foam and disconnected words dribbled from his mouth. Sometimes he kept moving from room to room, and only the light of dawn brought relief to his anxieties.

Whenever Filippo Maria had a nightmare, the morning after was spent in prayer; kneeling and beating his breast, he turned first toward the east then toward the west. He often made vows but kept them only occasionally. Seldom did he speak, and never would he look another person in the eye; his favorite topics were war, hounds, and horses. When he was in good spirits—which happened very rarely—he would tell dirty jokes, but he felt guilty afterward and went back to saying his prayers.

He loved good food and was an inveterate drinker but paid each time for his sins of gluttony with violent liver spasms, which killed him at last in 1447 so suddenly that he did not even have time to draw up a will and appoint a successor. Next day a group of noblemen shouting, "Long live freedom!" decreed the dissolution of the duchy and founded the Ambrosian Republic instead. The populace requested the reduction of taxes and took apart the castle of Porta Giovia. Several subject cities were inspired by the chaos to regain their independence; Venice, the old enemy of Milan, occupied Piacenza and Lodi.

The Ambrosian rulers entrusted their army to Francesco Sforza, a son-in-law of Filippo Maria and lord of Cremona. Son of the *condottiere* Muzio Attendolo, Francesco had also made a distinguished career as a captain of mercenaries paid in turn by Venice, Milan, and Florence. The greatest general of his time, he was tall, powerful, handsome, and brave. No one could wield the sword better than he, nor shoot an arrow more true. He slept under canvas with his soldiers and shared their meals, and when the battle was pitched, he was the first to join and the last one to leave it. He was a born military planner, and his bands defeated whole armies; sometimes his appearance alone sufficed to put the enemy to rout.

It is hard to believe that the newborn Ambrosian Republic could have chosen to place itself in the hands of this man, who, on top of everything else, was also the natural heir to the duke, having married his only daughter. Yet it did. And Francesco lost no time in winning back Piacenza and Lodi from the Venetians and then making a secret agreement with them by which he relinquished some of Milan's eastern domains to Venice as an exchange for recognition of his rights to his father-in-law's title. It was the year 1450. Francesco turned against Milan and laid siege to it. After a brief resistance the starved city opened its gates and crowned Sforza duke.

Francesco Sforza reigned until 1466 with an uninhibited magnificence that led the duchy to the rim of bankruptcy, from which it was rescued only by the loans of Florentine bankers. His policies encouraged immigration and prevented local trained workers from leaving; he gave prizes to the most prolific citizens and contributed in person to his planned population explosion by siring eight legitimate children and about twenty bastards. He bled the treasury but turned Milan into something it had never been before: a splendid metropolis, proud of its great buildings, among which the Sforza castle and the main hospital shone like jewels.

Francesco had a weakness for the weaker sex and betrayed his wife often—until, true to her Visconti heritage, she poisoned his mistress. Old age reawakened the rheumatic pains that had bothered him since youth: each summer he took to the watering places, went on strict diets, and had himself bled. Although wars and official business had left him with no time to pursue scholarship, he did encourage that of others; he invited the humanist Filelfo to Milan, supported literature and the arts, stimulated the sciences, and opened a school of painting. He died of dropsy in 1466, leaving behind a concert of sorrow and a pile of debts.

In Galeazzo Maria, the son who succeeded Francesco, the Visconti genes appeared to be dominant over the paternal ones. According to Corio, the "foul and lecherous" young duke surrounded himself with a harem of whores, attended orgies, and let himself go in the most reprehensible ways. A delusion of grandeur helped him to waste enormous treasures to embellish his court; he hired battalions of dwarfs, fools, comedians, and musicians and threw parties worthy of the *Arabian Nights*. When he traveled, a large escort of noblemen and courtiers were to follow him, dressed in sumptuous garb and riding superbly caparisoned horses bristling with feathers. In 1471 he visited Florence and his party included two thousand horsemen, two hundred mules, five hundred pairs of hounds, and hundreds of hawks and falcons. On that trip alone Galeazzo Maria spent no less than two hundred thousand golden ducats. When he was broke—and the way he lived he often was—he raised taxes and jailed or executed whoever objected.

His subjects hated him, and the nobility was not exactly fond of him either. On the morning of December 26, 1476, while he was attending mass in St. Stephen's, three young noblemen rushed Galeazzo, who died under a hail of daggers. One of the assailants was lynched on the spot by the duke's bodyguard; the other two were captured after long pursuit and quartered alive.

Galeazzo Maria left his seven-year-old son Gian Galeazzo under his widow's trusteeship, and she left the cares of government to an able minister, Cecco Simonetta, who was to rule with the assistance of the dead man's two brothers: Sforza Maria, Duke of Bari, and Ludovico Mauro, Count of Mortara.

Ludovico was the fourth son of Francesco Sforza. The Milanese called him *il Moro*, "The Moor," because of his dark complexion, black hair, and black eyes. Instead of taking offense, Ludovico was pleased by the nickname, and to make it more appropriate he adopted Moorish clothes and emblems and surrounded himself with Moroccan slaves. He could not have been called a handsome man. Although well-built and above average in height, he had sharp and irregular features: a long hawkish nose, a protruding chin, thin and drawn lips, the haughty expression of someone accustomed to giving orders. He was fond of beautiful women and a well-laid table but detested excess. One could find in Ludovico's personality ambition as well as effrontery, skepticism and superstition, generosity and diffidence. Because of Filelfo's classical tutoring, he could speak Latin and French, was able to follow a philosophical argument, and was sensitive to art.

Cecco Simonetta tried to rid himself of The Moor, but Ludovico roused the court against him with the help of his friends, one of whom enjoyed the duchess's favors. She, moreover, was persuaded to ask her minister to make peace with her brother-in-law, who in return had Simonetta beheaded and the duchess exiled, after which he took on his nephew's trusteeship—one can well imagine with what good intentions.

Gian Galeazzo, whom Guicciardini describes as "extremely incapable," was not yet nine years old. Weak, sickly, peevish and shy, he lived in a wing of the palace surrounded by preceptors; he was seen in public only during official ceremonies, holding a scepter and a sword, with the ring of ducal authority on his finger. He died for no good reason in 1494, relieving his uncle from his light yet uncomfortable presence.

Under Ludovico, Milan will reach the zenith of its splendor, but those times lie outside the scope of this history, so we shall now turn in the direction of Venice, which was rising beyond the Sforza outposts.

Chapter 18

THE MOST SERENE REPUBLIC OF VENICE

BY THE end of the fourteenth century Venice was the most powerful state in Italy; the lagoons on which the city is built had become a nursery of navigators and merchants. Venetian ships had been well known for some three hundred years, when they had begun to carry passengers and goods first across the Adriatic and then across the Mediterranean seas. Slowly, Venice's ships and sailors had transformed their city into the most important European harbor. On its wharves rugs, spices, brocades, and slaves were unloaded every day, while wool and manufactured articles left in return toward the east. The Balkan and near eastern markets were slowly conquered by the business sense of Venice's shippers, the initiative of her admirals, and the cleverness of her diplomats. In every foreign trading town, the Venetians built *fondachi,* little enclaves consisting of warehouses, hotels, hospitals, and churches that enjoyed immunity and various privileges from the host country. A bailiff appointed by the doge ruled the *fondaco* with powers of life and death over the inhabitants, and he also performed diplomatic functions. These commercial outposts made the fortune of Venice by assuring it a wide economic base.

But Venice's supremacy would have been very short-lived, had it not been sustained internally by a solid political constitution. Power rested, in theory, with the doge, but in fact he followed the desires of a moneyed aristocracy. From the middle of the twelfth century the doge was assisted by a Council of the Wise, or Major Council, originally consisting of thirty-five members, and this first council was soon supplemented by a more exclusive Minor Council, of six. The Major Council kept expanding with time; its members decided not only legislative questions but political and military issues as well. The doge and his committee of six Wisemen only had authority to approve the actions of those who had elected him, and they could be impeached at any time. In fact, the doge was really merely an exalted symbol given almost divine respect, in part also to discourage him from developing earthly ambitions.

The doge had the right to appoint the Patriarch of Venice and the Canons of St. Mark and had, among other titles, that of "Most Serene Prince." He lived in the Doge's Palace, surrounded by gold, marble, silk and tapestries, a setting of greater magnificence than the one the Emperor of Byzantium enjoyed. He followed an imperial ceremonial, down to the most finicky details; his every movement was a ritual. His clothes were extravagant; whenever he left the palace, trumpets blared, church bells rang, and heralds announced his coming. When he went through the city, trumpet players, flag bearers, and a covey of dignitaries preceded the doge who appeared on a golden throne, sheltered under a heavy and many-colored parasol. The Major Council walked behind him, followed by high officials of the state, foreign ambassadors, and the chapter of St. Mark's Cathedral.

A parade of such proportions was bound to impress the populace and to compensate it for the loss of those freedoms it had enjoyed when, in the seventh century, the islets of the lagoon had joined into a confederacy to defend themselves from the barbarian invaders. In fact, the first doges, as soon as they became elected officials rather than appointees of Byzantium, were appointed by a general public assembly. But when the population had grown beyond a certain point and broke up into various social classes, the so-called decisional power passed into the hands of the wealthy, and all pretense of democracy disappeared.

Toward the end of the thirteenth century, the constitution of Venice was pushed a step further along the direction to oligarchy. Previously, at least on paper, any citizen could be elected to the Major Council, even though in actuality only members of the two or three hundred families who controlled the republic's wealth ever made it: bankers, shipping magnates, great traders. These families constituted a moneyed aristocracy, which in Venice had higher status than an aristocracy based on titles. But the financial monopoly produced envy in those who were excluded from it, and therefore it was necessary to find a way to make it legitimate.

Thus, in 1297 Doge Pietro Gradenigo passed a law through the Major Council to the effect that its yearly elected membership was to be drawn only from families who had been previously represented in that body. Their names were inscribed in The Golden Book, a kind of Venetian social register. The screw was given another turn in 1319, when the yearly election to the assembly was abolished and its membership enlarged. Thus the Major Council became unwieldy and was forced to delegate many of its functions to more limited committees.

The Senate was established as an administrative body toward the middle of the thirteenth century, but its powers continued constantly to expand, until a hundred years later the Major Council transferred to it the management of all the political business of the state. The Senate set the rules for navigation and commerce, the army and the navy, and it appointed all ambassadors except the one to Constantinople, but its major task was that of shaping foreign policy. It was the Senate that decided on peace or war, that negotiated treaties and alliances, that gave instructions to ambassadors and received their weekly reports. The famous "relations" from diplomatic agents, which gave up-to-date pictures of the conditions at the various European courts, were read every week in front of the Senate. In effect, that body had acquired all the authority of the republic.

Another branch of the government was instituted in 1310. That year a nobleman, Baiamonte Tiepolo, had conspired to overthrow the government and establish a personal dictatorship in the city. Counting on the popular discontent caused by Pietro Gradenigo's *coup,* he gained some measure of support among the lower class. However, when his plot was discovered before it had matured, Baiamonte turned himself in to the doge, who spared his life but forced him to emigrate to Dalmatia. To prevent similar attempts from achieving success, the Major Council appointed something along the lines of an Un-Venetian Activities Commission: the Council of Ten. The Council of Ten's members were allowed almost unlimited powers and complete independence. They watched over every facet of the citizen's public and private life, investigated suspects, followed up anonymous accusations, gathered witnesses, rewarded informers. At first, councilmen were elected for two-month terms; later these were extended to two years. Selection of candidates was very rigorous; their loyalty to the republic and their incorruptibility had to be above all suspicion.

As soon as someone was appointed to the Ten, he became cloaked in mystery; he had to measure words and expressions, avoid parties and public ceremonies, and be, in fact, totally isolated from everybody except his colleagues, with whom he met every day in absolute secrecy. The Ten could not leave Venice except for emergencies, and three times a week they held audience for spies and informers. In other words, they were a real secret police, an early version of the NKVD.

The Council of Ten upheld the oligarchic constitution, but at the price of keeping the republic in a state of continuous terror. In 1355 it prevented the success of Marin Faliero's conspiracy, when Faliero, who had succeeded Andrea Dandolo as doge, got tired of holding only the symbols of power and decided to acquire for himself the reality of it as well. Like many before him, he tried to accomplish his design by arousing the populace against the nobility, to which he himself belonged. He hired a few hundred sailors and longshoremen, who, during the night between April 15 and 16, were supposed to spread the rumor through all the alleys of the city that the Genoese fleet was moving on Venice. This news would have moved the people to panic, and the nobles would have assembled in St. Mark's Square. Then the conspirators were supposed to move into the square from the surrounding lanes and slaughter everyone. Everything was carefully prepared when, shortly before the appointed hour, one of the conspirators revealed the plot to one of the Ten, but without implicating

Faliero. The doge was immediately apprised of the situation; he first tried to discredit the news, and then said that he already knew everything. But he soon had to admit his failure when the arrested conspirators began to confess. Next day Faliero appeared in front of a special tribunal consisting of the Ten and a jury of twenty judges. The sentence was death, and on the morning of April 17 he was beheaded on the step of the Giants' stairway on which he once had been crowned doge.

The spies of the republic also reported to the Ten. They were everywhere, but Genoa especially was thick with them, since that city had been for centuries the most fearsome competitor of Venice for dominance of the seas. Venice and Genoa contended for a huge stake: the markets along the shores of the Mediterranean, which both republics were trying to monopolize. Incidents erupted almost daily between Genoese and Venetians. The Venetian navy was defeated in 1298 in the waters of Curzola, but in 1379 almost all the Genoese galleons that had foolhardily penetrated the Chioggia lagoons were sunk by the ships of the Most Serene Republic. Next year a treaty that awarded naval supremacy to Venice was signed in Turin, thereby placing the city economically in a class by herself.

In the fifteenth century Venice was the wealthiest, most ostentatious city in Italy. The fabulous palaces on the Canal Grande, where merchants who had achieved the rank of nobility by means of their wealth lived, gave the city a unique charm. A magic architecture had wrought the buildings—thinly braided columns, slender rose-shaped balconies, binate windows—producing a precious lace-like effect that made the buildings look like a goldsmith's miniature chasings. The buildings were the perfectly blended synthesis of two very sophisticated styles: the Gothic and the Byzantine. The interiors were no less gorgeous than the fronts; they overflowed with exquisite articles and expensive furniture. The walls were enveloped with mosaics, tapestries, canvasses; the ceilings covered with frescoes, the woodwork gilded in genuine gold. The foremost Venetian artists were hired to build and decorate the mansions of great merchants, and patriarchs vied with doges to surpass each other in the magnificence of their homes.

The school of Bellini helped to make Venice into one of the foremost artistic centers of the fifteenth century. Jacopo, the founder of the school, had apprenticed with Gentile da Fabriano; then he worked in Verona, Ferrara, and Padua, where he met the great Andrea Mantegna, to whom he gave his daughter in marriage. Finally, Jacopo returned to Venice, where he set up a shop in which his two sons Gentile and Giovanni were to learn the first rudiments of their father's art.

Gentile and Giovanni became the two most charming painters of their times. Gentile began by following his brother-in-law's style in the outline of figures and the boldness of foreshortenings, but with the passing of the years he developed a completely individual touch. His first great work consisted of a series of panels for the great Council Hall, but they were destroyed in the fire of 1577. Fortunately, the sketches are still in existence, and they reveal an exquisite narrative line. Because of his fame as a portrait painter, Gentile was invited to Constantinople by the Sultan Mahomet II, whose features are now preserved on an extremely beautiful canvas. When he returned home, Gentile was overwhelmed by an avalanche of commissions. The school of St. John the Evangelist asked him to do three panels, one representing a miraculous healing, another the Corpus Christi procession, and the third a scene of the discovery of a fragment of the cross. Gentile developed these subjects into very complex compositions: each panel represents a scene of contemporary Venice filled with people, either parading around St. Mark's square or crowding on the bridges waiting for supernatural events to occur. The artist's touch is intense, the palette colorful and brilliant, the details are caught faithfully and with a flavorful realism. Gentile's last effort was a "St. Mark" preaching in Alexandria, but he did not live long enough to finish it. His brother, Giovanni, did it for him.

Two years younger than Gentile, Giovanni lived eight years longer than his brother. He, too, was deeply influenced by Mantegna, whose technique he refined chromatically. His main gift was one of color, but at his best he showed an extraordinary psychological depth and a true mastery of narrative style. He became the idol of Venice and its most popular painter. Dozens of his Madonnas were hung in churches, palaces, and monasteries; no major museum in the world is without one. As official painter of the republic, Giovanni had the concession for portraying the doges. After a while all those old men in fancy dress must have begun to bore him, because he changed his themes and found new inspiration in allegorical interpretations of classical mythology. In the "Feast of the Gods," he painted a picnic party of winsome ladies and disheveled and inebriated men; the picture, now in the National Gallery of Washington, faithfully mirrors the sensuously pagan zest for life of fifteenth-century Venice, which the Bellinis so admirably interpreted.

But the so-called minor arts also contributed to the pomp of the *Serenissima*. The mosaic laboratories produced delightful compositions destined to decorate the walls of churches and palaces. The glass works of Murano, the manufacturing secrets of which were jealously guarded by the state, turned out masterpieces of crystalware: vases, cups, stem-glasses. Another flourishing industry supplied the courts of Europe with helmets, armor, shields, and daggers finely chiseled and profusely inlaid in gold and silver.

This blossoming was not confined to the visual arts; it involved also literature, although humanism took roots in Venice later than elsewhere. If the *Serenissima* failed to produce a swarming of schools and academies such as followed on the heels of humanism in Florence, new ideas still found lively response and acceptance there. Culture had great status: there was no palace without its library, or that would not open its doors to writers and poets. Society ladies received theologians and philosophers in their living rooms. Schooling was available not only to the children of the aristocracy and the wealthy middle class but also to the sons of the poor.

The discovery of printing had enlarged the mesh of the cultural net by diffusing modern authors as well as the classics, and Venice became one of the publishing capitals of the world. The books that left its presses in the second half of the fifteenth century are authentic jewels for the elegance of their type-face, the quality of their paper, and the perfection of their printing. By the end of that century there had been 2,835 volumes published in Venice alone. Most of them bore the signature of a typographical genius: Aldo Manuzio. Born near Velletri in 1450, Manuzio, at a very young age, moved to Rome, where he immersed himself in the reading of the Latin classics. Then he lived in Ferrara for a while, where he translated the Greeks and gave scholarly lectures on Plato, Thucydides, and Cicero. He also taught for a while, and among his pupils was Pico della Mirandola, who was so beholden by his knowledge that he asked Manuzio to tutor his nephews Lionello and Alberto, two young men who later were to be the first financial backers of his extraordinary editorial enterprises. Manuzio set as his goal the printing of the Greek classics in a popular edition accessible to everyone. But cost was not his only obstacle: the texts had to be found, collated, and edited. Constant transcriptions had polluted the originals, and practically every line was the object of squabbles between experts. Finally, Manuzio also had to market his product, as one would say today. For all these reasons Manuzio moved to Venice, enlisted an army of philologists and other scholars, and entrusted them with the choice and the commentary of the texts. He made a fortune, and after his death the business was continued under the direction of his sons. Perhaps only in Medici Florence would such a venture have encountered a similar immediate success, for Florence was the only city that, in the fifteenth century, could compete with Venice in art and culture.

Chapter 19

Pater Patriae

No one has ever been able to explain convincingly why Florence should have been the foremost city, not only in Italy, but in the whole of Europe, in the fourteenth and fifteenth centuries. It makes no sense to say that its supremacy was the result of its wealth, since its wealth also needs an explanation—the city had no natural resources. It was built in the midst of a relatively poor countryside, without raw materials, without a favorable location, even without a good river: the Arno is too shallow for shipping during the major portion of the year.

Florence's political constitution might have been good for everything except for securing peace and order. The *signoria,* which is what the goverment was called, was eminently unstable; its various departments competed for power, instead of dividing it rationally, and succeeded only in paralyzing each other in turn. There was a "Standardbearer of Justice," who was responsible for carrying out laws and court sentences; there were eight "Priors" who functioned as a cabinet; and there was a Parliament where the "Council of the People" was assembled.

Such an organization seems, at least on paper, pretty efficient and democratic. But this semblance is due only to terminology; in effect the word "people" in Florence did not have the same meaning as it has now. It was reserved to designate only those who belonged to the *arti,* or trade guilds. The seven *arti maggiori* included the wealthy professions with high status: judges and attorneys, wool producers, silk producers, clothing manufacturers, merchants, bankers, doctors, and druggists. There were fourteen *arti minori* catering to less distinguished occupations: blacksmiths, gravediggers, carpenters, winemakers, bricklayers, and so on.

These two groups had fought for a long time, side by side, to dispossess the old landed aristocracy of their privileges, and by the end of the thirteenth century they had been successful. With the gradual destruction of the bristling castles in the countryside the city government had won its century-old struggle against the manor, and the urban classes with their industries took the lead from the rural classes.

But as soon as this victory had been achieved, the solidarity binding the *arti,* that is, the productive forces of the city, began to disintegrate. Only those registered on the guild rolls were full-fledged citizens, and such a limitation amounted to a rather drastic discrimination, since toward the middle of the fourteenth century only three thousand of the ninety thousand inhabitants could vote, if Villani's figures are correct. But even within this privileged minority there were deep inequalities, as shown by the names of "fat people" given to the major arts, and "skinny people" given to the minor ones.

The fat people controlled industry, finance, and trade and therefore held the reins of economic power very securely in their hands. They also controlled the levers of political power, because at least four of the eight priors and half of the Council of the People had to belong to the major arts. The much more numerous minor arts had therefore a very inadequate representation. Thus the Florentine constitution was far from being that model of democracy that some historians have claimed it to be; it was instead a corporate state in which the masses were not at all integrated. The imbalance resulted in recurrent uprisings: in 1345 Cinto Bandini and nine other agitators were executed because they attempted to revolt; in 1368 many other heads rolled for the same reason. Ten years later the wool-workers led by Michele di Lando took over the government, which they retained for a short time only because they ran it atrociously; the disquiet, however, remained.

And yet despite these social and political upheavals, the "economic miracle" of Florence had no equal in the whole of Europe. This small city had a yearly gross national product that surpassed that of England under the great Elizabeth; King Edward III of England had debts with some Florentine banks totalling 1½ million florins, or, in present currency, some 35 million dollars. Although Florence did file for bankruptcy like any private banker, its finances were not destroyed by a defaulting monarch; the city made up for its losses on other markets, thanks to the merchants' outstanding organization. Checks were invented in Florence and so were letters of credit and treasury notes, and double-entry accounting. What is even more important, however, is that banking became solidly tied to manufacturing by means of stock investments.

The Florentine textile industry had discomfited all foreign competition since it had developed chemical dying processes. Federico Oricellari derived his name from *orchella,* a lichen he discovered in the East that produced a purple pigment and brought him millions. The dyers used the capital made available by the banks in which they owned stock to tool up their workshops so that their wools underwent up to thirty successive manufacturing steps, each one supervised by specialized workers. The age of craftsmanship was giving way already to the age of industrial production.

This infant capitalism was growing into a moneyed aristocracy; in Dante's time already it had contested the leadership of the city by the blue-blooded aristocracy. The former were led by the Cerchi bankers, the latter by "Barone" Donati, and their struggle bloodied Florence for decades. Later these two dynasties disappeared from the stage, and their places were taken by a number of new names, all of bourgeois trading origins: Bardi, Peruzzi, Strozzi, Pitti, Rucellai, Ricci, Ridolfi, Valori, Capponi, Soderini, Albizzi.

The Albizzi family pulled the strings of city government for quite a while, but always through intermediaries; they were too shrewd to let others attack their influence by openly challenging the public institutions. They contented themselves with directing the government from backstage, thereby sparing the susceptibilities of the Florentines, who were very attached to their nonexistent democracy. Between the last decades of the fourteenth century and the first ones of the fifteenth, the Albizzi were the great masters of behind-the-scene government, and they used this power to keep the wealthy classes safe from the equalitarian reforms of the poor.

But Florence would not have been Florence had the harmony between the ruling classes lasted. In 1421 the capitalists watched with satisfaction the instatement of Giovanni de Medici as "Standardbearer of Justice." He owned a large bank, so he was "all right." But their complacency turned to incredulity first, and then to rage, when Giovanni decided to place a seven percent tax on capital. Considering our own experience with the internal revenue service, this sounds like small beer indeed, but in those times the tax was thought of as out-and-out thievery, and Giovanni was branded a traitor to the Manufacturer's Association.

Giovanni's was a recently enriched family. There is no sure indication as to the origin of the name—perhaps it was derived from a medical ancestor—nor of their armorial bearings, which consisted of six orbs in field or. There had been a Medici city counselor at the beginning of the thirteenth century, but the real founder of the dynasty and its wealth was Averardo, who a hundred years later embarked on the not too reputable business of appropriations. It happened in Dante's time, when the Blacks had wrested supremacy from the Whites; Averardo, who was on the winners' side, drew up a very comprehensive list of enemy collaborators and got for himself exclusive rights to the pillage of their houses. In Italy politics has always been used for such ends, but Averardo was one of its most creative pioneers. His enterprise launched the Medici dynasty, on the basis of a bank based on war spoils that produced millions—millions that resulted in political power, and power that multiplied the financial capital even further.

When Giovanni died in 1428, his son, Cosimo, found himself in the position of being the wealthiest capitalist in Tuscany (with a personal fortune of two hundred thousand florins, or about 4.5 million dollars), and, thanks to the taxes against the rich introduced by his father, the most popular leader of the Florentine proletariat. Cosimo was about forty years old, and he had spent his time, not only investing his capital soundly, but also spending it wisely, and he had learned to control his impatience and his ambitions. Then, too, he was careful not to display his power, which he employed through a relatively minor office, as a member of the Council of Ten, a kind of Defense Department that functioned only in times of war.

Luckily for Cosimo, a war was not lacking at the moment, since Lucca had revolted against Florentine leadership and had to be taught a lesson. Cosimo took over the direction of military operations and even paid all the expenses involved, as if the war had been his private business. And he won without spending a cent of the treasury. Thus the son of the man who had invented the income tax became a benefactor of the *signoria,* and his popularity increased dramatically.

The fat people realized that if he was not stopped in time, the game would be over for them. As it was to be expected, the counter-attack was mounted by the family whom the Medici success had harmed most; Rinaldo degli Albizzi accused Cosimo of dictatorial designs and succeeded in obtaining a warrant against him from Standardbearer Guadagni. Cosimo refrained from either resistance or flight, both of which he could have easily done; instead, he let himself be arrested with docility and even allowed a Parliament assembled in the *signoria* square to bring a sentence of death against him, under pressure from Rinaldo's armed braves. All he did was to send a secret bribe to Guadagni, who thereupon changed his mind and commuted the sentence to ten years exile.

Cosimo moved to Venice, where he had already transferred most of his fortune. That he must have invested his money well there, too, is witnessed by the fact that shortly after his arrival the doge in person implored Florence to recall the exile. His request was gladly accepted, since the *signoria* had already come to the same decision. Cosimo returned in triumph and showed himself sadly surprised at the fact that the Albizzis had fled the city: he repeatedly claimed that he would never have dreamed of avenging himself on them—which was probably true in that he would never have done it in person; he would have simply allowed his followers, whose number was constantly increasing, to take care of the *vendetta*. The man was cool, but he did not forget easily.

Although he could have done it easily, Cosimo refrained again from interfering with constitutional authority. In fact, after holding a few appointments, he retired from public office, claiming that power corrupted the soul and the body. However, all government positions were occupied by his men, the masses were with him, and a good portion of the plutocracy owed money to his bank.

Cosimo became a moderate and benevolent dictator. But when someone remonstrated with him that his friends the priors, having discovered a plot, had had its leader thrown off one of the towers, Cosimo answered with a sigh, "States are not ruled with the Lord's Prayer." Moreover, he did realize a basic concept: that a social revolution can be carried out without wasting a single drop of blood, just by manipulating the tax structure. He was probably the first European statesman to apply the graduated income tax, which in twenty years added almost 5 million florins to the treasury, or over 100 million dollars. Many wealthy families, especially those of landed origin, refused to pay and left the city to return to their country estates. They were the old aristocracy, the members of the "Society of Towers" who had given a high tone to Florentine life. But Cosimo was not dismayed by the exodus: "We shall provide," he said, "to find replacements. Today a few yards of red cloth are enough to make a nobleman."

As a banker, Cosimo never missed a deal and, above all, he never made a wrong investment. Once a partner reproached him for having loaned a large sum to the Bishop of Bologna, who had no security to offer. Sometime later that bishop became Pope Nicholas V, and he contracted the management of Vatican finances to Cosimo. To keep abreast of all his responsibilities, Cosimo rose at dawn and retired with the hens, ate and drank with moderation, and thereby remained youthful and active until he was seventy-five years old. His family life also was well ordered: only once did he stray with a chambermaid, and had an illegitimate son as a result. He was rather miserly in his personal life but did not spare expenses for the embellishment of the city. He spent four hundred thousand florins of his own on commissions to architects such as Brunelleschi, sculptors such as Donatello and Ghiberti; painters such as Botticelli, Gozzoli, Filippo Lippi, and Angelico; philosophers and writers such as Pico della Mirandola, Marsilo Ficino, and Leon Battista Alberti. When Niccolo de Niccoli, the greatest collector of books of his times, ruined himself financially because of his expensive taste in Greek manuscripts, Cosimo gave him limitless credit at his bank. Then after Niccolo's death Cosimo took over the eight hundred volumes that Niccolo had collected at the cost of six thousand florins and presented most of them to the library of St. Mark.

The Florentine intellectuals idolized him. Botticelli, Pontormo, and Gozzoli have all left paintings of him. Probably made somewhat more flattering by admiration and gratitude, they portray a man of average height, with a dark and furrowed face, deep and piercing eyes, a strong and prominent nose. Even historians with popular leanings have admitted that he was a most enlightened dictator, and Varchi sees him as the most important character in the cultural rebirth of Italy and Europe.

Cosimo was also a clever diplomat. Realizing that the future of Italy depended on the balance of power between its four major political entities—Milan, Venice, Florence, and Naples—he tried to preserve and strengthen their alliance by all means. When after the death of Filippo Maria Visconti the city of Milan seemed almost to fall apart and Venice attempted to step in, Cosimo immediately opened his purse to Francesco Sforza, enabling him to resist successfully. Venice made a league with Naples to avenge itself on Florence, but Cosimo avoided the threat by simply recalling his credits from the two cities, where most important firms found themselves suddenly on the brink of bankruptcy.

They called him "Father of the Country," meaning of the city of Florence. But Cosimo was the father of the rest of Italy as well. Perhaps Cosimo entertained dreams of a unified nation, but he must have realized its impossibility and therefore contented himself with the only goal a statesman of his times could have aspired to: that of an alliance between the "big four," preserving the country from foreign invasions.

Alliance, then, was the Medici policy till the end of the fifteenth century, and Italy owes to it those decades of relative peace and wonderful prosperity that enabled the miracle of the Renaissance to take place.

Chapter 20

LORENZO AND GIROLAMO

W HEN Cosimo died, in 1464, he was succeeded by his son Piero, who inherited his father's wealth and power, but also his gout, to which he owed the nickname "Gouty" and an early demise. A hard worker like his father, Piero did not inherit, however, his political tact and intuition. Thus he had barely returned from his father's funeral when he recalled all the loans by which the latter had cleverly bound the most powerful Florentine families to his cause. Threatened with bankruptcy, the debtors attempted to stage a revolution in the name of freedom: a holy cause that, as Macchiavelli later observed, was only used to cover their bad debts. But there were so many revolutionaries that Piero had a difficult time holding on to power until his death in 1469.

Cosimo had realized how frail his son's health was and, anticipating his short life, had taken great pains to give an appropriate education to his grandchild Lorenzo, a lad who promised well. Lorenzo was given the best tutors available: Argiropoulos in Greek, Ficino in philosophy, and Cosimo himself in politics and business. But Lorenzo was only twenty when his father died, and his brother, Giuliano, only sixteen. The Medici party, already fearful of being left without a strong leader, was seized by sheer panic when Lorenzo announced that his private business would not allow him to spend time on politics, and the citizenry, all people who owed their jobs and their wealth to the Medici, sent a deputation to entreat him to reconsider his decision to retire. Lorenzo let himself be convinced. In fact, as later events were to prove, that is what he wanted to do all along, but having learned Cosimo's lessons well, he had demurred, pretending the opposite. He offered to share his power with his brother, but Giuliano, who admired his older brother worshipfully, preferred to devote his time to poetry, music, jousts, and women and therefore refused.

Lorenzo had few physical attractions to offer. Tall and strong, he, like his grandfather, had a dark complexion, but his face had a somewhat coarse cast because of heavy jowls and wide nostrils. A broken nose, which looked like a prizefighter's, made his voice sound disagreeably nasal. But all those who knew him agreed that five minutes in his company were enough to be thoroughly charmed by his courtesy and his extraordinary gift for putting his interlocutor at ease. He became a poet when talking to a poet, a statesman when talking to an ambassador, and when talking to a ruffian, he was a ruffian and a half.

His mother, Lucrezia Tornabuoni, called by Cosimo "The only man in this family," married Lorenzo off at twenty to a Roman princess, Clarice Orsini, chosen for "her large size and whiteness." Worried about the hereditary gout that polluted the Medici blood, Lucrezia had chosen her daughter-in-law as one buys a heifer: Roman women had a reputation for being on the coarse side but for being better "nursers" than the Florentines. "We judge the young girl to be much above average," Lucrezia wrote back to her husband from the scouting trip. "Lorenzo has seen her. Find out from him whether he likes her."

Lorenzo did not like her much, but he agreed to marry her anyway, partly to please his mother, partly because he also was concerned with the genetic future of the lineage, and finally because marriage, then even more than now, did not entail any great sacrifice. After the wedding Lorenzo went on loving Lucrezia Donati, though at the same time doing his duty by Clarice, as witnessed by the six children she bore him: Lucrezia, Piero, Maddalena, Giovanni, Luisa, and Giuliano.

Lorenzo, like his grandfather before him, preferred to remain a private citizen and refused to take any public office. But to enable his men to rule with more ease he supervised the establishment of a new executive body, the Council of the Seventy, the members of which were elected to life tenure. His direction of foreign affairs did not have a smooth beginning: when the citizens of Volterra asked for royalties from the mines that Lorenzo had confiscated to benefit Florence, he punished the city with a violence that Cosimo would have surely avoided. At last, Lorenzo realized his hastiness and immediately tried to make amends.

His attempt to annex the town of Imola to the Florentine *signoria* was probably another diplomatic error, which almost cost him his power and Florence its independence. Sixtus IV, an impulsive and overbearing pope greedy for land to parcel out among his nephews, reacted by taking the management of the pontifical finances away from the Medici and giving them to the Pazzi, their worst enemies. Moreover, he encouraged the Pazzi to plot against and overthrow Lorenzo.

The coup was planned for the mass of Holy Saturday, 1478, in the Cathedral of St. Mary of the Flower. Lorenzo was there alone and unarmed. The conspirators convinced Giuliano, who had stayed home, to join his brother in church. At the moment of the elevation, while the priest was blessing the congregation with the consecrated host, the conspirators, among whom was Archbishop Salviati, threw themselves upon the two brothers. Giuliano was wounded by Bandini and finished by the dagger of Francesco de Pazzi. Lorenzo was able to shield himself with his forearm, and then, surrounded by friends, he was brought, only slightly wounded, into the vestry, the doors of which were then barred. Salviati, the Pazzi, and the other leaders of the conspiracy rushed into Piazza della Signoria trying to rouse the populace with the usual cry of "Freedom! Freedom!" But the people answered by shouting, "Balls! Balls!"—which were the Medici arms.

The punishment was harsh. Eighty heads fell; the archbishop who had unsheathed his dagger in church, during the most solemn moment of the mass, was hanged together with Francesco de Pazzi. (A young painter just turned twenty-six by the name of Leonardo da Vinci sketched them from below in the square as they dangled in space.)

The corpse of Jacopo, head of the Pazzi family, was dug up twice, dragged through town, and then dropped into the Arno. Lorenzo composed rhyming epitaphs for the victims and gave orders for Botticelli to immortalize their effigies in the Palazzo Vecchio.

It seems that Pope Sixtus had approved the plot, but had not agreed to the assassination. Now, however, the hanging of an archbishop gave him reason to excommunicate Lorenzo and the whole government of the city, to forbid all religious services, and to organize a kind of a holy war against Florence. King Ferdinand of Naples joined it and gave an ultimatum to Florence: either deliver Lorenzo to the pope, or have the Neapolitan army invade Tuscany.

With Medicean shrewdness Lorenzo advised the priors to accept the ultimatum and offered himself up as a scapegoat. But the *signoria* disdainfully refused, and the war was on. The Florentine army suffered a defeat at Poggibonsi, and taxes had to be raised to outfit another force. Lorenzo was aware that as time went on people would tire of sacrificing for his sake, so with generosity mixed with shrewdness he left the city alone and traveled in secret to Pisa, to board a ship for Naples, where he bravely delivered himself to the enemy king.

Ferdinand had an awful reputation: just a short time before he had invited the *condottiere* Jacopo Piccinino to be his guest and then had had him cowardly murdered. If that is how he treated his guests, one could well imagine what he would do to a foe he had declared war against and half-defeated. The Neapolitan army was in fact collecting one victory after another, and the pope kept insisting that Lorenzo be given up to him. But in a few days the Medici had developed strong friendships in Naples, thanks to his magnetic personality and to his bank account. The influential Count Carafa, Ferdinand's secretary of state, went over to his side: Lorenzo convinced him that weakening Florence meant a strengthening of the Church states, which were already pressing on the northern borders of Naples, and that war within Italy opened up the whole country to the greed of the Turks, who, after occupying Constantinople, were sending their fleets to conquer the Mediterranean.

Ferdinand, already impressed by the coolness and personality of his foe, ended by agreeing with his arguments. So instead of delivering

Lorenzo to the pope, Ferdinand signed a treaty of peace and alliance with him and sent him back to a triumphant welcome in Florence. Sixtus raged in vain. Finally, he, too, had to recognize the facts: a Turkish army had landed at Otranto and was threatening to overrun the country unless its internal differences were resolved. Lorenzo sent an embassy to the pope, with a message inspired by humbleness and devotion. Sixtus gave the ambassadors an embarrassing reception, reviling them in front of the court, but as soon as he finished playing the part required to save face, he made his peace with them and offered Lorenzo his friendship in exchange for fifteen armed galleons to send against the Turks. From that moment on Lorenzo's power was never again seriously challenged, except by Savonarola.

Girolamo Savonarola was born in Ferrara in 1452, and when still very young he left home to join a monastery. He was rather ugly, and what's worse, graceless—at a time when gracefulness was almost an eleventh commandment. He had a low forehead, dark, hollow cheeks, a thick and shapeless nose, and a large mouth with fleshy lips that rarely smiled. In that stormy face, closed as a tight fist, only the eyes were beautiful: dark gray, intense, now burning with rage, now delicately melancholy. Perhaps those eyes were appealing for sympathy, but the rest of Savonarola was not about to inspire any. Shyness and pride, which always go together, made him awkward and overly defensive.

After spending his novitiate at the monastery of St. Dominic in Bologna, in 1481 Savanorola was transferred to that of St. Mark's in Florence, one of the civic institutions that owed most to the Medici's largesse. Cosimo had commissioned Michelozzi to restore it, spending thirty-six thousand florins of his own money to do so. He had had Beato Angelico decorate its walls with frescoes and had bequeathed an extensive library to it, turning the monastery into a center of art and culture. Lorenzo had followed his grandfather's example, adding a stupendous park filled with some one hundred ancient statues, which Florentine sculptors were free to study and copy. Among those who came to the garden to study the secrets of the chisel in Savonarola's time was a small boy by the name of Michelangelo Buonarroti.

St. Mark's prior entrusted Girolamo with the job of training the novices, a position of great responsibility within the monastery. Savonarola was thought to qualify probably because of his success at a Dominican convention held some time earlier in Reggio Emilia. The assembly consisted of learned clergymen and scholarly laymen who had gathered to discuss questions of dogma. Among the laity Pico della Mirandola eclipsed all others. Only nineteen years old, he was already known as the "Phoenix of geniuses." As long as the arguments remained on a purely academic level, Brother Girolamo kept himself quietly wrapped in his robe, unnoticed by everybody, but when the debate strayed to the subject of the relationship between the Church and the world, he jumped to his feet as if released by springs and delivered a savage diatribe against the secularization and corruption of the clergy. The audience was dumbfounded, especially Pico, who, having been trained through humanistic studies in a very different kind of eloquence, was never to forget the friar's.

Flying into Florence on the wings of this success, the friar quite naturally was assigned to preach from the pulpit as well as to teach his apprenticing brothers. But the pulpit he was given shows that his reputation as a preacher was still not too high in the eye of his superiors. The great theaters where the stars of Florentine holy rhetoric shone were the *Duomo,* as the Cathedral of Santa Maria del Fiore was called, and San Lorenzo. One step lower were Santa Maria Novella and Santa Croce. Savonarola was assigned instead to preach jointly at a little convent church and at the Orsanmichele chapel. Yet even the unsophisticated lower-class public that attended those temples failed to appreciate the preacher who delivered his sermons "without planning, apostle-like," as a cronichler reported ungrammatically.

With time, however, Savonarola made progress, aided by constant phonetic exercises, undertaken to improve his voice and eliminate the traces of a thick Ferrara accent. It is clear that his ambition to become an orator was very strong. Fra Girolamo wanted to succeed, and the prior offered him the pulpit of San Lorenzo.

Savonarola's debut was a fiasco. The audience at San Lorenzo was composed of skeptical and sophisticated intellectuals who in a few weeks dwindled to only a couple of dozen persons, and the latter stayed on probably only for the typically Tuscan pleasure of embarrassing Savonarola with their ironic stares and mocking smiles. Presumably because of these failures, the prior of St. Mark's had him transferred, in 1486, to Lombardy. There, however, the friar abandoned the gruff and preachy style that had made him so unpopular in Florence and developed an open, passionate, and apocalyptic manner that was to turn him into a champion of religious oratory.

After four years of "exile" in the provinces, Savonarola was recalled to Florence by the Magnificent himself, on Pico's request. Once again the prior of St. Mark's put him in charge of training novices. But the news of his return at Lorenzo's special intercession had stirred much curiosity, and many laymen such as Poliziano and Ficino were also attracted to hear his lessons, their interest fanned by the wonderful stories that Pico was spreading in the intellectual circles. After a few days the crowd grew to such a size that Savonarola had to move his lectures to the shade of a grove of Damascus roses in the park, because there was no hall large enough in the monastery to contain the crowds.

Now that he was no longer intimidated by an audience, Brother Girolamo spent little time on his lessons and hurried instead to establish that magic atmosphere of which he became both creator and victim every time he opened his mouth in public. And the lesson changed into a sermon that, if it produced the most contradictory reactions in the listeners, still did produce reactions unfailingly. Consequently, the audience kept increasing each time. Many thought that Savonarola was rude and simple-minded; others felt that he was being rhetorical and melodramatic; but everyone was impressed by the strength, the warmth, and the sincerity of his speech, which borrowed its subjects exclusively from the Bible and had nothing academic or literary about it. Florence had not been accustomed for a long time, centuries perhaps, to hear such plain talk. It created scandal, it stimulated argument, and it gathered more listeners around the controversial preacher. And, finally, Girolamo was prevailed upon to take again to the pulpit.

His comeback was greeted by an overflowing crowd that literally laid siege to St. Mark's Church. Savonarola must have felt emboldened by the size of the crowd; times of tension were those best suited to his personality. He climbed the pulpit with assurance, opened his arms, and attacked the audience with vehemence and without hesitation. He had chosen the theme most congenial to his range: the Apocalypse. Perhaps he only repeated what he had been proclaiming across Lombardy for the past four years, but to the Florentines it seemed an improvised performance, such was the violence with which the tempestuous friar scourged the Church for its corruption and its vices and announced its punishment and imminent "renewal." At first the audience, accustomed to being flattered and seduced rather than assaulted and threatened, tried to resist the screaming and gesticulating lunatic, but soon it gave in to him, as if hypnotized. And when the sermon ended, the listeners were unable to express their emotion with cheers; the church was swept instead by a subdued murmuring more eloquent than an ovation.

But the difficulties were only beginning. Now that he had achieved success, Savonarola was bound to become a juicy target for the Florentine intellectuals. Even those who privately thought that he was an oafish ham who used shouts and threats to disguise a doctrinal void realized that it would be better to have him on their side and began to work on him. One after the other they called at the monastery, trusting that the enchanter of crowds would prove weak in a face-to-face confrontation. But private talks with Savonarola impressed the intellectuals even more than his sermons had done. They realized that the man despised culture, not for lack of education, but because he was convinced that learning perverted morality. And they discovered, to their surprise, that the monk was impervious to the corruption of worldly success: in that courtly era, he did not aspire to become a courtier, nor a darling of the salons and the academies. His mistrust of philosophy was only a reflection of his mistrust of man and of reason.

Brother Girolamo continued preaching in St. Mark's for a year and a half, until the end of the nineties. Finally the church could not contain the crowd and its enthusiasm any longer, and during the Lent of 1491 he was raised, by popular acclaim, to the pulpit of the *Duomo*. Some of Savonarola's followers were worried as well as pleased by this advancement: the cathedral was a platform of great responsibility from which one spoke to the whole city. But for that very reason, a certain amount of diplomacy was necessary if its holder was to prosper, and Girolamo had never shined at the art of mincing words. His friends tried to warn him that if he kept on foretelling doom and ill fate—a practice that had earned him the nickname "Preacher of the Bums"—he risked being taken for an evil-eyed jinx, and they admonished him that references to his "visions" could bring trouble with the Church, which frowned on all unauthorized supernatural experiences. Above all, they warned that he should not overstep the boundaries of religion and morality and stray into the field of politics.

The monk accepted and agreed to the advice, promising to follow it. His friends' misgivings must therefore have been great when, at the grand opening in the *Duomo,* they heard him embark on a tirade more savage than customary, clearly directed against temporal authority, that is, against the Medici: " . . . there is no longer any grace, any gift of the Holy Ghost that cannot be bought and sold, while the poor are oppressed by taxes, and with fifty florins of income they must pay a hundred in tolls. . . . Think hard, you wealthy people, because the punishment will fall on your heads. This city will no longer be called Florence, but turpitude, blood, a den of thieves. . . . I did not wish to speak in your name, O Lord, but you are stronger than I am, and your word has become a fire that burns the marrow of my bones that harbor it . . ."

Later, in his *Collections of Revelations,* Savonarola explained the abrupt change in plans:

> I remember that before preaching in the Duomo in 1491, I had decided not to use the sermon dealing with my visions, which was already prepared, and I further decided to make no reference to them in the future. God is my witness that I spent the entire Saturday and then the night after searching for another inspiration. But I did not find any. As it was dawning, and I was exhausted by the long vigil, I heard a voice as I was praying: "Foolish man, don't you see that the Lord wishes that you follow the self-same road?" As a result, that day I delivered a terrifying sermon.

His friends were confounded, but the popular success was enormous. It was the first time in half a century that anyone had dared to raise his voice against the government in public. And the government, surely on Lorenzo's suggestion, replied to the provocation by politely inviting the monk to preach in the Palazzo Vecchio to the representatives and officials of the *signoria*.

The move was worthy of the elegance and shrewdness of The Magnificent. It even flustered Savonarola somewhat, because he began his homily with a certain shyness: "In company of your Lordships I do not feel as sure of myself as I do in church. I shall better be urbane and controlled as Christ was in the home of the Pharisee. But I must tell you that the good and the ill of the city flow from its leaders, therefore great is their responsibility for even trivial sins." So far, the speech was in fact urbane and controlled, as Girolamo had promised it would be. But as if propelled by a mysterious force, he soon added: "Tyrants are beyond salvation, because pride devours them—they love flattery and refuse to return ill-gotten gains. They do not hear the destitute, they do not condemn the rich, they expect the poor to work for them without pay, they buy votes and sell tariffs to oppress the masses."

The full text of Savonarola's diatribe has not survived. Only the summary of it has come down to us. The summary must be pretty close to his actual words, however, and his listeners must have been left rather disconcerted. Among other things, Savonarola had said: "You must eliminate discord, do justice, bring back honesty." Those professional politicians trained at the Medicean school of disenchanted common sense must have smiled at those words and thought of their speaker as a witless visionary.

More skeptical but also more farsighted than his underlings, Lorenzo, on the other hand took the monk seriously. He asked five citizens of high status to talk informally with Savonarola, to warn him that if he continued in this direction he might even be exiled from the city. Although it was supposed to be private advice, the monk realized immediately where the warning originated: "I do not care," he answered, "let him do what he will. But tell him this: I am a foreigner and he is the first citizen of this town. Yet I must stay here and he must leave; *I* will stay, not *he*."

Lorenzo was probably more upset by the monk's rudeness than by his threats. Relying on his customary tact, once more he refrained from acting directly. Instead, he commissioned another monk by the name of Mariano to prepare a sermon attacking Savonarola. Goaded on by envy and obsequiousness, Mariano accepted his task with enthusiasm; it gave him a chance to please his lord and at the same time to clip the wings of a dangerous competitor.

As backstage gossip carried the news across Florence, a great crowd squeezed into the church of San Gallo to witness the confrontation. Everyone was there, from Lorenzo himself to Pico and Poliziano. Whether it was excessive eagerness that betrayed him, or the distinguished crowd that turned his head, the fact is that Mariano lost all sense of proportion and threw himself into a harangue fit more for a saloon than a church, spiced with unseemly accusations, vulgar insinuations, and rude name-calling. The audience was disgusted, Lorenzo first among them. But he was also worried, because he realized that Mariano's failure meant a superlative success for Savonarola, who might not have been a giant before but now would be so seen by everyone.

One month passed, and in July the prior's position at St. Mark's became open. There is no proof that the order cleared the new appointment with Lorenzo, but it seems unlikely that it could have turned a deaf ear to his veto if he had pronounced one, so it can be assumed that Lorenzo refrained from opposing Girolamo's appointment as prior, unless it was he who caused it in the first place. Savonarola showed his gratitude by refusing the courtesy call that every prior of St. Mark's had paid the Medici in recognition of their high patronage of the monastery. Those who reminded him of the custom he dryly answered: "Who do you think made me prior, God or Lorenzo? And I want to thank God, my Lord, not Lorenzo." When these words were passed on to Lorenzo, he shook his head and commented with a trace of resigned sorrow: "What do you say to that? A foreign monk has come to live in my house, and he would not even bother to come and say hello." Burlamacchi, a great defender of Savonarola, recorded the episode, thinking it redounds to the monk's honor; yet it rather shows the greatness of the lord and proves how wrong the monk was in calling him a tyrant.

The real feelings of The Magnificent for this unmanageable character will always remain a mystery. One cannot underestimate the fascination that the preacher worked on the crowds, but the Medici administration was solidly established, and Lorenzo had more than enough authority and prestige easily to eliminate any opponent, even one robed in a monkish cloak. In case Lorenzo needed it, he would have received support from the pope, who considered him to be "the compass needle," that is, the hinge of the coalition between the great Italian states that had given the country decades of peace and prosperity. And Florence was the city that had benefited most from it: what it had lost in freedom it had gained in order and even in social justice, because Savonarola notwithstanding, the Medici taxes were a model for their times, and the poor were less poor in Florence than anyplace else in Italy. Thus the opposition was left with few arguments, and its members were reduced to a wistful nostalgia for a freedom that had never existed or had been only the license of parties.

It is likely that assurance of his own power contributed to the tolerance that The Magnificent displayed in his dealings with the troublesome monk. But there must have been more to it, because Lorenzo did not stop at toleration; several times he went unofficially to St. Mark's and listened to the apocalyptic sermons of the preacher. It is not known whether Girolamo ever recognized Lorenzo sitting amidst the crowd; in any case Lorenzo's presence never slowed him down, because he kept on thundering relentlessly against the corrupt government, against feasts, games, the carnival (it was his nemesis), in other words, against everything Lorenzo stood for.

Despite the ceaseless harassment The Magnificent went on attending St. Mark's, and he never left without dropping an offering in the almsbox. Once the monks found a whole satchel of gold coins inside it. The prior, realizing immediately whence it came, sent the gift on to the goodmen of St. Martin for their "shameful poor" and indirectly acknowledged the present from the pulpit, saying that "the faithful dog does not stop barking in his master's defense after someone throws him a bone."

These provocations, instead of wounding him, seem only to have increased Lorenzo's curiosity. One day he came to stroll in the splendid garden of the monastery, ostensibly to admire the statues that he himself had donated, and which made a museum out of the park. In reality, he hoped to meet the monk, who still had not called on him. He was sure that a short private talk between them would have solved everything; nobody had ever resisted the warmth that The Magnificent radiated, his tact, his relaxed good humor, his contagious friendliness. Or perhaps he was also anxious to look into the eyes of the one man who seemed to contradict all his beliefs about men. Grandfather Cosimo had taught him with word and deed that friendship was only a question of fees. It was clear that the monk would not sell himself for gold. But a currency to buy his soul must also have existed. What was it?

For hours and hours Lorenzo dragged his swollen leg along the paths, though he was forced once in a while to sit down to relieve the pain. The novices in charge of gardening, as soon as they recognized him, rushed to the prior to inform him and entreat him to greet the illustrious visitor. "Did he ask to see me?" asked the prior. "No." "Then let him walk around some more."

The Magnificent kept at it all morning, then wended his way resignedly toward the exit. He realized that the monk knew of his presence and refused to show himself on purpose. He also suspected that their meeting would take place soon, anyway. During the past years his health had been worsening, and his condition left him with no illusions since it was the same illness that had destroyed his father, whose decline he well remembered. In April, 1492, he let himself be carried on a stretcher to the luxurious villa at Careggi, where he received a constant stream of politicians and writers eager to keep him company. They told him that brother Girolamo had already foretold his death, together with that of Pope Innocent and the King of Naples. For these latter two the prediction was safe, since they were old, but Lorenzo was only forty-three.

Poliziano records that at midnight on April 7, Lorenzo was told that a priest carrying the extreme unction had come to see him. "I can't allow," he said, "that Jesus should come into this room. Please

help me to walk so I can meet Him." His kidneys were already
blocked, so for him to get up was very dangerous as well as excru-
ciatingly painful. But his usual courtesy, if not faith, obliged him to
receive the Lord like a gentleman. He was carried to the salon where
he knelt in front of the priest and was given communion.

Immediately afterward a famous doctor, Ticino Logario, tried out
on Lorenzo a new drug he had just developed: a sort of a milkshake
made with ground jewels. One imagines how much good it did, but
the patient had already given up all hope, and appeared to be en-
grossed in different concerns. All of a sudden he mentioned Savonarola and sent people to summon him. His biographers have recorded
that when the prior of St. Mark's received the message, he hesitated
and objected; however, eventually he left for Careggi.

There are two versions of what happened during that historical encounter. Poliziano, the only witness of the event, tells that Lorenzo
had just taken leave of his son Pietro and was saying an affectionate
good-bye to Pico della Mirandola when Savonarola came in. There
was no time for pleasantries. The monk entreated the dying man to
hold firm to the faith, to live thereon outside sin, if God allowed him
to live, and to accept death with serenity, if God so decreed. Lorenzo
answered that his faith was strong, his rejection of sin irrevocable, his
courage unwavering. The monk then turned to leave, but Lorenzo
stopped him, asking for a blessing; with downcast eyes he devotedly
answered Girolamo's prayers, "according to the prescribed rites." After
the monk had left, Lorenzo finally received extreme unction and
waited for the end, kissing and fondling a crucifix. It was a silver
crucifix inlaid with pearls and precious stones; it must have given a
pleasant sensation to The Magnificent's fingers.

Savonarola's apologists are not satisfied with such a simple ending,
and they describe one that is much more dramatic. They say that the
monk required a full confession of the dying man and imposed three
conditions for his absolution. First, Lorenzo was to acknowledge faith
in God's mercy—which Lorenzo immediately did. Second, he had to
promise to give back all his ill-gotten gains, which were to be restored by his heirs; with this The Magnificent complied but only after

long hesitation and with visible effort. After this Savonarola is supposed to have stood up, and in a terrible voice ringing with a definitive
tone he is supposed to have enjoined: "Third, you must return freedom
to the people of Florence." The moribund prince looked at the monk,
who stared back at him without pity, and gathering his last strength
turned his back. And the monk refused to bless him.

It is probable that Savonarola's apologists—none of whom was present at the scene—were lying. One should hope so for the sake of their
hero: blackmailing a dying man would certainly not add to his stature. Unfortunately, it must be said that the story sounds only too true,
given Savonarola's character.

Chapter 21

The Medici Civilization and Its Protagonists

When the Medicis took over, Florence was already the unchallenged capital of European culture. Historians have long tried to explain the causes of this success: some ascribe it to geographic position, some to history, and others to industrial development, which itself needs to be explained. But none of the theories seem conclusively proved, and we would do better to stick to the facts.

Great poetry was born in Florence with Dante, great narrative prose with Boccaccio, great learning with Petrarch, great painting with Cimabue and Giotto, and great architecture with Arnolfo. There was obviously something in this city that led men to a vocation in the arts and in literature, but it is also a fact that when the Medicis realized this, they seconded the vocation with an eagerness, an intelligence, and a liberality that make them worthy of universal admiration. As Durant says, "No family on earth has ever equaled the Medicis in the patronage of culture."

It was Cosimo who inaugurated the tradition, by subsidizing literature, poetry, philosophy, and art. He spent a fortune on collections of original manuscripts imported from Athens, Constantinople, and Alexandria. But he did something else besides, something that later turned out to be a decisive element in the orientation of Italian and European thought: he established the Platonic Academy.

At the time, Italians knew next to nothing of Greek philosophy. A little Aristotle had come their way indirectly, through St. Thomas Aquinas and the other masters of Scholasticism. But those philosophers had absorbed only that part of Aristotelian logic that suited them; they discarded what embarrassed them. Philosophy in Europe was still the same as theology, and theology was a mixture of the Bible and of Aristotelian logic—or, rather, it was an attempt to put Aristotelian logic at the service of the Bible. The idea was to show that there was no conflict at all between the truth revealed in the sacred texts and reason, but that, rather, the latter was a confirmation of the former. As for Plato, he was even less known than Aristotle, and no one understood what were the basic differences between the two philosophers.

However, in 1439 something new happened. As we have seen, at that time and at Cosimo's request the Ecumenical Council met in Florence, to try to reunite the two branches of the Christian church— the Roman Catholic and the Greek Orthodox—that had separated four hundred years before. And what was nearly as important as the actual meeting was the fact that the emperor of the orient, John Paleologus, came in person and brought with him his best doctrinal scholars, among whom were Gemistus, Bessarion, and Scolari. And although the hastily contrived agreement on dogma triggered a rebellion among the Byzantine clergy and the attempt to reconcile the two branches failed, the Florentine intellectuals, who had followed the debates with passionate interest, were conquered by the dialectics of the Greek visitors, who quoted the two great masters of antiquity by heart and argued with a logic that in Italy was still unheard of.

The council was a revelation. The official losers became the cultural conquerors, especially Gemistus, who, having realized how ignorant the Italians were, published a popularized pamphlet in Latin to explain the difference between Plato and Aristotle. It was a rather partial explanation, because Gemistus was a fanatic Platonist, to the extent that he had assumed the pseudonym Pletone, and his Aristotelian colleagues retorted in very strong terms. The subsequent controversy then became downright vulgar when Trapezunzio joined in. Trapezunzio, or Giorgio da Trebisonda, did not stop at attacking Pletone, he went on to attack Plato, calling him a homosexual and a thief.

What was really striking (and somewhat comical) was the passion with which the Italian intellectuals, who were almost entirely ignorant of the matter, threw themselves into the debate. To talk of Plato and Aristotle was "in," and the majority of Florentines were usually in favor of whatever was new, that is, in this case, of Plato, whom they began to worship even before they read him.

Surprised and moved by so much zeal, Gemistus thought he should put it to good use. He went to see Cosimo and suggested that he re-open in Florence the famous Platonic Academy that had enjoyed such prestige in Greece. Cosimo immediately saw the convenience of the thing, and he also had available someone to fill the position of high priest of the new cult: a young man by the name of Marsilio Ficino, the son of Cosimo's personal physician.

Ficino showed an authentic vocation for philosophic discipline and embodied the characteristics of the perfect thirteenth-century humanist. He was so good-looking that all women fell madly in love with him, but he favored none, because he found none that to him was more attractive than his books. He was so infatuated with his intellectual master that he addressed his disciples as "brothers in Plato" instead of "brothers in Christ." Even though, at the age of forty, he did in fact become a priest and then a canon, he continued to light candles before Plato's bust, which he kept at his bedside instead of the crucifix.

Ficino passed for a great philosopher—which he was not, because he utterly lacked original ideas. His style was woolly and his critical insights limited. But he was very learned, and he was the first one to put down in Latin the whole work of exegesis of Greek thought done by the Alexandrians, thus throwing light on points of contrast between the two great schools. The Aristotelians maintained that nature works without knowing what it does, while the Platonists ascribed a spirit of consciousness to it. It was a question of deciding whether the world was ruled by reason or by chance, and only the first theory, Plato's, was compatible with the Christian view of creation—creation seen as the manifestation of the divine and universal spirit of the Creator. Aristotle saw creation as the result of blind laws governing matter.

Ficino, however, failed to see the seriousness of the rift on which had centered the dispute of the Greek scholars who had come to Florence. He tried to reconcile what was irreconcilable: paganism and Christianity. Borrowing from Confucius and Zoroaster as well as from the Greeks, he wrote a hodge-podge work, *Platonic Theology,* which only shows the great confusion that existed in Western minds at the time of their first contact with classical philosophical thought. A mindless enthusiasm for everything that the ancients had said or written pushed Ficino to justify them all, even if they contradicted each other. To Ficino, the most common banality seemed a revelation if it had been uttered by one of the ancients. And any revelation, including Christ's, had to be paralleled by some text of the ancients in order to be valid.

The Platonic Academy under Ficino's leadership became the arena for this new sport. It is almost impossible to imagine what a fever took hold of all the intellectual class of Europe. They flocked to Florence from all over Italy, France, Germany, and England. Everyone converged there—from Pico della Mirandola to Poliziano and the young Michelangelo. They met in the grand mansion of the Medicis, the one now called Palazzo Riccardi. Everyone took sides, backing this or that personage of Plato's *Dialogues* with an eagerness that often turned into aggressiveness and led to fights. It was difficult to make the ancients' theories agree with Christian teachings, but then Christianity was often forgotten, in spite of the presence of many prelates. When it was remembered, the solution was to utter some sophism or take refuge in twisted allegories. Every so often a speech was made or a hymn was sung in honor of the laurel-crowned bust of the Immortal who presided over the gathering from a pedestal. November 27, the presumed date of both the birth and the death of Plato, was celebrated as a religious holiday. Some of the academicians even proposed to ask the pope to make Plato into a saint.

Lorenzo had been Ficino's pupil, and he was among the most faithful followers of the Platonic debates and rites that made Florence the center of Western thought. He had the time to do it, because he had arranged his political affairs in a most clever way. After the trying test of the war with Naples, Lorenzo prevailed upon King Ferdinand, Galeazzo Sforza of Milan, and Pope Innocent to join him in a league for the safeguard of peace, and the small satellite states were pulled into the league as well, by the bigger ones' force of gravity. Only Venice remained outside the league, but it was kept in check by the strength of the four-way coalition. Internal politics Lorenzo left in charge of the Seventy, and they took turns in the various offices. He limited himself to general supervision. His real concerns were the arts, literature and scholarship, and Florence's social life, of which he set the tone. This is where he got the title by which he is known in history: The Magnificent. *Magnifico* was a title given to every lord in those days, but Lorenzo was the *Magnifico par excellence*.

Florence became wildly excited about culture, and also about parades and masquerades, to the point that the carnival became a national event. Lorenzo encouraged these happy pastimes and continued to perfect their style. He hired the best artists to paint the floats on which the youths wearing extravagant and allegorical costumes rode from Ponte Vecchio to Piazza del Duomo. And he personally supervised the production of the *Trionfi*—the shows with which the parades ended. He even composed songs for these occasions: the famous *Canti Carnascialeschi*, which later were so much to enrage Savonarola, who took them for a Satanic incentive to moral perversion. *Carnascialismo* —carnival merriment—became a natural vocation of the people. It flourished in other places as well as Florence, but Lorenzo raised its level almost to the point of art.

Lorenzo had the knack for organizing great popular festivals, and he enjoyed them. His many-sided personality allowed him to be interested in the philosophical problems he debated with Ficino, and at the same time to give equal attention to a discussion about crops with his farm steward, or about architectural problems with Leon Battista Alberti, or about music with Squarcialupi. However, it seems that the strongest component of Lorenzo's character was his down-to-earth popular characteristic, as is shown by the preference he always showed,

among all his friends and protégés, for Luigi Pulci, the author of
Morgante Maggiore.

Pulci was a plebeian Cervantes who smelled of the tavern, and his
famous poem satirized the high-minded heroes of the *chansons de
geste.* Like the true Florentine he was, Pulci had a lively sense of the
grotesque, a biting polemic spirit, a foul tongue, a bubbling, roaring
Rabelaisian laughter, cutting and colorful answers, and coarse, rough
manners. But Lorenzo liked him for just those characteristics. "Gigi"
was his carousing companion. The family chaplain wrote to Lorenzo
reproachfully, concerning Pulci: "He is the spirit in your balls"—of
course, he meant the balls on the Medici coat of arms. The truth is
that even though Lorenzo favored the study of Greek and Latin and
financed the Platonic Academy, The Magnificent realized the danger
that erudition might stifle culture, by making it consist wholly of a
rehash of the classics—which is, in fact, the doom that eventually befell
Florentine culture. And Lorenzo loved Pulci because he was an exception in being free from the slavery of erudition. The Magnificent
himself avoided the display of learning in his poems, which are among
the very few of the period to have a popular inspiration and an exquisite feeling for nature. And such poems are hard to find in Italian literature, which remained academic, professorial, and courtly until jour-
nalism came along to stimulate and revive it.

It was due also to Lorenzo that Italian retained its status as a cultivated language that Dante had achieved for it, and which probably
would have been lost if the Latin-fans and the humanists had had their
way. More than that, it was at Lorenzo's court that the language received those finishing touches that made of it the richest, most refined,
and sweetest of tongues, not only in all of Italy, but—in those days—
in the whole world. The Magnificent, even though he read and wrote
the ancient languages well, spoke only Italian and wanted no other
language spoken at his table, where all the great scholars of the day,
infatuated with Greek and Latin, sat as habitual guests.

Among those learned guests was Poliziano, who was Lorenzo's
creditor on two accounts: he had taught Lorenzo the art of making
poetry and he had saved Lorenzo's life. It was he who pulled Lorenzo

away from under his would-be murderers' daggers and pushed him into the vestry, barring the door, when Lorenzo was attacked by the Pazzi in the cathedral. Poliziano was a perfect courtier, in the best sense of the word: a cultivated and refined man of the world, an enchanting conversationalist, a confirmed parasite bred in the hothouse that was the Medici palace. But all his life long he remained sincerely attached and utterly faithful to his lord. He was the incarnation of the melancholy spiritual adventure of the humanistic *nouvelle vague* of the time. He had be n considered a young prodigy when, hardly twenty, he had comp sed some wonderful octaves about Giuliano de Medici's tournament, which had made of him the heir apparent to Petrarch. But, l ke his teacher, Poliziano succumbed to the fever of classicism that had infected everybody, and the poet in him deteriorated as the scholar developed. He started writing poems in Latin, which were imitations of Greek models; he became an excellent professor of metrics and philology, and he never again produced anything original. But he remained an accomplished gentleman and a devoted friend until the end, exempt from pettiness and envy.

We owe to Poliziano's pen the best and most admiring portrait of another champion of the Medici elite: Pico della Mirandola. Poliziano describes him as being very handsome, tall, with delicate features and gentle manners, touched by an inner light that had something divine in it. An aristocrat who instead of court life had chosen a life of libraries in Bologna and Paris, Pico was considered the phenomenon of his time. They called him the "Phoenix of geniuses," because his extreme thirst for culture, his desire for universality, had pushed him to study everything. Later generations found out that though he knew indeed something of everything, that something was little and inaccurate. He prided himself on knowing twenty-seven languages, but actually of some of them he knew only a few words. However, his extensive reading and his iron memory enabled him to sprinkle his talk with quotations that brought him general admiration in the society of erudites in which he lived.

Pico chose Florence as his country of election, and there, under Lorenzo's patronage, he worked on an attempt to condense into nine hundred propositions all human knowledge, of which he (mistakenly) believed himself to be the depository. He also declared that he was ready to defend his work in an oratorial tournament, but no one picked up his challenge.

Such, then, were the chief protagonists of the Florentine cultural life that had its center at the Medici Palace and the Platonic Academy. In these centers the fires of doctrinal dispute blazed with a violence that in our day hardly seems justified. And from these centers the controversies spread to private sitting rooms, to the streets, and even to taverns. The city, miraculously free of political strife, used up its exuberant energies in ideological orgies. What is the soul? An idea, as Plato said, or a form, as Aristotle asserted? And how can damnation be eternal, and therefore infinite, if it is the requital of sin, which is finite?

These were the problems that preoccupied the citizens of Florence under Lorenzo. But they were just intellectual games of dialectics, nothing more. Women also took part in the discussions, and some of them composed essays and poems in Latin or even in Greek. All this was not limited to the higher classes. Lorenzo fostered the spreading of culture—this, indeed, was his great merit as a statesman. Against the advice of Poliziano, who in the typical fashion of Italian intellectuals wanted to keep culture a high-caste monopoly, Lorenzo opened his purse to Bernardo Cennini, when the latter opened the first printing press in Florence. He gave a palace to Christoforo Landino who later ruined himself by publishing the complete editions of the works of Horace, Vergil, Pliny, and Dante, with commentaries. Lorenzo had the education of the people at heart, and he understood how much the new techniques of diffusion would contribute to raise its level.

It was under Lorenzo that the tradition of the learned artisan was born, a tradition that still exists in Florence. While the great painters, sculptors, and architects worked in the palaces and churches, every small workshop of goldsmith or etcher had its "maestro," such as Finiguerra, Baldini, or Raimondi, who invented new methods of workmanship and discussed the ancient methods with their disciples. They made comparisons between the various schools and styles; they discussed Vitruvius, whose *De Architectura* had been published with Lorenzo's help, and Leon Battista Alberti, the first Italian art critic.

Alberti was born in Venice, of a family of Florentine exiles. He was handsome, tall, and strong. He studied the classics and could quote Plato and Vergil; he had an extensive knowledge of mathematics, astronomy, music, and geometry; he rode well and practiced archery. When he was invited by Cosimo to move to Florence, his sparkling, learned, and sophisticated conversation conquered Florence's sitting rooms, and high society ladies competed for him and went out of their way to cover him with favors. Leon Battista repaid them gallantly, but he lost no occasion to make fun of them with his friends. He liked women, but he preferred the pleasures of the mind to those of the alcove. He spent his nights bent over Aristotle and Lucretius, reading by candlelight, wrapped in a fur coat. He used to say that "Man can do anything, if he wants to," and he himself was the best proof of that saying. He explored every branch of knowledge and was a very prolific writer. He wrote an essay on painting that was studied by Piero della Francesca and Leonardo da Vinci.

Alberti has been likened to Leonardo because of his encyclopedic and protean genius. He was also a fair painter, demanding and meticulous. When he finished a painting, he showed it to the children on his block, and only if the children found it beautiful did he exhibit it. But it was his work as an architect that made Alberti famous. A great lover of antiquity, he made many long stays in Rome, where he carefully studied the ruins, took measures of monuments, and reproduced the friezes and decorations of the Pantheon, the Colosseum, and the Theater of Marcellus. With fantastic speed he sketched ideas on paper, for later use for the façade of a cathedral or the interior of a palace. When he was called to Rimini to remodel the church of St. Francis, he transformed it into a splendid pagan temple. But most of Alberti's works are in Florence. The marble façade of Santa Maria Novella bears his signature, and the Rucellai Chapel in the Church of San Pancrazio was built according to his design. Many other Italian cities commissioned him to design lay and religious buildings. For Mantua he designed the façade of the Church of Sant' Andrea, which he embellished with a great triumphal arch of Roman inspiration. In fact, Vasari, in his *Vite*, praised Alberti as one of the most ingenious architects of his time, second only to Brunelleschi.

Filippo Brunelleschi was for the fifteenth century what Michelangelo was for the sixteenth: the inventor of a new architectural style. The new style rejected the traditional Gothic canons but kept some of their elements, which it assimilated into a new and vital concept of space. "It must have been heaven," Vasari writes, "that sent us Filippo Brunelleschi; he gave architecture a new form after centuries of stagnation."

Brunelleschi was born in Florence in 1377, into a well-to-do family. His father was a lawyer, and he wanted his son to follow the same career. But the boy spent whole days drawing and looking at churches and palaces. When he was ten years old, he became a goldsmith's apprentice, and he learned the difficult art of chiseling. Also during those years he came to know Donatello, and he learned to sculpt. What moved Brunelleschi most, however, was architecture. He visited Rome with Donatello several times, inspecting the ruins with the patience of a monk and the eagerness of an archeologist. Seeing the two artists rummaging among the ruins of the Forum so intently, the Romans took them for treasure-hunters and referred to them as "those guys of the treasure." Brunelleschi was impressed by the size and proportions of the Pantheon's majestic cupola, and he used it as a model when he was called upon to build the cupola of the *Duomo*.

The roofing of the cathedral had become a real headache for the Florentine architects and engineers who worked on it. Their orders were to build a dome that would be tall, elegant and majestic. It had to tower above all the other buildings in the city; it had to stand out against the sky as the emblem of the spiritual greatness of the city. The base of the dome had to rest on the octagonal apse of the cathedral, which was almost 151 feet wide but had no outer buttress or inner beams. The weakness of the supporting structure seemed to rule out a high dome, on the grounds of danger to the safety of the church and the worshipers. Brunelleschi, however, designed a dome with curved, ogival lines and showed it to the Florentine architects. They said that it would never stand up. Filippo had someone fetch an egg for him and then he brought it down on the table with some strength. One end was smashed, but the egg stood. Someone objected that a dome was not an egg, but most of those present agreed that Brunelleschi had made his point. It took Brunelleschi fourteen years, from 1420 to 1434, to build his dome.

More difficulties than he had foreseen came up during the construction; the high cost of materials and the jealousy of rivals were among the contributing factors. But when the dome, which rose almost 145 feet above the supporting walls, was finished, the whole population of Florence and many foreigners flocked to admire it. Michelangelo found his inspiration for St. Peter's cupola in Saint Mary of the Flower, and he wrote that his dome was "larger, but not finer" than Brunelleschi's.

The dome of the *Duomo* is undoubtedly Brunelleschi's masterpiece; however his name is linked to a quantity of other architectural endeavors. The Pazzis, who were the Medicis' relentless antagonists, charged him with the building of their family chapel in the cloister of Santa Croce. Filippo designed a portico, with a slender arch in the middle and columns on the sides, articulated inside by pilaster strips covered with a sort of marquee and topped by a small dome. He designed the Church of Santo Spirito in the same classical style: in the shape of a Latin cross and with three naves. This was Brunelleschi's last project, and he died before it was finished. His body was laid out under the dome of the cathedral, and Florence gave him a solemn funeral, which was attended by all the artists of the city, including Donatello.

Donatello is short for Donato di Niccolo di Betto Bardi. He also was born in Florence, five years after Brunelleschi. Little is known about his family and his childhood. We find him as a youth in the shop of Ghiberti, the man who decorated the doors of the baptistry. But Donatello's apprenticeship did not last long, because as soon as he had learned the first rudiments of the art of sculpting, he left his master and started work on his own. By the time he was twenty-two, builders and patrons vied for his services. The heads of the greater corporations invited him to decorate the Church of Orsanmichele— the priceless shrine of fifteenth century Florentine sculpture. In it the artist left two mighty statues of the evangelists. When Michelangelo saw the one representing St. Mark, he exclaimed: "It would be impossible not to believe in a Gospel preached by such a man!"

When Donatello was twenty-three, the chapter of the Duomo ordered from him a statue of David, and from then on David became a frequent subject of Donatello, and his favorite one. Among the many existing Davids by Donatello, the one in the Bargello museum reached an unequaled degree of perfection. The conqueror of the giant Goliath is represented holding a long sword in his right hand, a Greek helmet and the enemy's head lying at his feet. The left arm is bent, pivoting on the hand that rests on the boy's waist, the elbow projecting out at the side. The left knee is slightly bent so that the body's whole weight rests on the right leg. The body is the focus of attention: naked, smooth, flexible, modeled by the shadows of *chiaroscuro*. One feels in it the influence of the Greek sculpture of Phidias and Praxiteles.

Donatello worked on the baptistry and on Giotto's Campanile. He visited Rome, Siena, and Venice, and in 1444 he moved to Padua, to model the first Renaissance equestrian statue: a likeness of Erasmo Gattamelata that recalls Marcus Aurelius on horseback in the Campidoglio, but it is more dynamic and more dramatic. The Venetian *condottiere* is portrayed in all his strength; he has sharp features, a manly expression, and his arm is set in a gesture of command. The statue, on the Piazza del Santo, took six years to make and cost 1,650 golden ducats.

After twelve years of absence Donatello returned to Florence, summoned by Cosimo who flooded him with orders for the Churches of San Lorenzo and Santa Croce. The artist and his patron became inseparable friends, and they spent whole days together discussing sculpture, poetry, and philosophy. Cosimo paid a handsome salary to the artist; Donatello put the money into a basket which hung from his workshop's ceiling and let his friends take from it freely, when in need. He lived happily under the protection of the Medici house until he was eighty, and when he died he was buried with great honors in the crypt of San Lorenzo.

Donatello was the greatest artist of plastic forms in the fifteenth century. He opened up new frontiers for sculpture, especially in the portrait genre; he rediscovered the nude, which religiously inspired and moralizing medieval art had repudiated; and he was the founder of the realistic tendency that in painting was best represented by Masaccio.

Masaccio's real name was Tommaso Guidi, and he was born at San Giovanni Valdarno in 1401. The name Masaccio, a pejorative distortion of Tommaso, was tacked onto him to connote his slovenliness and absentminded carelessness. He began to paint at a very young age and became a pupil of Masolino da Panicale, who taught him the rules of perspective, in which he excelled. He attended also Ghiberti's studio, where he studied anatomy.

Masaccio left behind few works, because he died at the age of twenty-seven. His masterpiece is the cycle of frescoes illustrating St. Peter's life that decorates the Brancacci chapel in Santa Maria del Carmine. The "Tribute to Caesar" is a splendid digest of Masaccio's pictorial qualities: nobility of design, majesty in the figures, unity of composition, measure in perspective, and psychological intensity. Vasari called "modern" the style of this genial and solitary artist who smoothed out the path for all the following Tuscan painters, for the Brancacci chapel became the school of the major artists of the time, from Beato Angelico to Lippi and Botticelli.

Guido di Pietro di Vicchio di Mugello was called Beato Angelico because of his piety and sweet temper. At twenty he entered the Dominican order. After a period as a novitiate in various convents in Tuscany he was assigned to the convent of St. Mark, where he spent most of his life praying and painting. He painted frescoes in the common room, the cloisters, the dormitory, and the cells, portraying scenes from the Gospels and the lives of the saints. He took communion and said his prayers before picking up his paint brush, and he never accepted a commission for a painting unless the prior agreed.

His paintings are suffused with a sweet, mystical idealism. His figures, especially female ones, radiate mildness and humility. The flesh is soft and white; profiles are delicate; hands long and tapering; eyes languid; attitudes composed and devout; garments bordered with golden tassels and richly embroidered.

Pope Nicholas V called Beato Angelico to Rome, to put him in charge of the decoration of his private chapel, but life at the Curia, luxurious and depraved, did not agree with the quiet and timid monk, and after a year he returned to Florence. He died in 1455, aged sixty-eight, and the humanist Valla coined his epitaph: "Let praise go to me not because I was a second Apelles, but because I gave everything I had to those faithful to you, O Christ."

Angelico's mystical and edifying style acquires a subtly mundane flavor in Filippo Lippi. The son of a Florentine butcher, Lippi was orphaned at two and brought up by an aunt. The aunt shut him up in a convent when he was eight, and there Filippo studied painting. His first works are lost, but Vasari says that they equaled in beauty and perfection Masaccio's frescoes in the Cappella Brancacci. At twenty-six Lippi left the convent but not the cassock. However, the cassock did not protect him from temptation: he was a robust sinner, ever ready to run after a skirt. Once when Cosimo ordered a painting from Lippi he noticed that the artist could not stick to his work because he was distracted by the women in the house, so Cosimo locked him into the studio. During the night, seized by an erotic fit, Lippi escaped through the window by using a rope made of bed sheets, and betook himself to a brothel.

Lippi's main clients were religious institutions, and he had a preference for the female orders. In the convent of Santa Margherita at Prato he met a nun, Lucrezia Buti, whom he seduced and carried off with him. Lucrezia became his model, and her features and body are reproduced in many of Lippi's splendid madonnas, which are among the sweetest and most delicate of the Renaissance. In 1461, on Cosimo's request, Pius II freed Lippi from his religious vows. Filippo, who had not lost his youthful vehemence, repudiated Lucrezia, who had become fat and sickly, and fell in with a "Lolita." However, when he seduced the young girl, her parents poisoned him in revenge. Lippi left many works behind, scattered in churches, convents, public buildings, and private mansions, and he also left a pupil who became more famous than his master.

Sandro Filipepi was born in Florence of a modest family. Because he seemed to have little inclination for work, his father had put him as an apprentice with the goldsmith Botticelli. Then, however, the young Sandro learned the art of chiseling so well that people started calling him by his master's name—the name by which he went down in history. Filippo Lippi, who knew Sandro, describes him as being elegant, with long curly hair, but being crabby and sensuous, having irregular and graceless features.

When he was twenty, Sandro opened a studio, of which the Medicis became the most assiduous customers. He painted scores of pictures with mythological subjects and a heathen inspiration for Lorenzo and Giuliano Medici, whose friend and carousing-mate he was. In his most famous work, the "Primavera," Botticelli celebrated admirably the Renaissance dream of beauty and joy of life that Lorenzo had sung in his hymn to Bacchus. But the Epicurean grace of those pictures disappears in his later works, due, it seems, to a spiritual shock. Sometime, around 1485, while listening to Savonarola's preaching, the artist was so overwhelmed by the monk's apocalyptical oratory that he decided to put his art at the service of religion. He illustrated the *Divine Comedy* with eighty-eight drawings, and he painted madonnas, saints, and apostles. Unfortunately, as Gide said, good intentions are not enough to make good works of art: Botticelli's brush became hagiographic and declamatory; the vigor and brilliance of old were blurred as he lost in talent what he had gained in faith. Savonarola's death embittered Botticelli's old age, and he died at sixty-six, alone and forgotten by everyone. He was the last great painter of the era; with him the Florentine art of the fifteenth century reached its highest peak.

Chapter 22

THE ESTES AT FERRARA

Este was a small county that around the end of the eleventh century was given by Emperor Otto I as a fief to a certain Count Azzo di Canossa, descendant of the famous Matilde of Toscana. Count Azzo's heirs cleverly managed to survive between papacy and empire, both of which for centuries claimed a theoretical sovereignty over these lands at the center of the Bologna–Milan–Venice triangle. As a matter of fact it was by playing the one against the other, papacy against empire, that the Estes became lords of Ferrara at the beginning of the thirteenth century and later governed the city as marquises.

Ferrara was hardly more than a village at the time. But it was in a good geographic position, and the Estes used this advantage very adroitly. Like all the lords in those days, they were burdened by few scruples; nor did they feel themselves bound by the laws that they themselves issued. The use of poisoned cups or the daggers of hirelings to get rid of their internal enemies or troublesome neighbors and then to annex their lands was a commonplace occurrence—a family custom. But this never became a mere vice or pastime. The Estes killed with moderation and almost always for state reasons— which however were the same as Este reasons.

Rather than bloodthirsty, they were eager for money; they didn't, however, stuff it into a mattress. They spent it generously, but often for works of public voluptuousness rather than public utility. No matter how heavily taxed, the people did not resent those squanderings, which resulted in feasts for the eyes and flattered civic pride. Thus, when, at the beginning of the fourteenth century, Pope Clement V wanted to expel from Ferrara these unruly vassals, the city rose in rebellion, and the next pope had to revoke the "purge." The Estes came back triumphant, agreed merely to pay a monetary tribute to the Church. And from that time the dynasty climbed toward ever greater glory, hatching among other things two of the longest-lived and most prestigious European royal families: the Brunswick and the Hanover.

The Este lord who best embodied the characteristics of the house was Nicholas III, who governed for almost fifty years, from 1393 to 1441, fighting, spending, and marrying with the same generosity. It was said of him that his wars extinguished fewer lives than the number brought into the world by his loves, and it is partly due to him that Ferrara acquired the national record for the number of illegitimate births that it has kept up to our days. But trouble came to this remorseless womanizer just from the alcove, when, after being widowed for the third time, he married the lovely Parisina Malatesta, who was some twenty years his junior, for she fell desperately in love with her stepson Ugo, who was her own age. Nicholas, following the Italian tradition of masculine behavior, reacted to his wife's adultery with a furor equal to the lightheartedness with which he himself had always practiced adultery. Not only did he have the two lovers beheaded, but he promulgated a law condemning to death all wives convicted of unfaithfulness. The town shivered with terror and resigned itself to becoming an all-male town. Actually the absurd law was applied only once, to the wife of a judge, who couldn't convince the marquis of her innocence because she happened to be his own mistress. After that the law was revoked, to the great relief of the husbands of Ferrara who, like most husbands, would rather be cuckolds than widowers.

Aside from this dramatic and bloody conjugal episode Nicholas was a magnanimous prince, brilliant and epicurean. Instead of increasing taxes, he reduced them, and this measure started a blossom-

ing of commerce and industry in Ferrara that made the city a dangerous competitor for Venice and Milan. Nicholas was not a cultivated
man: war and women took up all his time. But he respected culture,
or at least he perceived its importance and usefulness. Ferrara already
had had a university, but it had been closed for lack of funds. Nicholas
reopened it, and he filled all its chairs in the various disciplines with
scholars of prestige, making it one of Italy's most important universities.

The marquis's luck was good also in respect to children: he had
three sons who were all successful and valuable, even though—or perhaps because—they were illegitimate. Leonello, the first one to succeed
him, was a rare combination of speculative intelligence and practical
wisdom—the perfect Renaissance man. As a statesman and a diplomat
he was first and foremost concerned with peace, and he was able to
establish it even beyond the borders of his marquisate. Somewhat as
Lorenzo de Medici would do later, Leonello played, with great discre-
tion, the role of an arbitrator in the midst of the endemic struggles
by which the Italian lords kept the country in constant turmoil. But
glory came to him from yet another source: he was greatly admired
by the men of culture, the humanists, who considered him as their
main patron.

One of the most renowned humanists, Filelfo, declared that he
was nonplussed by the ease with which the marquis handled Greek
and Latin. Leonello, in fact, was the first scholar who denounced as
apocryphal a collection of letters from Seneca to St. Paul that were
thought to be authentic at the time. He was able to govern through
laws alone, without having recourse to poison or dagger. When he
died, barely forty, in 1450, all Italy mourned him as the most enlightened lord of his era.

Leonello's brother, Borso, who took his place, was perhaps less
well-rounded and certainly less amiable. He knew little or no Greek
and Latin. His interests were strictly political, and his character was
resentful and domineering. But he also successfully pursued a policy
of peace, and he continued to protect the men of culture that Leonello
had brought to Ferrara. He was shrewd enough to know that culture

was a necessary tool in building up his status. An ambitious man, he yearned for a higher title than the one he had. Consequently, when he failed to obtain from the pope promotion to Duke of Ferrara, he bought from the emperor the title of Duke of Modena and Reggio, cities that his father Nicholas had annexed.

The negotiations were expensive, long, and complicated, but finally they succeeded, in 1452, and the new duke celebrated the acquisition of his title with huge festivities. For months the city was kept in a state of jubilant activity. Nobility came to take part from all corners of Italy, dressed in flashy costumes and accompanied by jaunty followers. In fact, the celebrations had such repercussions in the world at large that when, some years later, Borso was acknowledged also Duke of Ferrara, many foreign rulers sent him congratulations and presents addressed to the "King of Italy."

Borso died in 1471, and his brother, Ercole, succeeded him. Munificent and magnificent, Ercole spent fabulous sums to continue the Estes' tradition of epicureanism and revelry. He was well educated, brilliant, and refined, and he generously subsidized artists and men of letters, whose company he enjoyed. He gave freely also to the clergy; he financed the building of churches and convents and protected monks. He married by proxy Eleonora, the daughter of the King of Naples, and celebrated her arrival at Ferrara with fireworks and public dancing. But when his father-in-law, prodded by the pope, declared war on Florence, Ercole did not hesitate to take the side of the Medicis. In 1482 the pope revenged himself by besieging Ferrara. Ercole was kept in bed by an attack of gout and could not defend his city, but the citizens put up a desperate resistance and were able to preserve their independence.

Since war had depleted the finances of the duchy, Ercole raised taxes and stiffened the fines against blasphemers and those who profaned sacred places—fines that each year contributed six thousand crowns to the state treasury. Ercole also needed money to build new dwellings in Ferrara, where the population had grown at a breathtaking rate. Indeed, the population explosion was threatening to paralyze the city. Ercole had engineers and architects design a new plan, and the city walls were extended to include many outlying districts. Neighborhoods were renewed, streets were widened and sometimes rerouted. In a few years Ferrara became one of the most modern and rationally functioning cities of Europe. However, the urban renewal did not change the life-habits of the citizens: the people continued to meet in the Piazza del Duomo and the nobles in the castle built by Nicholas. Below the palace there were underground labyrinths used as jails, while the floors above ground sheltered sumptuous halls with stucco-decorated ceilings, frescoed walls, and softly carpeted floors.

Court life went on in a relentless round of parties, banquets, masked balls, and concerts. Generals mingled with midgets, state officers with jesters, artists with minstrels. Ladies received knights in their apartments and had the *chansons de geste* sung to them, and Eleonora received Ferrara's café society in her drawing rooms.

The intellectuals met in the halls of the university and in Guarino's studio. Guarino, born in Verona but an adoptive son of Ferrara, was one of the most cultivated men of his time. Born in 1370, he had studied Greek in Constantinople, where he had spent five years and whence he returned with trunks full of manuscripts. The story goes that during the passage home one of these precious trunks was lost at sea, and Guarino's hair turned white with grief. Before moving to Ferrara he had taught in Venice, Verona, Padua, Bologna, and Florence. Nicholas charged him with his children's education and named him professor of rhetoric and Greek at the university.

Students flocked to Ferrara's university from everywhere in Italy, and also from abroad, attracted by Guarino's renown; his classes were always crowded and students had to stand in line to get in. He revived interest in classical drama; he translated the comedies of Plautus and Terentius and staged them himself. Despite his fame he lived very modestly in a plain house, spending his earnings to help needy students, with whom he shared roof and table. His meals were very frugal: according to one chronicler, he only ate once a day, and then often it was a simple dish of beans. Nevertheless, he supported a wife and thirteen children and gave up his teaching only when, in 1460, aged ninety, he passed into the grave. Thanks to Guarino, Ferrara became one of the intellectual capitals of the renaissance, a center to which men of letters and artists were attracted: Boiardo and Tura, Cossa and De'Roberti, among others.

Matteo Maria Boiardo, Count of Scandiano, ambassador of the Estes, belonged to one of the most powerful families of the duchy. He had a broad humanistic education, and between missions he composed madrigals addressed to the ladies of the court. He had a weakness for them and they seem to have been crazy about him. However, after he married Taddea Gonzaga, he stopped composing madrigals and he wrote an epic poem, the *Orlando Innamorato,* which tells of Roland's tormented love for Angelica. The poem consists of sixty thousand lines filled with duels, jousts, and scenes of battle and death. It is populated by fantastic heroes and wonderfully beautiful women. The author read each canto as he finished it to the court, and taken in small doses the poem is not that bad. It served as a model to Ludovico Ariosto, who found in it his inspiration for the *Orlando Furioso.*

Cosmé Tura was court painter from 1458 to 1495: he painted the portraits of whole generations of Estes and decorated the splendid palace of Schifanoia, the summer residence of the dukes. Raphael's father, who was court painter for the Montefeltros, admired Tura's austere, dignified massive figures and listed him among the best artists of the time. Francesco Cossa distinguished himself among Tura's pupils, and two very beautiful paintings by him are preserved in one of *palazzo* Schifanoia's halls: "The Triumph of Venus" and "The Races."

Around these masters there gathered a crowd of lesser artists and artisans—tapestry-makers, miniaturists, goldsmiths—who left their mark in the churches and palaces of a city that was in a perpetual state of festivity. The holiday atmosphere reached its peak during carnival, but it was still present in Lent, because even the religious services had something worldly and theatrical about them.

Chapter 23

THE KINGDOM OF NAPLES

WHEN Robert of Anjou died in 1343, his niece, Giovanna, succeeded him, and she ruled, or rather *mis*ruled, over the kingdom of Naples for forty years. Her uncle had her married at sixteen to Andrew of Hungary, a coarse, vulgar, squint-eyed prince. Giovanna, in contrast, was very beautiful and sensual, and she detested her husband, even though she had known him from childhood when they had played together at court. It was said that at night she locked herself into her bedroom and wouldn't let her husband approach her. He must have been a repulsive man indeed, for she accorded practically anyone else the favors she denied him. Pages, grooms, butlers, dignitaries, generals and ministers took turns in her bedroom, where she had a trap-door installed, through which indiscreet lovers disappeared after she had poisoned them. It is amazing that despite all this she always managed to find new lovers, but she did.

For conjugal bliss Andrew had to turn to his wife's maids, and Giovanna used this pretext for having her husband strangled. Surely it was not because of jealousy; rather, she had to get rid of Andrew because she was pregnant and wanted to marry her new lover, Luigi, Prince of Taranto. The people of Naples were indignant over Andrew's murder, and even though they knew that Giovanna was to blame, they asked that the assassins be punished. Giovanna, afraid

215

that she might lose the throne, ordered the arrest of her maid Filippa la Catanese and the lawyer Melizzano, whom she had implicated in the murder plot. These people were sentenced to be skinned alive; Giovanna in the meantime produced a baby boy, whom the pope himself held at baptism.

When the King of Hungary, Louis, heard of his brother's murder, he marched on Naples to avenge him. Giovanna flew from the city when Louis entered it with a large army thirsting for vengeance and plunder. Indeed, the resulting sack of Naples would have gone on for God knows how long, had not an epidemic of plague forced Louis to make a sudden retreat.

Giovanna, therefore, returned to Naples, this time on the arm of the Prince of Taranto, whom she married against the court's advice and without the consent of the pope. A few years later, however, Luigi died, exhausted by his wife's sexual appetites. Giovanna consoled herself by marrying the Prince of Majorca, a handsome, manly, likable, and penniless playboy. His manly powers were such that it seemed as if they would last forever, but after seven years with Giovanna he fell victim of the same disease that had killed his predecessor.

The insatiable queen then married again, but her new husband, Otto of Brunswick, wary of ending his life like the others, limited his effusions so much that Giovanna, even though she was well past menopause, felt authorized to take on an official lover, whom she soon dismissed so that she could replace him with a younger man.

The people of Naples were growing unhappy with their queen. They had never loved her, not because of her dissoluteness, over which they were willing to close an eye, but because of her cruelty, which ran against their good nature. Therefore when Carlo of Durazzo mounted a coup in 1381 and deposed Giovanna and had her strangled, the populace rejoiced.

Carlo, however, died in 1386, and the throne went to his son, Ladislas, who kept it for fifteen years before dying wretchedly. His sister Giovanna held power next, and she inherited her namesake's insatiable lust. After her coronation, Queen Giovanna married Giovanni della Marca, who, to prevent her from ruling, relegated her to one wing of the royal palace and kept her imprisoned there for years, freeing her only when the mob, who felt sorry for their queen, forced him to do so.

Once free, Giovanna set about getting Sergianni Caracciolo as her lover. Sergianni was an athletic and ambitious young man, but he was also very shy. He was so shy that each time he met Giovanna, he blushed and avoided her. But Giovanna trapped him. She knew that Sergianni was afraid of mice, so she invited him to her apartments to play chess and during the game let two mice loose in the room. Caracciolo was seized by panic and ran into the bedroom and found refuge under the bedspread, where Giovanna promptly joined him. From that moment on he became the queen's most trusted counselor, and she never took any decision without his consent. He made her adopt Alfonso of Aragon, King of Sicily, as her legitimate heir in order to reconstitute the old kingdom, only to induce her later to reverse the nomination in favor of Renato of Anjou.

Finally, however, Caracciolo's interference alarmed the court, and Giovanna herself tired of him once her enthusiasm waned. She therefore decided to get rid of him. In August, 1432, while a great party in the queen's honor was in full swing in the palace, Sergianni was stabbed from behind, and his body was later found lying in a pool of blood at the foot of a bed. Giovanna herself died three years later, and the crown passed on to Renato. However, Alfonso, King of Sicily, expelled Renato from Naples and took his crown, thus reuniting southern Italy—the mainland and the island. The Aragonese dominion, which would last until 1501, thus began with Alfonso in 1442.

Benedetto Croce wrote in his *History of the Kingdom of Naples:*

> The people of Naples never loved Alfonso of Aragon with the same love that they bestowed on their Anjou kings, even on the last queen, toward whom they felt protective. Alfonso remained a stranger and he kept alien ways and the manners of a conqueror. He made his royal power felt, and he was the ruler of vast dominions which he controlled with overwhelming strength. He was surrounded by a crowd of Catalan, Aragonese, and Castilian men on whom he conferred offices that had traditionally gone to local people; and those retainers were hated because of their "haughtiness, nasty ways and

very great tyranny"—they were hated and they caused the king to be hated.

Nevertheless, Alfonso was a splendid king. He was shrewd and enlightened, and he made a gay and efficient capital of Naples. He demolished old slum neighborhoods and called the best architects of his time to build new houses for the people; he commissioned fashionable painters and sculptors to decorate palaces; and the Maschio Angioino was rebuilt during his reign with the addition of a majestic triumphal arch designed by Luciano Laurana. The wharves were enlarged, the arsenal restored, streets widened, new sewers built, the low-lying and humid sections of town called the *bassi* reclaimed. Alfonso beautified the court with luxurious tapestries, paintings, carpets, and damasks. He had a penchant for parties and gave some fabulous ones, spending enormous sums on them; at the same time he loved culture and helped writers, poets, philosophers, and artists in general. Among his famous protégés were Filelfo, Manetti, Fazio, and the greatest of them all: Lorenzo Valla.

Valla, who was born in Rome in 1407, studied at the school of Leonardo Bruni, who had directed him toward the study of the classics. Valla was infatuated with Latin to the point that he wanted to abolish the use of Italian and go back to the language of Caesar and Quintilian. For a while he taught rhetoric at Pavia, but he had to leave the university because of a quarrel with the jurist Bartolo. He took to writing polemic pamphlets and learned treatises, and in 1431 he published a dialogue called *De Voluptate et Vero Bono,* in which he wanted to prove that all pleasures are healthy as long as they don't become excesses. Valla condemned chastity, judging it useless and inhuman; he said that a hundred nuns are not worth one courtesan, and that continence is bad for health and does not improve society.

Lorenzo lived according to his preaching: he surrounded himself with mistresses, and he loved luxury and debauchery. He was violent and quarrelsome and made many enemies. Often unemployed, he wandered across Italy looking for work. He found it at the court of Alfonso, who received him with great honors and gave him a good salary. At Naples he wrote the *De Falso Credita et Ementita Constantini Donatione,* his most famous work, in which he showed in irrefutable terms that Constantine's transfer of power was a hoax, a colossal mystification contrived by the Church to justify and make legitimate its temporal rule. Moreover, Valla maintained that even if Constantine had really given the Church this power, the gift was now void because of the crimes, the avidity, and the corruption of the clergy.

Valla was a fierce anti-clerical. "I attack the living as well as the dead," he used to say, and he flung himself against the popes with unprecedented violence, pointing to them as the source of all the evils that afflicted Italy. When he invited the Romans to take arms for the overthrow of the papal government, Eugene IV denounced Valla to the Inquisition. Valla destroyed other myths as well: proofs in hand he showed that Abgarus's letter to Christ was a vulgar fraud, and that the Apostles were poor, half-illiterate fellows, ignorant of theology. The humanist Valla was certainly not shy about voicing his ideas; however, it would never have occurred to him to set them down in writing, had King Alfonso not prodded him to do so.

The king hated the pope, a feeling that was amply reciprocated. However, Alfonso was a good politician, and when he needed the pope's help he did not hesitate to effect a reconciliation. Valla was nobody's fool, either, so when he perceived that the situation was changing, he retracted everything he had written against the Church and wrote a letter to the pope asking forgiveness. Eugene refused, but his successor Nicholas V not only pardoned Valla but named him secretary of the Curia and put him in charge of translations from Latin and Greek. Calistus III made him parson of San Giovanni in the Lateran, and the former clergy-hater died there in 1457, surrounded by priests, a priest himself.

Alfonso followed him into the grave the next year, mourned by men of letters and artists who had nicknamed him "The Magnanimous" because of his patronage of the arts. In spite of the arguments with the church, Alfonso was, in his own way, a good Catholic, especially in his last years after his reconciliation with the pope. He was a scholar of sacred history; he kept the Bible by his bedside, had read it

forty times, and knew long parts of it by heart. Women were another
of his passions—all women except his own wife, Mary of Castile. He
had a great number of mistresses, but he loved one of them in particular: Lucrezia d'Alagno, a shapely eighteen-year-old beauty from
Amalfi. Alfonso, who was much older than Lucrezia, would have
married her if the pope had allowed him to divorce Mary. As it was,
he brought her to court, where he treated her as a queen and kept
her at his side during official ceremonies. Capaccio called Lucrezia
"the most chaste Venus," and Pope Piccolomini wrote that "Alfonso
never united himself with her," but this is hard to believe, given Alfonso's temperament and the large brood of illegitimate children he
brought into the world, from among whom he picked his successor,
Don Ferrante.

Don Ferrante's mother was called Margarita of Hijar, and she was
a woman of doubtful morals. According to Pontano, who was the
king's secretary for many years, Ferrante wasn't Alfonso's son at all,
but the son of a converted Spanish Jew. Physically he was not handsome: stocky and clumsy, he had a large face with loose-hanging
cheeks, small piercing eyes, and a long knobby nose. He was suspicious, sullen, domineering, but not without political qualities. A wise
and careful administrator, he rearranged the state's finances, which
had been exhausted by Alfonso's prodigality. He encouraged private
initiative and helped develop commerce; he reduced taxes and abolished, for a few years, custom duties on exports. He encouraged Gen-
ovese, Venetian, Florentine, and Catalan to settle in the kingdom of
Naples and admitted even Jews, who were promptly ostracized by a
population that never missed an opportunity to harass them. In fact,
in 1490 some fanatic monks stirred up the populace against the Jews,
and a riot broke out in which a man lost his life. However, when
Neapolitans asked their king to chase out the Jews, Ferrante refused.

With the arrival of foreigners, the opening of warehouses and commercial enterprises, and the influx of baron-oppressed farm workers
from the country into the city, Naples's population grew to more than

one hundred thousand inhabitants. The king had to have the city walls enlarged to include as yet unbuilt districts. The kingdom prospered, thanks also to the state of peace that Ferrante was able to maintain through a shrewd policy of matrimonial alliances. He gave his natural daughter Maria in wife to the Duke of Amalfi, Antonio Piccolomini; he obtained the hand of Ippolita Sforza for his son Alfonso; and established a link with the Hungarian monarchy by marrying another daughter to Matthias Corvinus. Indeed, although Ferrante reigned for thirty-six years, his throne was endangered only once, by a conspiracy of barons.

The barons were the feudal nobility of the kingdom. Descendants of Longobard, Norman, German, French, and Spanish knights, they lived in the country entrenched in hilltop castles. The wealthier ones owned huge amounts of property, but most of them lived off a few hundred acres of land worked by hungry peasants reduced to a state of slavery. The barons despised urban life, snubbed the bourgeois, and looked down on commerce and the arts. Their only occupation was war: they fought each other, and they united in coalitions against the king.

Violent and quarrelsome, the barons, according to Machiavelli, were "enemies of every form of civilization." They harassed the kingdom with small fratricidal wars, insurrections, and coups. Indeed, many of the evils that still today afflict southern Italy can be traced back to these ambitious, meddlesome, unruly squires who weakened the state to the point of collapse. In order to pacify them, the kings relieved them from many obligations such as military service, exempted them from taxation, and recognized their right to be judged by their own courts.

The barons' anarchy was almost tamed when Frederick II had their castles destroyed and forbade their reconstruction. But when Frederick died, the barons reared up their heads again, nor did they bow down again when order was restored under the Anjou. Alfonso of Aragon gave the barons numerous privileges, among which was the permission to torture guilty parties "for an unlimited period of time," and to administer punishments greater than the ones established by the law. As for Ferrante, he exempted the barons from some taxes in 1485, but they tried to oust him anyway.

The army of the barons clashed with the king's army and was defeated by it, and the leaders were given up to the king. At first, Ferrante seemed to show himself magnanimous toward the rebels. A few days after the battle he invited the baron leaders to celebrate the reconciliation, and they all accepted and went to his palace. Ferrante escorted them in person to a great hall, where at a sign from him the doors were locked and the guests disarmed and thrown into prison. The next day Ferrante confiscated their estates, and after a week he had them tried and sentenced to death. The first baron whose head fell under the executioner's ax was a certain Francesco de Petruciis. He was first beheaded and then dismembered: his left leg was exposed to the public on the Maddalena Bridge, one of his shoulders was hung by a hook on the Casa Nova, and the other at Chiaia Street.

From then on until Ferrante's death in 1494 the kingdom was never troubled by baronal uprisings. It was only a truce, however, and under Ferrante's successor internal strifes flared up again.

Chapter 24

ROME AFTER AVIGNON

As we have already seen, the papacy's exile to Avignon was a catastrophe for Rome. At the dawn of the fifteenth century the city covered an area ten times smaller than it had been under Aurelian, twelve centuries earlier. With a mere sixty thousand inhabitants, Rome was less populous than Milan, Venice, or Florence. Walls were crumbling and had gaps in them; towers were chipped; and the roads were flooded with polluted, stinking puddles. The clogged aqueducts were inadequate to supply the city with water, and many Romans were reduced to drinking the Tiber's water. Hence pestilences killed more people than war.

The state of decay and abandon was not limited to the poor neighborhoods on the outskirts of town; it extended to the center. The Forums were fetid basins; the Colosseum and the Theater of Marcellus were used as garbage dumps; Capitol Hill was studded with evil-smelling, crooked huts. Cattle, sheep, and swine grazed in the churchyards. Many churches looked like ruins, even though they were still used for worship, and the apostolic palaces had lost their brightness and majesty. No one dared to walk the streets at night for fear of being waylaid by the bandits who infested the city. Night supervision by the authorities was very scant, and the officers could easily be bought.

Each of the major clans, such as the Orsini, the Colonna, and the Caetani, had its own army of thugs, castles, fortifications, and "reasons of state." Thugs were ever ready to start fights, to plot intrigues, and to stir up the poor, who were always willing to get into a brawl if there was hope of getting a chunk of bread. The struggle of rival factions was the only flourishing industry in a city that produced nothing and lived exclusively from sheep herding and marginal trade. In Rome the great communal revolution had not taken place, and thus there was no mercantile middle class with a private initiative that could have been used to thrust Rome into the vast and dynamic economic circuit of which Florence, Milan, and most north Italian cities were already a part. The populace lived on charity; the nobles had incomes from their lands and from plunder; the clergy received tithes and practiced usury and simony.

When the pope moved to Avignon, many treasures and much capital also left for France. When Gregory XI decided to return to Rome, the finances of the Church were in a very bad way, and the Church could certainly not count on Rome's resources, since it had none. On the other hand, there was the *Stato Pontificio*—the Papal States: a vast territory that included Latium and large slices of Umbria, Marche, Romagna, and some thirty cities ruled by papal legates. The Papal States had also feudal rights over the kingdom of Naples and the lands of Matilde in Tuscany. This meant tributes, but to collect them the popes often had to use the threat of excommunication. When even this failed, they called in mercenary troops, because the Church had no regular army, and the few guards the popes kept in the city were hardly enough to protect Christ's Vicar from the violence of the nobles and from popular riots. Thus, it was thanks only to the energy, courage, and wisdom of Gregory's successors, Nicholas V, Pius II, and Sixtus IV, that Rome regained her rank of capital and started on the way to become one of the greatest centers of the Renaissance.

Nicholas V's name was Tommaso Parentucelli, and he was born in Pisa, the son of a surgeon. He later studied at Bologna and received a degree in theology. At Bologna he met the archbishop Niccolo degli Albergati, who gave him the important office of supervisor and took

him to Florence, where Tommaso came into contact with the humanists and engulfed himself in classical studies. He hungrily read Greek
and Latin authors, took part in literary and philosophical discussions,
and spent all the money he made on manuscripts. Impressed by his
erudition, Cosimo hired him as librarian and assigned him a good
salary.

It is only because of his cultural merits that he was made first a cardinal and then pope, in keeping with a trend that had developed inside
the Church. The humanists exulted, and Nicholas recruited them in
mass, transforming the Vatican into a true Academy. Lorenzo Valla
was entrusted with translating Thucydides into Latin; Guarino da
Verona translated Strabo; and Niccolo Perotti was paid five hundred
ducats for the translation of Polybius. Filelfo was the luckiest of them
all, because in exchange for the Latin version of the Homeric poems
he received a most beautiful house in Rome and a large country estate.

In his travels Nicholas was escorted by a troop of scholars, artists,
translators, and scribes, with whom he familiarly discussed Horace,
Vergil, and Aristotle. He took them along also when he left town because of epidemics, and at his court gave them precedence over the
prelates, to whom he was not very close. Ecclesiastic questions interested him less than philosophical and literary ones, and he preferred
Catullus's *Carmina* and Ovid's *Metamorphoses* to the Bible. At night
he locked himself up in his study to read until dawn the translations
that the humanists brought him, and then he had them bound in red
velvet and ranged them on elegant shelves.

Like all the Renaissance lords, Nicholas had an itch for building
and spent enormous sums to return Rome to its old shape. The city
walls were repaired; convents, churches, and palaces were restored;
new buildings, sewers, bridges, and aqueducts were built; and streets
were repaved. He gave Leon Battista Alberti the task to plan *piazzas*
and palaces; Bernardo Rossellino was charged with the restoration of
San Giovanni Laterano, Santa Maria Maggiore, San Paolo, and San
Lorenzo. The doors of the Vatican were opened to Andrea del Cas-
tagno and Beato Angelico so that they should decorate its walls. He
spent all the income from the 1450 Jubilee on the beautification of the

city, which on that occasion received one hundred thousand pilgrims, and in order to make the access to St. Peter's easier he had many houses torn down after he had evicted their dwellers.

Nicholas was uninhibited when it came to getting money, and when he needed it, he did not hesitate to stiffen taxes. The Romans were always hostile to him. Led by a certain Stefano Porcaro, whom Nicholas first exiled to Bologna and then beheaded, they staged violent manifestations to demand the return of the republican regime.

This affair was the only dramatic event in an otherwise smooth pontifical term. Nicholas died, aged fifty-eight, of gout and of heartbreak, after he had failed to persuade the European princes to reconquer Constantinople, which had fallen into the hand of the Turks. A chronicler dedicated the following epitaph to him: "He was just, wise, benevolent, magnanimous, peaceful, affectionate, charitable, humble, and virtuous," thus mistakenly attributing to him virtues he did not possess and failing to mention the ones he did.

The next pope, Pius II, was Enea Silvio Piccolomini, from Siena. Pius came from a family of impoverished nobles and again was trained not in a seminary but in the humanistic studies of Florence. When he was twenty-seven, Enea became the secretary of Cardinal Capranica, whom he accompanied on long and delicate diplomatic missions in Italy and abroad, in which he revealed outstanding qualities as a negotiator. He was refined, brilliant, and ambitious; spent all the money he earned; and shared his time evenly between libraries, taverns, and brothels. Women were mad about him, but he carefully avoided those that expected marriage, because the very idea of marriage frightened him. A host of concubines gave him a multitude of children, whom he passed on to his father, having neither the time nor the inclination to raise them himself.

Writing was an outlet for his sensuality, and he wrote scurrilous verse and short stories in Boccaccio's style. He also wrote a pornographic novel, which his enemies kept bringing against him as long as he lived, but which he very likely never regretted having written. He tried his hand at the most diverse literary activities and was a prolific, lively, elegant, and pleasant writer. He left behind a huge quantity of poems, epigrams, dialogues, novels, memoirs, travel impressions, and essays, most of which were in Latin. His conversation was not less brilliant and delightful than his prose, and the fashionable *salons* fought for him. High-society ladies went into raptures at the witticisms of this Talleyrand of the fifteenth century, who did not sleep more than five hours each night and could never stay idle.

Piccolomini had become Emperor Frederick's favorite, and in 1455 the emperor sent him as ambassador to Rome, where he captivated the Curia and became a priest. The hagiographers say that from then on he lived in chastity, even though he had hardly reached forty. At the papal court he put his exceptional diplomatic talent to good use and reconciled the German clergy with the Roman. As a reward, the pope named him bishop of Siena, and in 1456 made him a cardinal. When the pope died, the Holy College closed an eye over Enea Silvio's past and made him pope.

Pius was only fifty-three, but he looked much older. He was pale, emaciated, full of wrinkles and infirmities; he suffered from gout, from kidney stones, and from a chronic cough. Platina says of him, "At times no one would have known that he was alive if he had not spoken." His youthful excesses had left their mark, and diets, blood-letting, and other remedies were of little use. Whenever he could, he retired to the country, followed by a troop of humanists, where he organized pastoral gatherings along the banks of little streams or in the shadowy quiet of a grove. Like Nicholas, he disliked priests and preferred philosophical or literary discussions to theological ones, and he loved pre-Christian writers best, especially Cicero.

He slipped his relatives into all kinds of jobs, and created new ones for them when the existing positions were not enough. Thus the Vatican was made into a Piccolomini colony. But he was a good pope: he tried to stop the Turks' forward thrust into the Balkans, and in 1459 he summoned the European princes to Mantua to induce them to take arms against the Infidels. But no one came to the meeting, and since he could not stop Islam with the sword, Pius tried to do it with the pen. He wrote to Mohammed II:

> If you should become a Christian, there would be no prince on earth superior to you in glory or equal in strength. We would recognize

you as Emperor of the Greeks of the Orient, and that which you have obtained through violence and keep with injustice would become your legitimate possession. If you joined us, the whole East would turn to Christ, and one will—yours—would give peace to the whole world.

Even though, according to some sources, Mohammed II was born to a Christian mother, he did not accept the pope's invitation. The pope, therefore, again called the Christian princes to arms, but again he had no luck. Only Venice answered the summons and sent a small fleet to Ancona, where a few weeks earlier, in July, 1464, the pope himself had landed at the head of his own fleet. Upon seeing the Venetian ships approach, Pius felt such strong emotion that he died, and the utopian dream of a last crusade was buried with him.

Pius' place was taken by Sixtus IV, formerly Francesco della Rovere, born into a family of humble Ligurian farmers. Francesco adopted the surname della Rovere from a noble family whose children he had tutored. Little is known about him before he became pope; only that he studied philosophy at Pavia, Bologna, and Padua, and that for some time he had been a teacher and enjoyed the well-deserved reputation of being a great scholar. At the age of fifty-seven he was elected pope, but he was not able to give as much time to his studies as Nicholas V and Pius II had, because his papacy was burdened with conflicts and difficulties. He, too, cherished plans for an expedition against the Turks, but the growing strength of the enemy dissuaded him from action. Instead, all his energies were spent in strengthening and enlarging the pontifical state, and in reducing to obedience Rome's riotous nobility and turbulent populace. At such tasks he was very successful, but his success was marred by the hatred of his subjects, who also resented his shameless nepotism. Perhaps only Alexander Borgia bestowed as many offices and rents on relatives, close and distant. For example, in 1471 Sixtus appointed his twenty-five-year-old nephew, Pietro Riario, a cardinal, and he assigned him four episcopal sees and a yearly income of sixty thousand ducats. He appointed Pietro's brother to be the head of the papal army, and another nephew became Rome's prefect.

When he took over the papacy, Sixtus found the treasury well stocked with gold, but in thirteen years he spent it all, down to the last penny. The money that he didn't spend on war or give to his nephews he spent on works of art. He embellished Rome with new public buildings and churches; he had the hospital of Santo Spirito restored and enlarged and reorganized the university. His name is tied to the Sistine Chapel, which was begun under him according to the plans of the architect Giovannino de Dolci, and he had its walls decorated by Perugino, Signorelli, Rosselli, and Cosimo with scenes from the life of Moses and Christ.

Many humanists gathered around Sixtus, and he added over a thousand books to the Vatican library, which already contained more than twenty-five hundred volumes. The mathematician Regiomontano was commissioned to reform the Julian calendar, a work that remained unfinished because of the scholar's premature death. Sixtus invited John Argiropulos to Rome to give a cycle of conferences on Greek literature, and he encouraged every initiative aimed at the diffusion of art and culture. Sixtus's dream was to bring Rome back to the splendors of the time of Augustus, but malaria killed him in 1484.

Rome owes her rebirth to these three magnificent popes. The Church has perhaps less reason to be grateful to them, because they were decidedly instrumental in changing the Church into a great artistic-cultural enterprise, and shifted its concerns to the plane of temporal interests at the expense of spiritual ones. During their reigns the Renaissance entered the cathedrals of Rome, and God left.

Chapter 25

At the Mercy of the Mercenaries

As we have followed the fortunes of the major Italian cities through the fourteenth and fifteenth centuries, we have passed over the infinite little wars that accompanied their development. The fact is that these struggles did not affect the fate of the country, which was already partitioned into five large states—the Viscontean, the Venetian, the Florentine, the Papal, and the Angevin-Aragonese—and into a galaxy of tiny ones. Often the little wars were simply skirmishes aimed at taking over a castle, or at rectifying a borderline, or at conquering a stronghold. But by the end of the fifteenth century the *comuni* and the *signorie* had long stopped employing regular troops, because these were very expensive to recruit, and also because they disrupted life by taking people away from their civilian activities, and had turned to mercenary troops instead.

The mercenaries were first formed when feudalism began to crumble, and the towns triumphed over the castles. Many noblemen who had some soldiers, rather than becoming sedentary bourgeois town-dwellers, preferred to hire themselves out with their men to this or that *comune* or lord. They enlisted into their gangs ex-convicts, outlaws, crusaders who had been ruined by the holy wars, and soldiers left behind from the imperial armies after a rout. Mercenary troops, in fact, cropped up all over Europe, but they prospered most in countries such as Italy and Germany where there was no central power.

Each mercenary company was made up of a few thousand foot soldiers and cavalrymen divided into squadrons; the men had helmets and armor and were armed with swords, daggers, and javelins. Each company had its own motto and its own flag and took its name from its commander. Fra Moriale's company even had treasurers and judges who had the task of arbitrating the fights that broke out among the soldiers when booty was being shared.

When, in time of peace, there was no booty, the mercenary companies blackmailed the towns. Only if they paid large sums would they be spared from attack and plunder. Pisa and Florence, for example, used to have to pay sixteen thousand and twenty thousand florins, respectively, every two years to keep Fra Moriale's troops away from their walls.

The mercenary companies, greedy for gain, moved by an unquenchable thirst for plunder, immune from legal sanctions, took the service of the town or lord that paid the highest price, and they didn't hesitate to betray their temporary master if the enemy lured them with more attractive wages. Giovanni Acuto, for instance, fought under the colors of Pisa, Milan, the pope, and Florence, with many changes of side, becoming the most powerful and most feared army leader of the fourteenth century. And the life history of this captain is a good example of the chaotic situation that prevailed in Italy.

Giovanni Acuto's real name was John Hawkwood, and he was born in a village in Essex, England, in 1320. Of above average height, he had square shoulders, a bull's neck, and powerful arms. He had a long nose of irregular shape, thin and nervous lips, high-colored cheeks, and hard-set jaws. His curly brown hair fell to below his ears, and his thick eyebrows shadowed deep, brown eyes. He had been mad about weapons since early childhood, and an uncle of his had taught him to ride and to wield the sword and use the bow. His father was a tanner who, when he died, left his son a small hoard. With that money John bought a horse, a suit of armor, and a sword, and then he joined the army of King Edward III, who was crossing the channel to attack France.

As part of the English army Hawkwood took part in the battle of Crécy in France, where the English used artillery for the first time. Ten years later he was made a knight on the battlefield of Poitiers. After the peace of Bretigny he crossed over to Italy with some hundred followers and he signed up with the German troop leader Albert Sterz, who headed the famous "White Company."

No day went by when these men did not raid the fertile plains of Piedmont and Lombardy, destroying crops, seizing herds, robbing cottages, and raping the women. That was the life that Giovanni Acuto had always dreamed of living. Sterz made him his deputy, and when Pisa hired the White Company to fight against Florence, it was Acuto who dictated the conditions of the contract. And he led the military operations as well. When the fighting was over, Acuto obtained an agreement from Pisa by which the booty taken from the enemy would be assigned to the company and his men would be free to move about the territory of the republic, and spend the winter there. The troops were so pleased by his negotiations that in appreciation they deposed Sterz and acclaimed Acuto their new leader. Pisa, moreover, put a bodyguard and a number of pages at his disposal.

When the hostilities against Florence resumed, Acuto recruited new troops and hurled them against the Florentines with such strength that they, unable to hold their own, sent ambassadors to the English leader to induce him to come over to their side. When the ambassadors stopped before the leader, they pulled out large wine flasks filled with florins; Acuto weighed them for a long while, and then he called his soldiers around him and asked them what they wanted to do. They all went over to the enemy side, except for Acuto himself and eight hundred Englishmen, who remained at Pisa's service. But this was not done out of loyalty. A short time before, Acuto had been offered much more favorable terms for his services by a rich merchant of Pisa, Giovanni Agnello, who, taking advantage of the confusion into which the city was plunged, meant to seize power in Pisa. Acuto was to re-

ceive three thousand florins for his help. The coup was successful, and
the Englishman received a fat tip besides the agreed fee.

Acuto needed the money, because hard times were about to come
for the mercenary companies. Pope Urban V declared them anathema
and invited the princes of Europe to make a coalition to fight them.
Many princes answered the call, and a powerful league was formed.
However, when the time for action came, most of the league members
turned around and went home. The pope himself, worried by the
news that came from the Holy Land, set aside the idea of a crusade
against the mercenary troops.

In the meantime, Acuto had scraped together a few thousand men
and had had a secret meeting with the agents of Bernabò Visconti,
who wanted him for his service. The English leader willingly accepted,
both because the Duke of Milan paved his way with gold and because
he was engaged in order to fight the pope, the mercenary captain's
mortal enemy.

In any event, the company, more than four thousand men strong,
fell upon the Papal States, wracking them with sword and fire. Acuto
ordered his men to set fire to churches and convents and to slay the
inhabitants regardless of sex or age. The raids ended only when Bernabò recalled Acuto to Milan to send him to conquer Florence and
Pisa, an undertaking that failed because Florence and Pisa had a much
larger number of mercenaries at their service. The fiasco, however,
induced the ambitious duke to reduce Acuto's salary, and Acuto, out
of spite, went over to the pope's side, partly, of course, because the
pope gave him the fiefs of Bagnocavallo, Cotignola, and Conselice,
between Rimini and Bologna, and also the title of Lord.

Acuto surrounded his territories with walls and erected towers and
from his outpost carried out with admirable zeal his duties as the pope's
policeman. When an insurrection against the pope broke out in Faenza,
for example, Acuto ordered his men to sack the town and to deport the
inhabitants, except for the young women, on whom the soldiers performed all sorts of abuses. The chief himself indulged in wild violence.
One day, seeing two mercenaries fight over a nun, he had her brought

into his presence and then split her in half with his sword, saying to his men: "Now each has his piece." After his Faenza raid Acuto went back to his lands, but he didn't stay there long. The town of Cesena had revolted and had to be punished. Acuto assaulted Cesena, massacred twenty-five hundred people, and razed the town.

Acuto's relations with the pope became cooler after a while. The pope did not pay, and the company was giving signs of discontent. Moreover, both Bernabò Visconti and the Republic of Florence sought to take advantage of the situation by luring Acuto away from the pope. The Duke of Milan went so far as to offer the mercenary his daughter, Donnina, in marriage, with a dowry of ten thousand florins. The offer was too good to resist, and Acuto accepted, even though he was nearing sixty.

Acuto was still a vigorous man, and he had not lost his youthful boldness. His hair had turned white, but it was concealed under his war helmet or a velvet cap. He had lost some teeth, and wrinkles had appeared on his forehead, but on the whole he had a youthful appearance. Donnina was very beautiful. She had black hair and eyes, long, slender hands, and a sweet, intense expression. The wedding was celebrated with great pomp, the duke presiding, and it was concluded by a picturesque tournament that sealed the new contract between Acuto and Bernabò.

However, after a year Bernabò and Acuto were again at loggerheads, and Acuto moved to Florence, where he was named general captain. He paraded along the festively decorated streets of the city, amid the ring of trumpets and bells, holding a small scepter. The city government assigned him a splendid dwelling in the city, exempted him from taxes, and for some ten years employed him to make inroads and lead skirmishes up and down the peninsula.

A new war with the Visconti broke out in 1390. For Acuto it was his last and also his least successful battle. The duke's army, twenty-six thousand men strong, defeated the English company, which numbered only seven thousand men. Yet, even though he was beaten, Acuto was honored by Florence, and the city raised his salary and granted Florentine citizenship to all his relatives.

By that time Acuto was seventy years old, and he had spent more than fifty years on battlefields. He was tired and felt a yearning for peace. Then, too, he had two daughters of marriageable age and wanted to see them settled. However, when he had married one to the Count of Porcia and the other to a German mercenary captain, he felt homesick for England and for his native village, and he thought of going home. He had never forgotten England, and when his country was mentioned in his hearing, he was moved to tears. Indeed, he had kept his English customs, refusing even to learn Italian.

Everything was ready for John Hawkwood's departure when he died of a heart attack. Florence prepared solemn services: the standard bearer, priors, and all the prominent citizens followed the bier in mourning. After a long procession through the city, the party reached Saint Mary of the Flower, where a requiem mass was celebrated. The bier remained in the center nave for a few days, and then it was buried in the choir, whence it was later removed on request of King Richard II, who had the body transferred to England. Some decades later Paolo Uccello immortalized the famous leader by painting a horseback portrait of him on one of the walls of the Duomo.

When Acuto died, Francesco Bussone was four years old. He was born in 1394 in Carmagnola, a small town south of Turin, on the right bank of the river Po. A shepherd's son, he would probably have gone on herding sheep all his life if the mercenary captain Facino Cane had not enlisted him among his men.

Bussone was a stout and lively lad, with rough features, big brown eyes, and pink cheeks. His father had not been able to send him to school, nor did Francesco feel the need for it. Weapons were his one passion. The first time he picked up a sword he almost ran through a cavalry man. In Facino's company he was singled out for his exceptional courage and for the number of enemies he had stabbed.

Eventually, the young soldier's renown reached the ears of Filippo Maria Visconti, who was preparing to recover the territories he had lost on the death of his father, Gian Galeazzo. The Duke of Milan summoned Bussone to his court, hired him, then sent him out to reconquer fortresses, castles, and cities. Bussone, who had been rebap-

tized Carmagnola by his soldiers, won such victories that Filippo
Maria made him Count of Castelnuovo Scrivia and Lord of Vespolate,
assigned him large properties, and made him his confidant. The condottiere from Piedmont became a sort of gray eminence—feared and
envied by the plotting dukes and ambitious courtiers who thought of
him as an intruder, and hatred of the brilliant officer became more intense when it was announced that he was to marry Antonia Visconti,
bastard daughter of Duke Gian Galeazzo.

Antonia had been wedded in a first marriage to one of her father's
bodyguards, and she was rich, young, and beautiful. After the wedding, which was held with great pomp in the Duomo, the couple
went to live in city hall, where not long after Carmagnola received
the news that he had been named governor of Genova. The promotion was really a removal from the command of the army, and the
condottiere could not see the reason for it. Taking along only a small
escort, he went to the castle of Abbiategrasso, where the duke was, and
asked to see him. He was answered that Filippo Maria couldn't receive him. Carmagnola was indignant, and he became even more
angry when, as he was leaving, he saw the duke's grinning face peer
at him from one of the tower's windows. He wanted to go back to
Milan, where he had left his wife and children, but on the road he
learned that Visconti had made them prisoners. He could only flee.

At first Carmagnola offered his services to the Duke of Savoy,
Amedeo VIII, who refused them for fear of Filippo Maria's wrath.
Then Carmagnola turned to Venice, who was Milan's rival in the
bid for supremacy over northern Italy. Doge Francesco Foscari and
the senators received him with great honors, made him the commander
of all their land troops, and gave him St. Mark's insignia—but they
also put two commissars at his side: to follow and protect him, they
said, but also to spy on him.

When war with Milan broke out, Florence and Venice joined in
a league to repress the expansionistic aspirations of the Visconti.
Carmagnola moved against Brescia at the head of an army of sixteen
thousand horsemen and six thousand foot soldiers, and the town ca-
pitulated after a weak resistance. Back in Venice, Carmagnola was

carried in triumph on the Grand Canal. But when the doge ordered him to leave again for the front, he asked for a delay. Some months earlier he had fallen from a horse and had badly hurt his back. The pain was flaring up and was so severe that he couldn't ride, and the doctors advised a thermal cure. After a few weeks of mud baths he wearily took up arms again, only almost immediately to retire from service. In April the senate ordered Carmagnola to march against Lombardy, but he answered that the grain wasn't high enough in the fields to feed the horses, and that therefore they had to wait for summer. Finally, in June, he began his campaign, but in September he again gave up. This time, however, the doge lost his patience and threatened not to pay the troops, and Bussone had to give in and attack the enemy.

The two armies clashed in the plain of Maclodio on October 11, 1427. The Venetians won a smashing victory: ten thousand of the duke's men were made prisoner and all their weapons were piled up in front of Carmagnola's tent. The Visconti flag also was captured and laid at the foot of the Venetian one. Mauroni, who described this battle, which marked the highest peak of Carmagnola's military fortune and also the beginning of his ruin, in a bad tragedy makes much of the *condottiero's* generosity, because he set his prisoners free on the very evening of the victory. Others, however, say that the reason he let them go was simply that he didn't know where to put them, and still others say that he did it to ingratiate Filippo Maria.

In Venice the defeat of the Visconti was greeted with exultation. The Great Council gave Carmagnola a splendid palace on the Grand Canal and offered to make him commander-in-chief of the army for another two years. Bussone hedged at first but later accepted. He had just reached thirty-seven, and except for the bruised back he was in the fullness of his physical vigor. But something had changed in him. He had become taciturn, he avoided friends, he was almost never seen in public; he had no commerce with women and didn't go to the sumptuous balls given at the ducal palace. He spent long hours reading the messages that Filippo Maria had begun to send him; messages in which the Visconti duke gave him news of his wife and children and promised to reintegrate him into his domains. Carmagnola handed those letters over to the senate, but the suspicions that had begun to accumulate on him since Maclodio only grew stronger. Why did he keep up a correspondence with the enemy?

The Venetians thought they knew the answer when, in later battles with Milan, their own armies always lost. In March, 1432, the doge called together the Council of the Ten to judge the disconcerting behavior of Carmagnola, who was at Brescia at the time. They decided to recall him to Venice on some pretext. Carmagnola, suspecting nothing, went. When he arrived in Venice, he was greeted with great honor by a delegation of nobles, who escorted him to the ducal palace. But once he was inside, guards surrounded him and pushed him into the underground dungeons. They threw him into a filthy low-ceilinged cell, hardly three feet long, where he could neither lie down nor stand up. For three days he refused food; on the fourth they took him to a torture chamber where he was undressed, hanged from the ceiling by his wrists, and scorched with red hot irons. Finally he "confessed," whereupon he was sentenced to death for high treason.

Francesco Bussone climbed the scaffold with faltering steps, hands tied behind his back and with an iron bit between his teeth. He was pale and disheveled, and his body was covered with welts and bruises. His favorite dog, a pointer that had followed him to prison, came behind him. The square was overflowing with a silent, stunned crowd, while a chorus of priests sang funeral hymns. At a signal the executioner made Carmagnola kneel, setting his head on the block. Then he lifted the ax and let it fall three times. At last the head came off and rolled away amid a splatter of gushing blood. The dog whined and began to lick it. That evening Carmagnola's remains were put into a rough coffin and sent to his wife.

Machiavelli, in *The Prince,* had this to say about Carmagnola:

> The Venetians, knowing him to be very valorous, as under his leadership they had broken the Duke of Milan, and on the other hand knowing that he was waxing cold in the war at hand, judged that they couldn't win with him anymore, because he didn't want to

win; nor could they dismiss him, because that could mean losing what they had already conquered; therefore for their own protection they were forced to kill him.

It seems, then, that Machiavelli found it entirely logical and even inevitable that Carmagnola should end as he did, even though he judged him innocent and "very valorous." Machiavelli, as a good Renaissance Italian, considered murder motivated by "state interest" to be entirely legitimate.

If moral judgment had fallen so low in Italy it was at least in part due to mercenary practices. The mercenary companies had exempted the Italians from military service, and by doing so they had made men pusillanimous. They had destroyed in the Italians that sense of values that can be kept alive only by a national army. Acuto's and Bussone's lack of ideals, their lust for power and money, their readiness to double-deal and betray were no scandal to a people who had forgotten, or rather, had never known, what fatherland meant—or honor and loyalty, for that matter—simply because they had lacked the institution in which these virtues are developed and trained: the army. Italy was the paradise of condottieri because it had no soldiers. But a country without soldiers is also a country without citizens.

Part IV

THE NEW WORLDS

Chapter 26

THE FALL OF CONSTANTINOPLE

AT THE end of May, 1453, Christian Europe was stunned by the news that Constantinople had fallen under the vigorous blows of the Turkish armies of Mohammed II, "The Conqueror." What struck people's imagination most was the dramatic and symbolic aspect of the event. At the time nobody realized the catastrophic political implications of the fall—not even the Italians did, although they were the ones destined to suffer most from them. Only the Venetian ambassadors had a lucid premonition of things to come.

Like its Western counterpart, the Eastern Roman Empire had also amply deserved its fate. For two centuries before 1453 it had outlived itself, intent only on enjoying the delights of a splendid sunset. The decline had begun with the Crusaders' invasion of Constantinople in 1204. After dethroning the *Basileus* Isaac Angelo, they partitioned the country into a cluster of tiny independent states that were always fighting each other: the mini-empires of Trebisond and Nicea, the despot-ruled Epyrus, the principates of Philadelphia and Rhodes, the empire of Constantinople, the kingdom of Thessaloniki, the duchy of Athens, the principate of Acacia, and the cluster of Venetian domains scattered along the archipelago.

In 1261, after fifty-seven years of chaos, the powerful Paleologus family restored the monarchy. But the long interval had caused irreparable damage. The economy was falling apart: agriculture, which was its backbone, had not been able to adapt to "technological progress." Farming was still tied to archaic and unproductive methods of cultivation and caught in the system of large landed estates that produced an unruly rural sub-proletariat full of class hatred and easy prey for egalitarianist demagoguery. The landowners, on the other hand, were hostile to any reform that might threaten their feudal privileges, and they were firmly decided to maintain the status quo.

Another menace came from the continuous incursions by neighboring peoples: the Ottomans, the Serbs, the Bulgarians, who when short of food—which they regularly were before harvest time—erupted into the Byzantine provinces with the voracity of locusts, devouring crops and animals. Moreover, the imperial armies were moved by the same lust for plunder as they moved back and forth through the empire, even in times of peace. The *Basileus* looked on, powerless to stop these depredations, limiting himself to issuing sanctions that were never enforced.

Commerce, which had been the empire's main resource and had dominated the Orient for centuries, was not in much better shape. At first, although the oilslick-like expansion of Islam in the Mediterranean had struck a hard blow at the Greek maritime merchants, the powerful Byzantine mercantile fleet had modernized itself and in less than a century was able to cope with the new reality and to recover its old supremacy. However, real decline set in with the Crusades, in the wake of which followed Venetian, Genoese, and Pisan commercial colonies, which sprouted like mushrooms along the Greek coast after the year 1000. These colonies enjoyed franchises, tax exemptions, and countless privileges that made of them states within a state, with their own neighborhoods, courts, and churches. The bailiffs that ruled these foreign enclaves in the names of their home countries did not hesitate to foment and sometimes even personally to lead uprisings against the emperor when they came into conflict with him. The *Basileus* did not dare repress these riots for fear of retaliation from the maritime republics, and these disorders often caused war among the Greek population itself, which was deeply xenophobic.

Eventually, the slack agriculture and the loss of trade to foreign merchants hastened the financial collapse of the empire, which had drawn its main income from land taxes and custom duties levied on the big landowners, who were supposed to pay the former but had no trouble bribing the fiscal agents charged with tax collection, and by the Venetian, Genoese, and to a lesser extent by the Spanish and French merchants, who were exempted from paying custom duties, at least the heaviest ones.

To make ends meet, the Paleologi emperors reduced their military budget and cut back their army, unaware that by doing so they were heading for suicide. By leaving their borders unguarded, they emboldened the land- and conquest-hungry Slavic and Turkish peoples hovering on the edges of the empire, ready to cross the borders at the bidding of a leader. And yet in reaction to every defeat the *Basileus* in Constantinople gave banquets and festivities worthy of the *Arabian Nights.*

To finance such affairs, the emperor drew blindly on the funds of the state and soon exhausted them, but at least the court's life style was splendid, as spectacular as it had been in the golden age of Justinian and Theodora. Inflation and court parties progressed at the same reckless speed: new buildings went up all the time in the imperial enclosure, old ones were repainted and decorated. The Holy Palace was a fantastic assemblage of gold, mosaics, tapestries, damasks, and gem-studded rings. The emperor and the empress wore dazzling garments covered with precious stones; the dignitaries and courtiers displayed the same luxury.

One chronicler tells us that on the occasion of John Paleologus's wedding, in 1347, food was served on earthenware dishes and tin plates, and that the crowns the bride and the groom wore were adorned with worthless stones and broken glass. But this account does not square with those that have been left us by most of the historians of the time, who were unanimous in denouncing the imperial display of pomp.

What the rest of the city looked like on the eve of its fall is described by the Spanish diplomat Ruy González de Clavijo: "The capital is choked with impressive buildings, churches, and monasteries in a state

of complete abandon." This image recalls Rome at the time of the
Goths and the Longobards, when the streets had turned into sewers,
the piazzas had become pastures, and the churches had changed into
barracks. The outskirts of Byzantium were reduced to stinking slums,
infested by mice and lice, peopled by waifs and tramps. Famine and
epidemics took turns in gnawing away at the population, which had
shrunk to little more than one hundred thousand.

Society was in full decay; only philosophy and the arts had not entirely lost their shine. Some schools had to close down for lack of
students but the majority kept running, even though students were
becoming more and more scarce. Learned philosophers held learned
debates about Plato and Aristotle, taking sides with fierce opposition,
and *Basileus* John VI Cantacuzene, by far a better scholar than a
ruler, thought Aristotle to be superior to Plato.

Against the background of general decline, art had a last flicker of
life. The themes and motives from which it took inspiration were still
the same religious ones—the Old and New Testaments and the lives
of saints—the tone was still edifying and hagiographic, but a breath
of naturalism had begun to permeate it and make it less pompous.
The Byzantine artists now portrayed sketches of daily life in colorful
large frescoes as well as scenes of the Passion and miraculous legends.
But all such activities were not enough to shield the empire from the
sword of Islam brandished by the warlike Ottoman Turks.

The Ottoman Turks were originally from central Asia, whence they
had drifted south. After long, wearying marches across mountains and
plains they had settled in the Anatolian highlands. They lived in tents
and in coarse straw huts. Sheep raising was their main occupation,
but they had rudimentary notions of farming, and they were fine
horsemen. When they came to settle in Asia Minor, they were
heathens, and the Byzantine missionaries did not succeed in convert-
ing them to Christianity. Instead, it was the Arab caliphs who, arriving on the crest of Islam's great expansion, converted them to Islam,
which was a creed much more congenial to the Ottoman Turks'
temperament, since it was practiced with the sword.

In the second half of the fourteenth century the Ottoman Sultan

Orkhan asked for and obtained the hand of a Greek princess. Around 1350 his son Suleiman was enlisted by the Byzantine emperor of the then ruling Cantacuzene family to fight against the rival dynasty of the Paleologi. Thus the Turks first experienced the empire's troubles, and from that time until the empire's final collapse, the Turks never stopped taking advantage of the constant fratricidal fights that bloodied the throne of Byzantium. And in the meantime they began making advances on their inheritance by annexing one by one the Balkan provinces of the empire.

The star of this northwestward movement of expansion was the Sultan Murad, the true founder of the Ottoman Empire, one of the most fearless warriors of his time. Warlike virtues were combined in him with exceptional political and diplomatic qualities. He divided his subjects into two categories: in the first he put the Turks and all those who adopted Islam, and in the second the Christians, who continued to live according to their own customs and laws, on condition of paying a special tax. In wartime, if a city resisted, its male inhabitants were made slaves and its women concubines. Since being a slave or a concubine or a second-class citizen had many inconveniences, and precluded advancement, there were many conversions.

It was thanks to Murad's religious policies that the Ottoman Empire found cohesion and unity in spite of its heterogeneous and colorful cosmopolitanism. This farsighted and open-minded ruler also was responsible for the Janissaries, a select corps of guards whose members were recruited at a very early age—were brought up according to a rigid military discipline that required absolute loyalty to the sovereign, and were trained in the use of all weapons. The Janissaries enjoyed special privileges and received a special pay, much higher than the one regular career soldiers were paid. They were the first organized corps of the Turkish army, which until the beginning of the century had been hardly more than a horde.

When Mohammed II became sultan in 1451, the Ottoman Empire was already prosperous, powerful, and feared. It dominated a good part of the Balkan peninsula and a large slice of Asia Minor. Only Constantinople remained independent, but in the way a castle under

siege would be. On paper it was still the capital of an empire, but its
borders coincided with the city walls.

On Easter Eve, 1453, the city was alerted by the news that a Turkish army of one hundred forty thousand men in full combat gear was
approaching. Some people fled to the nearby countryside, fearing that
a siege and a long famine would kill them, but most people stayed and
began to prepare for the city's defense. On April 2 the enemy van-
guard appeared threateningly over the horizon. The Emperor Constantine XI Paleologus ordered one cavalry squadron to sally, but after
they had brought some confusion to the enemy's ranks, they caught
sight of the rest of the enemy army and beat a hurried retreat. All the
drawbridges were pulled up, and the gates of the city were sealed. To
prevent Turkish ships from mooring in the Golden Horn, the harbor's
mouth was blocked with a barrage of floating logs tied together with
iron chains.

On April 5 the sultan with his colorful following pitched their tents
in an open field a mile and a half from the city. The next day he moved
his camp a few hundred yards forward. Constantine appealed to all
the foreigners living in Byzantium, asking them to help defend the
city, and so they did. The Venetian and Genoese merchants took arms
and, under the command of their respective bailiffs, took up the positions assigned to them. Monks, too, were mobilized and used as liaison
officers. Priests were invited to hold themselves ready to confess the
living and bring the last sacrament to the dying.

The commander of the city ordered the cannons to be fired at the
enemy camp, but the recoil after the first volley made several deep
cracks in the towers on which the guns were enplaced. Consequently
the cannons couldn't be fired again, and the Turks advanced another
few hundred yards. When the sultan moved his red and gold tent
forward for the third time, he offered the Greeks a truce, but they disdainfully rejected it. Then he ordered his artillery to fire at the walls,
which soon collapsed in several places. Then, as the defenders repaired
the gaps as best they could, the Ottoman guns went on booming for
six weeks. Whenever the cannons stopped, battering rams and other

heavy war machines were pushed against the wall, while the besieged showered boulders, boiling oil, and tar from above.

On May 28 Mohammed II ordered the trumpets, drums, and fifes to give the signal for attack. In Constantinople all the churchbells began to ring a full peal, spreading panic among the people who left their homes to seek refuge in St. Sophia's naves or churchyard. All the forgotten relics were exhumed, and the intercession of the most popular saints was invoked. Someone even remembered an old prophecy according to which an angel bearing a long sword would drive back the infidels and free the city.

But the prophecy did not come true. After a desperate resistance, Byzantium was overcome and a battalion of Janissaries erupted into the city with the violence of water breaking a dam. Constantine, seeing himself lost, took off his imperial emblems and, holding a spear, together with a few companions, threw himself against the Turks. The chroniclers of the time don't tell us if he survived the skirmish. Most likely he perished in it, as he sealed with a brave and noble deed the liquidation of a dynasty that in two centuries had done nothing of that nature.

Mohammed waited a few hours before entering the city, to allow his soldiers time to satisfy their urge for plunder. And when he entered, the massacre and the robbing ceased—but by then there was little left to kill or steal. The city's streets and squares were paved with corpses, many of which were horribly maimed. Convents had been sacked and their inmates, regardless of sex, brutalized and slaughtered. Some nuns had drowned themselves by jumping into convent wells to avoid falling into enemy hands; others had shattered themselves by leaping out of windows; still others took poison. After profaning the holy places, the Ottomans had invaded the libraries, wreaking havoc in the immense, priceless collection of codices and manuscripts preserved there: tens of thousands of volumes went up in flames or disappeared into the sea.

When, after three days, things began to calm down, the sultan started to reorganize. He decreed that a certain number of churches should be changed into mosques: the *Ulema* climbed the pulpits and announced that Allah was the true god and Mohammed was his prophet. Then the sultan summoned his generals and divided the booty while they were present, keeping a generous share for himself. The take was not only arms, jewels, trophies, silver, and other precious objects; it included also the surviving members of the imperial family and a certain number of officers, dignitaries, and court ladies who had escaped the massacre. Mohammed generously let the less pleasing women go free and added the more beautiful ones to his harem.

Then he proceeded to restore some order in the city. He named the theologian Gennadio as the new patriarch and entrusted Byzantium's Christians to his charge—he was to watch over them as the sultan's representative. In the beginning of January, 1454, Gennadio received from Mohammed's hands the emblems of his high office: the long dress, the staff, and the pectoral cross. After the ceremony the patriarch mounted a white horse, which was the sultan's present, and rode to the church of the Holy Apostles, where he was crowned by the Metropolitan of Eraclea. To end the ceremony he led a long procession through the streets of the city.

Together with the title of patriarch, Gennadio also received many privileges from Mohammed: personal inviolability, fiscal exemption, unlimited tenure in office, and the right to transmit these prerogatives to his successors. Moreover, he obtained broad judiciary concessions, insuring to the Orthodox Church the right to judge not only religious controversies but also cases dealing with marriage, divorce, and the guardianship of minors.

After the religious settlement came the economic one. Mohammed elected Constantinople to be the new capital of the Ottoman Empire, instead of Adrianopolis. He invited the Greek merchants to reactivate commerce, and the craftsmen to open up their shops again; he appealed to the Armenians, Jews, and Turks living in other parts of the empire to come to live in Byzantium; he recruited a group of competent architects and commissioned them to restore the city and to erect a royal palace in the center, and when it was ready, he moved into it with the court and a populous harem. In a few years' time the city was reborn: it quadrupled its population and reacquired the rank and tone of a capital.

When Constantinople fell, the people then living failed to realize that the history of Europe had taken on a new course. The fall of Byzantium not only destroyed a capital—one which had done nothing to preserve itself—but the last Roman (and therefore Western) outpost in the Balkan peninsula and in Asia Minor. The great loser, however, was the Christian church, which saw itself definitively replaced by Islam, which it had fought for centuries and had tried to suppress through the Crusades. Islam's sword, moreover, had taken its revenge by sinking its blade deep into the borders of most Christian Hungary.

The Ottoman revenge was both religious and economic. Economically it was mainly the maritime republics of Venice and Genoa that suffered from the take-over. These republics had had free rein in the Adriatic and the Aegean seas since the eleventh century, monopolizing commerce, enriching themselves beyond measure, making and breaking treaties, and, by their greed for gain and quarrels, helping to wreck the weak and corrupt Empire of the Orient.

However, not all the values of the great Byzantine civilization were lost to the West. Constantinople's surrender caused the exodus to France and Italy of a great number of Greek philosophers, writers, and artists, who acquainted the West with the cultural and intellectual treasures of their fatherland. And it was these men who brought to Italy the seeds of that humanistic revival which characterized the golden centuries.

Chapter 27

THE DISCOVERY OF AMERICA

THE FALL of Constantinople closed the Mediterranean trading routes for Europe, and forced Europe to look westward. Popular imagination saw the West as an endless stretch of water lying beyond the straits of Gibraltar, which were known as "Hercules' Pillars" and marked the limits of the known world. Those who went beyond never returned, swallowed by the untamed waters of that mysterious sea. What did its abysses conceal? How far did its farthest limits reach?

The most bizarre and fantastic answers had been given to these questions. Philosophers, theologians, and scientists had maintained for many centuries, without giving plausible reasons, that the Ocean (this is what they called the Atlantic in antiquity) was not navigable. But in 986 the Vikings had dared to set out on it, thrusting as far as the coasts of Greenland, and in the year 1000 they had discovered a new continent, but finding it deserted, they had turned around and headed back for their home ports.

These deeds, which were preserved in northern legends, did not find much acceptance in the rest of Europe. However, they fired the imagination of a young Genoese seaman who heard them when, during one of his voyages, he touched those Scandinavian shores from which the Viking ships had sailed five hundred years earlier.

Christopher Columbus was born in Genoa in 1451, to a family of poor Jewish weavers who had come to Liguria from Spain, and who had been converted to Christianity. When Christopher was a child, to escape his creditors his father had had to move the family to Savoy. And there he had found work as an innkeeper. Poverty had prevented him from sending his sons to school, and so when they reached puberty, the boys were shipped out to sea on some old merchantman.

By 1471 Columbus had reached the rank of captain. Five years later while he was sailing toward Lisbon, his ship was attacked by pirates and sunk. Christopher survived, miraculously managing to swim for six hours while holding onto a plank, and in 1477 he visited Scandinavia, when he heard about the transoceanic exploits of the Vikings. He did not believe that they had discovered a new continent but thought that they might have found a western route to India and China, one that would circumvent the barrier raised by the Ottoman conquest of Constantinople.

During the long hours of idleness at sea Christopher had read the *Imago Mundi* of Peter d'Ailly, the *Historia Rerum Ubique Gestarum* of Pius II, the Italian translation of Pliny's *Historia Naturalis,* and Marco Polo's *il Milione.* In particular, Marco Polo's fabulous descriptions of China and Japan had taken hold of his vivid imagination. Marco Polo estimated that the nearest island of the Asiatic continent lay five thousand miles west of Lisbon. The Florentine physician Paolo Toscanelli gave the same figure for the shortest distance between the Portuguese coast and India. Columbus's biographers tell us that it was these estimates that put the idea of challenging the ocean into the Genoese navigator's mind.

Columbus had taken a wife in Lisbon after his shipwreck, so it was to the king of Portugal that he turned first with his project. He wrote to the king asking him for three caravels, and he stressed how much the Christian faith stood to gain from the conversion of Asia's inhabitants. The king submitted the request to a commission of geographers, who judged it unacceptable, because, according to them, the distance between Portugal and the easternmost edge of Asia was much greater than what Columbus had indicated (and no one then suspected that there was another continent in between). The sea captain then turned to Genoa and Venice, but they refused to give any aid. Next he knocked at the door of the Spanish monarchs, Ferdinand and Isabella, who appointed a commission of experts who confirmed their Portuguese colleagues' opinion. Disappointed, but not discouraged, Columbus thought of going to France to the court of Charles VIII. But a friend of his, the Abbot Perez, prevailed on him to wait and obtained for him an audience with Queen Isabella. At the same time he also was helped by a Castilian cabinet minister, Louis de Santander, a baptized Jew who advised the queen to give her support to the enterprise. Failing royal support, Santander promised Columbus that he would finance the expedition himself. But at last Isabella and Ferdinand decided to give their consent.

In a few days' time two million *maravedis* were collected, and three caravels were armed: the *Pinta,* the *Niña,* and the *Santa Maria.* The *Santa Maria* was the flagship, with a displacement of 233 tons, and a length of about 115 feet. All three had guns, large ones charged with granite balls and small ones that shot lead. On the masts flew pennants emblazoned with the cross. The holds had been filled with wine, water, and foodstuff. Each sailor had a right to a daily 350 grams of crackers, 280 grams of meat or fish, and 2 liters of wine. There were also tons of vegetables, onions, and cheese, and cases of glass beads, mirrors, many-colored caps, needles, and pins to distribute to the inhabitants of Catai and Cipango (China and Japan).

Columbus took command of the *Santa Maria;* he put Martin Alonzo Pinzon in charge of the *Pinta* and Vincente Yanez Pinzon, one of the best Spanish navigators of the time, in charge of the *Niña.* On August 3, 1492, the small fleet sailed from the port of Palos amid the cheers of the festive population. After a few days of navigation the *Pinta* was damaged and had to be towed until the Canary Islands were reached. There Columbus stopped and had the *Pinta* repaired. The stop lasted a whole month because the wind had died down or blew from the wrong direction. But at last the three ships were able to sail onward toward the West, that is, toward the unknown.

At sunset the men gathered on the bridge to say their "Hail Marys" in chorus and to sing slow Castilian and Andalusian songs. As the days went by and the vessels pushed forward on the ocean, the men became restless and doubting. Every now and then a man would fall prey to despair, and collapsing on his knees, he would stretch his arms to the sky and pray for land to appear, or seeing a mirage, he would madly point his finger at the horizon, only to fall into deeper dejection after the vision was gone. Those were moments of terrible anxiety for the admiral. One evening some of the sailors told Columbus that they wanted to turn about and sail for home. "You are wasting your time," he answered, "because I have left for Catai and I shall continue to sail until, with God's help, I shall reach it." Since the sailors couldn't convince him with arguments they tried to organize a mutiny. The plot was discovered, and Pinzon advised Columbus to hang the rebels. "If you won't do it, then I shall," he said. Only then did the sailors of the *Santa Maria* again become obedient.

On October 11 the *Pinta's* crew fished out of the sea a reed, a carved stick, and a clump of grass. At this sign the sailors sang a *Te Deum,* and the admiral ordered the night watch to keep a very sharp lookout for the landfall that must be near. At 2:00 A.M. a cannon blast from the *Pinta's* deck aroused the crews of the three ships. A certain Rodrigo de Triana had sighted land, thus earning the thousand *maravedis* that King Ferdinand had promised to the first man to set his eyes on Asia.

At dawn the caravels lowered anchor in the waters of a luxuriantly wooded island rimmed by a beach of very fine sand and inhabited by exotic birds and naked men. Columbus had a launch lowered and took his place in it with the Pinzons, the notary, and the inspector of the fleet, and they rowed toward the shore. Columbus held the royal banner in his right hand, while the other two captains waved a flag with the cross. They were all dressed in gorgeous gold-and-silver-embroidered garments, and they wore hats with rich feathers. When they touched ground, the admiral declared that he was taking possession of the island in the name of Ferdinand and Isabella. Then he opened a bag and handed out its contents—glass beads, rattles and bells, red caps, and other trinkets—to the natives who had gathered around the Spaniards, and who were fascinated by the latter's clothes and shining swords.

Columbus called that land Guanahani, and he was convinced that it was in Asia, not far from the Great Khan's city. For a few days they wandered about the surrounding islands, baptizing them with the Spanish names of saints and princes: Santa Maria de la Concepcion, Fernandia, Isabella. And he set down in his diary what he saw. What struck him most, besides the beauty of the spot and the warmth of the climate, was the tameness of the natives. Two days after his arrival Columbus entered in his diary: "These natives must make good servants. If the sovereigns so desire, they can have them brought over to Castile. Or they can have them held prisoners on the island, because fifty armed men can easily keep them all under control"—not bad, as an example of Christian charity!

The admiral ordered his men to arrest a certain number of natives, especially women, and had them baptized. Then he had a huge cross manufactured and planted it at the harbour's mouth so that it was visible from many miles away. Some days later he wrote again in his diary:

> I say that Christianity and especially Spain, to whom all must be subjected, will make good business with these people. And I say that our Highnesses should not allow any foreigner to set foot on this island, unless they be Catholic Christians, because the reason and the end of this enterprise is to enhance the growth and the glory of the Christian religion, and no one should come here who is not a good Christian.

Columbus continued to explore the archipelago, and on October 28 he landed in Cuba. A crowd of natives surrounded the Spaniards and joined them in singing when, as they did each time they took possession of a new territory, they intoned a "Hail Mary." Some even tried to imitate the Spaniards when they crossed themselves, provoking the latter's laughter. The headman of the natives pronounced the word Cubanacam, the island's name, which meant interior Cuba, and Columbus exulted, because he understood the man to be saying "Kublai Khan," and he thought he had finally arrived at the home of the great lord of China. He sent two ambassadors to seek out the elusive monarch, and the two men came back a few days later with a detailed account of what they had seen. Instead of the Great Khan, they had found only more dark, naked natives, but these blew smoke from their noses and they had long, rolled up leaves stuck in their nostrils. They said that the natives had welcomed them with much friendliness, and that they themselves had tasted the aroma of those leaves, deriving a strange pleasurable sensation from it. Those two Spaniards seemed more impressed by the discovery of tobacco than by that of the New World. We don't know whether Columbus stuck those leaves into his own nose as well, and if so, whether he liked it. Knowing him, one would tend to doubt it. He was an ascetic man, almost a monomaniac, dominated by a single idea: to discover Catai and to multiply the followers of Jesus Christ and the subjects of the King of Spain.

Because of Columbus's single-mindedness his relations with Martin Pinzon had deteriorated. The *Pinta's* commander was after a different ideal, and leaving behind the *Niña* and the *Santa Maria* he went to look for gold in the countless islands surrounding Cuba. Naturally, Columbus didn't despise gold either. He had found some of it in the island of Haiti, where he had landed at the beginning of December, and he continued to look for it. Then, however, one night, during a storm, the flagship became stranded and sank. Most of the cargo was salvaged and loaded onto the *Niña,* which had rushed in to help. The sailors and officers swam to the shore of the nearest island where they were fed and sheltered by the natives.

Columbus left a small garrison in Haiti, and then on January 16 he gave orders to the *Niña* and the *Pinta* to set sail for Europe. It was a long crossing, often troubled by violent storms. When the caravels came in sight of the Azores, Pinzon went ahead by himself, with the *Pinta,* leaving Columbus and the *Niña* behind. He wanted to reach Spain first, to carry the news to the sovereigns that Asia had been reached.

Because of some repairs that had to be made, Columbus was delayed. In the meantime, some of his sailors went ashore to carry out a vow they had made during a particularly violent hurricane that had almost sunk their ship. However, when the men arrived in town, they were surrounded by Portuguese soldiers and put in jail. They were released only after four days and went back to the *Niña,* which was now ready to sail, but again the ship was caught in a storm, which shattered her sails. The crew made a vow to fast for a whole day if they escaped ruin.

On March 3rd the *Niña* sighted the shores of Portugal. Since the sails of his caravel were in shreds, and the port of Palos was still 220 miles away, Columbus decided to land in Lisbon to repair the damage. At last, however, on March 15 the *Niña* anchored in the bay of Palos, Spain, where it was greeted by an exultant crowd. Columbus found a message from Ferdinand and Isabella inviting him to Barcelona. The monarchs had already learned from Pinzon about the happy outcome of the undertaking, but, with kingly propriety, they had refused to receive Pinzon before Columbus.

Columbus presented himself at court followed by a small crowd of natives carrying boxes of gold and brightly colored parrots. When the king asked to whom he should give the prize he had promised to the man who first would sight land, Columbus answered that it was to him the prize was due.

For the next six months Columbus lived at the court collecting funds for a new expedition. This time he was able to outfit a fleet of 17 ships and 1,200 men, and besides food, drink, and ammunition, he also took along a number of animals, which he intended to breed on the islands to enrich the fauna of those lands, which a papal bull had baptized "Indias." Finally he also embarked five confessors, who were to convert the natives.

The convoy sailed from the port of Seville on September 25, 1493, and less than forty days later it landed on the shore of an island that Columbus called Dominica, because they reached it on a Sunday. From there it penetrated into the Lesser Antilles, which Columbus called the Virgin Islands, and then the sailors discovered Puerto Rico. At last the expedition went back to Haiti, where the small Spanish garrison had been left, but they found only one man alive: the others had either been killed by the Indians for stealing their women or slain each other.

Columbus appointed a new garrison in the island of Isabella and set out to circumnavigate Cuba, but a storm pushed back the ships to their point of departure. There he found his garrison again destroyed. The Spaniards, it appeared, had captured some youths to make slaves out of them, and in retaliation the natives had attacked the settlers' encampment, killing most of them.

Columbus stayed in the West Indies for two and a half years, recruiting slaves, and returned to Spain in March, 1496. A chronicler reports that of the five hundred natives who had begun the crossing of the Atlantic, two hundred had died during the crossing, and the others within a few years, incapable of adapting to the Old World's climate and habits. Then, in May, 1498, Columbus crossed the ocean again, looking for new lands to discover. He planted two more settlements in Haiti, and he authorized the settlers to kidnap and subjugate the Indians with no regard for sex or age. This caused many violent revolts, which Columbus smothered in blood, raising gallows all over the island.

The great admiral was a very bad governor: choleric, cruel, and revengeful. His collaborators began to detest him, and they bitterly criticized him in each report they sent to Madrid. Ferdinand and Isabella became worried, and in 1500 a royal commission with full powers was sent to the Indies to investigate.

Of this power Francisco de Bobadilla made very poor use. He arrested Columbus and flung him into jail, then sent him back to Spain handcuffed and in irons. In Spain he was kept prisoner for six more weeks, and then was led into the king's presence. Ferdinand reproached him for his errors as a governor and took that office away from him but left him his possessions in the New World. Columbus countered the accusations, and as he took his leave, he asked the king to provide him with a new fleet, to continue his explorations.

Columbus sailed for the fourth time in May, 1502. This time he visited Honduras, Nicaragua, Costa Rica, and Jamaica, where the ships suffered such damage during a storm that they couldn't leave for a year. When help finally came from Santa Domingo, the Spanish castaways were at the end of their strength, and the admiral, tortured by arthritis, couldn't wait to get home. He got there in November, 1505.

Columbus was fifty-eight, but he looked considerably older. His hair had turned white, he had dark rings under his eyes, and his sun-baked face was furrowed by deep wrinkles. He could hardly move because of his many infirmities, and his incapacity plunged him into dark melancholy. As soon as he arrived in Spain, he asked for a new audience with Ferdinand, who received him at the court of Segovia. Columbus begged the king to return him his old privileges and his governorship, but the king would only offer him a large estate in Castile. Columbus answered that he had no use for that, and he was right. A few months later death put an end to his bitter and solitary decline.

Columbus is not one of the most colorful and fascinating figures among the great men in history. His disappointments were due not only to other people's ingratitude but also to his own narrowness of spirit, aridity, and greed. However, his achievement remains one of the greatest and most crucial of all times. Fourteen-hundred-ninety-two is really a fundamental date, and many scholars have adopted it as the line that separates the Middle Ages from modern times. Certainly, it also marks the shift of the world's center of gravity from the Mediterranean to the Atlantic. The great adventure of the Italian maritime republics was over; now was the turn of Spain, Portugal, and England, and the new geography left Italy in a position of secondary importance.